VOCABULARIES OF PUBLIC LIFE

Perhaps more so than at any other time this century, cultural analysis lies at the center of the human sciences. Written both for the specialist and for scholars in a variety of disciplines, these essays explore the revolution which has taken place over the last twenty-five years in our understanding of contemporary culture, and decodes a number of the symbols which now dominate public life.

Wuthnow divides the essays collected here into three distinct "vocabularies" Part I examines the ways in which religious and scientific languages function as vocabularies of conviction in public life, Part II focuses on music and art as vocabularies of expression, and Part III considers law, ideology, and public policy as vocabularies of persuasion. The contributors discuss such diverse subjects as American spiritualism, the syntax of modern dance, and the social context of number one songs. What unifies the book is the common concern with the concrete, everyday manifestations of culture and the importance of understanding its basic structure.

Robert Wuthnow is Professor of Sociology at Princeton University.

Vocabularies of Public Life

Empirical Essays in Symbolic Structure

Edited by
Robert Wuthnow

London and New York

First published 1992
by Routledge
11 New Fetter Lane, London EC4P 4EE

Simultaneously published in the USA and Canada
by Routledge
a division of Routledge, Chapman and Hall, Inc.
29 West 35th Street, New York, NY 10001

Typeset in 10 on 12 point Bembo by Fotographics (Bedford) Ltd
Printed in Great Britain by The University Press, Cambridge

British Library Cataloguing in Publication Data

Vocabularies of public life: empirical essays in symbolic structure.
  1. Wuthnow, Robert
  306

Library of Congress Cataloging in Publication Data

Vocabularies of public life: empirical essays in symbolic structure/edited by Robert Wuthnow.
    p.   cm.
Includes bibliographical references and index.
1. Communication—Social aspects. 2. Symbolism in communication.
3. Discourse analysis. I. Wuthnow, Robert.
HM258.V63   1992
302.2—dc20   91–19122

ISBN 0-415-07636-6   ISBN 0-415-07637-4 (pbk)

Contents

Notes on contributors

Albert Bergesen is Professor of Sociology at the University of Arizona. He is currently completing *The Ritual Order*, a book on the sociology of ritual and discourse in the reproduction of modern society.

Gene Burns, an Assistant Professor of Sociology at Princeton University, is completing a book on ideological change in the Catholic church. Part of that research appeared in a recent article in the *American Journal of Sociology*. He intends to continue to study the role of ideology in social revolutions, applying the approach adopted in his chapter in this book to the Iranian Revolution.

Karen A. Cerulo received her PhD from Princeton University and is an Assistant Professor of Sociology at Rutgers University. She has contributed articles to several journals, among them the *American Sociological Review*, *Communications Research*, and *Social Forces*. Her research interests include symbolic communication, methods of enhancing communication effectiveness, and social structural influences on decision-making processes. She is currently writing a book entitled *National Symbols: Bonds and Boundaries*.

Frank Dobbin is an Assistant Professor of Sociology at Princeton University. His interests include comparative public policy and organizations, and his work is historical and constructivist in orientation. He is currently finishing a book on nineteenth-century railway policies in the United States, Britain, and France that chronicles the rise of different national industrial policy styles. Other projects include an analysis of the effects of public policy on foundings and failures among early American railroads, and a collaborative study of postwar changes in organizational personnel practices.

Timothy Jon Dowd is a doctoral candidate in the Department of Sociology at Princeton University. Specializing in sociology of culture, organizations, and stratification, he is writing a dissertation on popular music.

Eva Marie Garroutte is completing her PhD studies at Princeton University. Her dissertation on nineteenth-century religious movements reflects her interests in the sociology of religion and historical sociology. Other areas of interest include the sociology of knowledge, of science, of language, and feminist theory. She is a Ford Fellow and a member of the Cherokee nation of Oklahoma.

Benjamin Gregg is a doctoral candidate in the Department of Politics at Princeton University. He has also received a PhD in philosophy from the Free University of Berlin and is the author of several articles on nineteenth- and twentieth-century European social thought. He is currently studying the shifting patterns of legitimacy of normatively ambiguous legal systems.

Susan Harding is Professor of Anthropology at the University of California, Santa Cruz. Her chapter is part of a larger project on narrative and politics in the Reverend Jerry Falwell's fundamental Baptist community in Lynchburg, Virginia. She has been a fellow at the Institute for Advanced Study in Princeton and a member of the Religion and Culture Workshop at Princeton University.

Allison Jones is a doctoral student in the Department of Sociology at the University of Arizona. She is working on a project in cultural sociology, specifically in the area of dance.

Joan Morris is a PhD candidate and lecturer in the Department of Sociology at Louisiana State University. Her research is concerned with culture and knowledge in its various forms. This includes issues such as: community formation in scientific texts, the veneration of science in American culture, and the organization of technological knowledge. She is currently examining the nature of class culture as a knowledge system and its consequences for working-class Americans.

Richard L. Rogers is a doctoral candidate in the Department of Sociology at Princeton University. His principal interest is in the sociology of religion. His current research is on early nineteenth-century American evangelicalism.

Marsha Witten is an Assistant Professor of Rhetoric and Communication at Temple University. She is currently researching the effects of secularity on the discourse of contemporary Protestant sermons in the United States.

David E. Woolwine is a Visiting Professor in the Department of Sociology at Hamilton College. He received his PhD in sociology from Princeton University, where he also studied history and philosophy of science. His interests include sociological theory, the sociology of science, and the sociology of religion. He is currently working on a book on the development of transcendent languages in response to the AIDS crisis.

Robert Wuthnow is Professor of Sociology at Princeton University. He is a founding member of the University Center for Human Values and director of the Center for the Study of American Religion. His most recent books include *Acts of Compassion* (Princeton University Press, 1991) and *Communities of Discourse* (Harvard University Press, 1989).

Introduction:
New directions in the empirical study of cultural codes

Robert Wuthnow

Over the past quarter century a revolution has taken place in the way in which social scientists understand and think about culture. It was once commonplace for theorists and researchers in the human sciences to speak of culture as if it consisted of deep norms and values, beliefs and orientations, predispositions and assumptions – all with an implicit stability and orderliness to which speech and action merely gave expression.[1] Now, an increasing number of scholars question the fixity, even the reality, of these unobservables. Increasingly, speech and action themselves have risen to prominence, losing the superficiality of their earlier reflective character, and becoming the constitutive features of social reality itself.[2] The world is at once more transparent and more precarious. Speech and action are no longer the surface manifestations of firmer, deeper, and more dependable foundational values. For values themselves are now said to be constructed in speech and action.[3] No meanings exist apart from their symbolic carriers. And these carriers can be constructed and reconstructed, giving meaning and value a more fluid, dynamic, and situational character.[4]

But what does this transformation imply? For some, it signals the end of positive knowledge as the human sciences have conceived of it for more than a century. Everything – even the researcher's own claims – must be bracketed as reflexive constructions more dependent on their own internal relations than any relation with absolute truth or a reality that precedes symbolic mediation. When language becomes reality, the quest for social structure must cease as well. Statistics about the occupational and income distributions of social classes cease to be of vital importance in their own right, because all statistics, all definitions of occupational categories, all meanings of income, and all concepts of social class are the result of language games. All research becomes interpretation. Wordplay replaces knowledge. The social sciences must revert to literature.

Such a view cannot, however, be sustained. If the worlds in which we live are increasingly composed of symbols and symbol manipulation, these

1

worlds are nevertheless the realities to which we attribute, and from which we derive, meaning. And this meaning, just as the traditional beliefs and values with which it was associated, is no mere resident of the inner being, but is a product of the regularities present in speech and action themselves.[5] We may be at the mercy of wordmongers who deliberately construct the realities in which we must live, but the wordmongers themselves depend on the rules of symbolic use of which culture consists, if only to violate them. In other words, symbolism can be allowed to come to the forefront of attention in the human sciences without rendering these disciplines nothing more than cynical exercises in subjective interpretation. Symbolism is itself a reality that can be subjected to systematic investigation.[6]

It is thus understandable that a host of new approaches, theories, perspectives, and methodologies for the analysis of culture has arisen in recent years. Perhaps more so than at any other time in the present century, cultural analysis lies at the center of the human sciences. Semioticians seek the ways in which language and meaning intersect. Historians rediscover the richness of folklore and personal narratives. Communication specialists explore the rhetorical vehicles used to disseminate information. Writers and literary critics attempt to break down the boundary between high culture and popular culture and to shock us into greater awareness of the ways in which our lives depend on the facilities of language. Students of religion, and even theologians, are increasingly mindful of the complexities of symbolism, ritual, and myth. Though the particularities of these approaches differ, they all assume the importance of studying culture as an entity in itself and the possibility of gaining valuable insights into its composition and functioning by examining its internal structure.

So rich and varied are the current perspectives that crowd uneasily together under the rubric of cultural analysis that petty disputes, turf wars, and miscommunication are almost inevitable. Hackles can be raised on some necks by suggesting that anything at all is new; on others, by slight nuances in the ways in which words like meaning, value, and symbolism are used; and on others, by subtle variations in preferred genres signaled by the length of sentences, choice of adjectives, and formal construction of paragraphs. The temptation is often strong simply to throw up one's hands and abandon the field altogether, or else drift into the safe havens of narrow empirical topics. And yet, to do so abrogates responsibility for such a vital area as the study of human values to an overly cautious set of technical virtuosi, on the one hand, or to the esoteric ruminations of grand interpreters, logicians, and pundits, on the other.

At the risk of driving away nearly everyone who remains wedded to the complete rectitude of his or her own particular approach, some effort must be made, therefore, to set forth the premises on which not only the present collection of essays but a whole line of inquiry within what is perhaps best known as cultural sociology is based. Or to put it a different way, various operating assumptions need to be spelled out as a vision of what cultural sociology *could be* and of what it *could contribute* to the human sciences, even if there is sparse agreement in any quarter at present about these particular assumptions. What follows, then, are assumptions that underlie at least most of the essays herein, that (in my view) can be advanced with integrity as a firm basis for ethically-guided empirical work in the human sciences, but that are also likely to be so readily assented to by some practitioners that any hint of novelty or originality will be questioned, and so bitterly contested by other practitioners that little hope may be seen of moving beyond theoretical disputes at all.

Operating premises for a sociology of culture

(a)   The realm of values, ideas, knowledge, and symbols of which culture is composed is of vital importance to the understanding and advancement of the human condition. Few, I suspect, would be willing to dispute this premise, particularly because the very act of engaging in disputation is predicated on the assumption that ideas matter. Furthermore, the scholarly enterprise itself is generally regarded as a contribution to the realm of ideas and values rather than being worthwhile simply for its potential achievements in the realm of technical mastery. Nevertheless, it is important to state this premise as straightforwardly as possible at the start of any discussion involving the social sciences, for there is still a widespread view in these disciplines that culture is an epiphenomenal, if not an effete, subject worthy of little attention at all compared to such robust and consequential topics as power, institutions, and social stratification. Sociology of culture, on the contrary, is based on the premise that even these preoccupations must be viewed as having a very strong cultural component. Culture, then, is not a separate realm, somehow removed from the realities of ordinary life, but a feature of all human behavior and interaction.

(b)   Culture is not only a vital feature of the human condition, but a particularly problematic topic deserving special consideration in our time. Serious debates exist everywhere about the nature of the human condition, its capacity to survive on this planet, the bases on which ethical and moral decisions must be made, and the values and commitments on which social order and cohesion must be founded. Perhaps it has always been so. But whether ours is a uniquely perilous time in human history, or whether all ages have faced such challenges, the imperative to confront ourselves and our collective understandings is not diminished. The study of culture should, for this reason, be more than an idle exercise in intellectual speculation. Even when the nature of values and truth is seriously in question – and perhaps especially when it is – the study of culture should be concerned with the clarification of value and truth. It should be more than a narrow technical endeavor, linking technical considerations to larger questions about the nature of what is desirable and beneficial for the good of society and the growth of the individual. In short, it should address both the long-standing concerns that have become more problematic in our time, such as the bases of ethics in a pluralistic society and the nature of commitment in a climate of individualism and relativism, and newer concerns that have arisen because of the times in which we live, such as the authority of science and technology and the relations between human societies and the global environment. It should address these concerns empirically and analytically with an eye toward describing and explaining serious social problems and their causes. But it should also have the courage to take normative stands on these issues, including the formulation of critical treatises and the advancement of visionary alternatives.

(c) The sociological study of culture should be guided more by a recognition of the need for interdisciplinary borrowing and cooperation than by a desire to uphold rigid disciplinary boundaries. Sociologists can rightfully be proud of their own contributions to the study of culture. The major founders of the discipline, Max Weber, Karl Marx, Emile Durkheim, all devoted serious attention to questions of culture. Their legacy has been carried on in the significant work of more recent sociologists: Daniel Bell, Peter Berger, Robert N. Bellah, and Jürgen Habermas, among others. At this juncture, the work of a generation of sociologists concerned with the empirical study of cultural issues has also begun to bear fruit. The studies of Paul DiMaggio, Wendy Griswold, Ann Swidler, Jeffrey Alexander, Joseph Gusfield, Michael Schudson, Gary Alan Fine, Richard Peterson, Vera L. Zolberg, and Michèle Lamont, to name a few, testify to the important work that is being accomplished within sociology.[7] At the same time, the more significant features of this work can often be attributed to cross-fertilization from reading and collaboration with scholars in other disciplines. Anthropology, literary criticism, political philosophy, religious studies, cultural history, and cognitive psychology are all rich fields from which new insights can be derived. Indeed, it is probably safe to say that common concerns are bringing the human sciences together in a way that has not been witnessed for many decades.

(d) A sociology of culture nevertheless has a distinct niche to occupy relative to various other approaches to the study of culture. One has only to read the contributions of scholars in the various disciplines concerned with culture to see that different issues and different traditions continue to animate these discussions. Sociologists may borrow from other disciplines, and yet must recognize in doing so that the distinctive contributions of those disciplines may not be transferrable. What makes an analysis of a diary from the eighteenth century interesting, for example, is not likely to be the same as what might make such an analysis of a twentieth-century diary important. Sociologists may engage in close analyses of conversations and texts, and yet

4

to call this work "discourse analysis" would be to point toward a separate sub-field in communication studies that often raises questions of little interest to sociologists. In part, then, sociologists of culture must be concerned with the symbolic identity of their own niche. In borrowing the language of other approaches, they must be wary of confusing the issue by selling short their own identity. More important, though, sociologists must be aware of what they do have to offer that is distinctive. There will, of course, be disagreement about this, but in my view several distinctive features of sociological work on culture give it a clear niche to occupy. Among these, I would briefly enumerate: (i) a strong emphasis on the relations between culture and social structure, including questions about the shaping influences of the latter, and the ways in which culture may effect changes in social structure; (ii) central concern with the production and dissemination of culture and, thus, with the ways in which cultural products are influenced by the availability of social resources; (iii) a continuing emphasis on the relations between cultural phenomena and social actors, especially the processes by which actors interact with and internalize their symbolic worlds; and (iv) a renewed emphasis on what can be learned about social interaction and social structure through the examination of textual form and content.

(e) Any sociology of culture will inevitably be an interpretive venture, but should also strive toward rigor and systematization in the use of evidence. It is to be regretted, I believe, that so many valuable empirical studies in the sociology of culture in recent years have generated discussions, not about the substantive merits of these studies, but about their presumed location within some larger debate between positivism and hermeneutic approaches to the human sciences. Because this sub-field has sometimes become a preserve for those disdainful of the positivism implicit in more dominant quantitative sub-fields, any call for rigor and systematization has been met with suspicion that the positivists were readying themselves at the gate for a full-scale assault. As in any sub-field, those with narrowly-focused empirical interests have, for their part, registered suspicion about the broader theoretical orientations from which hermeneutic claims have been advanced. The appropriate response, in my view, is to be properly cautious about any empirical claims one might make, drawing on the hermeneutic literature to go ahead in the face of interpretive limitations, but to go ahead nonetheless, doing empirical work with as much attention to rigor and systematization as any unrepentant positivist might give. The value of rigor and systematization is not, as some might believe, that it yields a kind of positive knowledge, but that it leaves "tracks," so to speak, of one's decisions, assumptions, procedures, and methodologies, and therefore of one's biases. The value of recognizing that interpretation is always present is that one is then prompted to make these interpretations explicit. The ideal, it seems to me, is a blend of the two, resulting in cultural studies based on a high density of empirical observations and a rich interpretive framework that puts these observations into a broader context and explicates some of the various meanings.

(f)   Much of what sociologists of culture are concerned with studying is, in fact, amenable to rigorous and systematic observation.[8] It may be fine, some readers will perhaps argue, to call for rigor and systematization, but surely this goes against the very grain of cultural studies, for culture is concerned with the meanings of things, and those meanings are inherently subjective. Certainly there is some validity to this objection. Meanings are often not only subjective, but situational, idiosyncratic, and unstable. But this is only one way to look at meanings. They are also structured by the contexts – the symbolic contexts – in which they appear. One cannot read the sentence "my love is like a rose," and come away with just any meaning. Each word is constrained by the others, leaving the reader with only a possible range of meanings among a much larger universe of meanings that might attach themselves to these words in different settings. The same can be said for other kinds of settings as well; for example, if this sentence is uttered in a honeymoon suite as opposed to its being uttered before a crowd of poetry buffs in an auditorium. In either case – the text itself or its social context – the setting is composed of symbolic elements and these elements are arranged in a way that imposes a certain order on the communication process. They render the sentence meaningful in the first place. They also delimit its various possible meanings. These symbolic elements – their arrangement – are observable. Even the interpretation given the sentence by one reader or listener is observable insofar as it is recorded or otherwise turned into a text. What makes cultural sociology a branch of the human sciences concerned with observations, therefore, is that it is essentially a study of texts: texts of all kinds, including the printed word, graphic images, spoken utterances, and even the messages "given off" in social settings by such behaviors as bodily movements and positions (which we correctly refer to as "body language"), gestures, facial expressions, or the public "face" of organizations and institutions. To the extent that these texts vary in scope and origin, this means also that a sociology of culture should be methodologically eclectic. Qualitative historical studies, quantitative surveys of opinion statements, ethnographic research, and close analyses of written and oral texts are all needed for the hard work of developing a rigorous and systematic sociology of culture.

(g)   Beyond merely accumulating empirical evidence, the tasks of a sociology of culture should be centrally concerned with theoretical reflection about the social characteristics of culture. This ideal derives in part from what I have already said about the problematic features of values and beliefs in our time. But it also points to a need for what might bluntly be called a heightened level of seriousness among cultural sociologists toward their topics of interest. It is perhaps endemic in an era when the grand historic designs of an earlier generation of social theorists have fallen into disrepute, when the positivist hopes of scientifically-oriented social theorists have been dashed – when the idea of "local knowledge" seems to turn everything into immediate, situational, idiosyncratic stimuli – that there is much uncertainty about what the "big questions" are, let alone what the answers to these questions may be.[9] If everything is local and situational anyway, then why should not I study the things of interest in my backyard, you study the things of interest in yours, and the two of us agree simply to tolerate one another's obsessions? To be sure, there is much to be learned from studies of "little" topics (like the culture of drag racing enthusiasts or the underlife of a local beer parlor). Each may be the grain of sand in which a universe is inscribed. But we are likely to see that universe only if we are looking for it. Were we enthusiasts of drag racing and beer parlors ourselves, we might well be content to describe everything about how these subcultures work – who the key actors are, how they became involved, where their finances come from, what their aesthetic standards are, and why they continue to do what they do. As sociologists we must, however, go beyond these questions to ask others, many of which have as their repository the reflective theoretical works of our discipline. Is modernity changing in such a way that certain values and lifestyles are imperiled? As cultural traditions adapt to modernity, are they selling their soul as the price of success? What are the cultural ingredients from which our definitions of our selves are constructed? How do communities come into being, maintain themselves, service their members, and in the process give plausibility to certain cultural codes? Has pluralism fundamentally altered our capacity to communicate with one another? Is the symbolic texture of our society largely a reflection of its economic and political processes? Can we find underlying rules of dialogue and expression that will help us address the major challenges facing our society and our world? What are the links between symbol systems and power? How are inequality and oppression perpetuated by cultural constructions? These, in my view, are questions of vital importance that must be confronted anew by each generation of scholars in the human sciences. None of them rules out the study of topics that may spring from aesthetic concerns or even from purely autobiographical origins, except that scholarly work, like all work, requires an expenditure of personal and social resources, and resources are always limited. For that reason alone, we must pay careful attention to our priorities. All inclinations toward cynicism aside, what we do matters a great deal. It matters not because of some game we are playing to see who can amass the most academic toys in the shortest time possible, but because ideas do make a difference in the conduct of our lives, individually and collectively. Even the pursuit of large questions in small arenas contributes to the keeping of those questions alive. Our hope of finding answers may indeed be small. But if the questions themselves are left unasked, and thereby cease to be a part of our collective memory, then we are all surely the losers. Cultural sociology, together with its kindred fields in other disciplines, must be vitally committed to these higher pursuits.

7

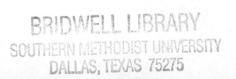

The problem of public discourse

What I have just sketched is a highly personal statement about what the sociology of culture should be. It reflects concerns that I believe are widely shared among practitioners in the human sciences. And yet it represents a vision that I have seldom seen expressed in published form. It is a kind of prolegomenon to which I often refer in my own work when questions begin to plague me about the reasons for working in this field at all. It sets forth assumptions that can guide, but never be fully realized in, concrete empirical studies, and certainly not within the scope of a single volume, given the range of significant questions that need to be addressed.

Of these questions, I consider the problem of public discourse among the most important for sociologists of culture to address. How can we communicate with one another about the basic values, the collective symbols on which our society rests, the goals and ambitions to which we aspire as a people? Our way of life, our future as a society – the future of any democratic society – depends on arriving at effective answers to this question. Our freedom depends on being able to contribute to the public debate over collective values, rather than having the essential decisions that guide our society determined bureaucratically. The quality of our freedom depends equally on our ability to engage in collective deliberations, rather than letting the blind forces of economic markets and self-interest dictate the limits of our freedom. The determination of collective values, moreover, can never be turned over to the voting booth alone, or to the mass media, if a healthy society is to survive. It must involve statements of opinion, expressions of value, and the sharing of sentiments, whether these be about personal interests, groups, or whole segments of the society.

What makes the study of public discourse of particularly vital importance in today's world is a widely shared perception that we are increasingly talking past one another, letting bureaucratic and technical concerns predominate, rather than finding effective ways of reaching consensus on matters of the common good. To cite but a few of the indications that this is a valid perception: the debate over abortion is mired in a polarized rhetoric that masks deeper differences in worldviews and seems incapable of leading toward creative solutions; environmental crises loom with increasing intensity and yet public officials seem incapable of mobilizing popular opinion toward any measures that may have a considerable effect; after years of educational programs and policy initiatives designed to curb racial and ethnic discrimination, the relations among racial and ethnic subcultures in our society seem to be on the verge of erupting into violent confrontation at any moment; for all the talk about changing conceptions of gender, the public arena seems to be filled with grave uncertainties about the nature of families and the balance between child-rearing and work demands; old religious divisions have been reduced only to reveal new tensions dividing religious liberals and religious conservatives; a generation of value neutrality and ethical relativism has given way to new discussions of values and ethics but without any authoritative basis on which to make normative assertions; and so it goes.

Each of these issues deserves scrutiny by social scientists. And yet there is an even more fundamental contribution that social scientists can make: learning better how to approach the problem of public discourse and, thereby, discovering the rules by which it operates. A seemingly simple act of public discourse, such as a sermon, a direct-mail solicitation, or a popular song, contains a vast inner structure of form and content. If we are to know why we are convinced by a particular sermon, repulsed by a letter asking for money, or moved by a popular song, we must begin to pull apart these inner structures to see how they are composed.

Communication specialists have led the way in studies of public discourse. Beginning with early work on radio and propaganda, and then progressing through studies of television and other mass media, they have called attention to intricacies of these texts. Content analysis has played a major role in unearthing themes and trends, and recent work has paid increasing attention to the use of rhetorical devices. And yet this is one area in which my admonition about sociologists of culture having something unique to offer holds true.

The sociological study of public discourse is distinguished from communication studies primarily by placing greater emphasis on the social world depicted within the text and the relation between that depiction and the social world that constitutes the context of the text. Whereas communication studies may well emphasize the performative aspects of a public utterance, sociological studies are more likely to focus on the ways in which form and content convey messages about social understandings. And whereas communication studies may stress the themes and arguments being advanced in public discourse, sociological studies need to be attentive to the complex codes, distinctions, rules, and interplay between form and content that permit a public utterance to articulate with its social environment.

Although the sociological study of public discourse is still a relatively underdeveloped sub-field, this way of characterizing its basic emphasis is by no means original or new. Its roots can be traced backwards at least to the early part of this century, especially if one recognizes its affinities with the vision spelled out by Mikhail Bakhtin (1986) for a "sociological poetics" and carried forward (or rediscovered) by neo-Marxist literary critics such as Raymond Williams, Terry Eagleton, and Frederic Jameson. The insight that distinguished this tradition qualitatively from the more prominent Marxist perspective that became known as the sociology of knowledge was that culture is not simply a reflection of social structure but contains an elaborate internal structure of its own that borrows from the social world, textualizes that material, and in the process transforms it. Literary texts are thus mirrors of social reality that present images which come alive, engage in dialogue, refigure the social world, create actors, and send these actors back into the external environment to transform it in creative ways.

What can be said of literary texts can also be said of public discourse (which may in part be composed, of course, of literary texts). Although the typical utterance of which public discourse is composed may not be as elaborate as a work of fiction, it is nevertheless an intentional construction. It therefore must follow certain rules, employ certain devices, and utilize certain strategies for it to accomplish its purpose. It does not simply articulate a theme, but couches that theme in a framework of parallels and contrasts, frames it within certain categories that deny others, and implies various relations between the speaker and an audience. Without knowing anything directly about the context in which it occurs, we can nevertheless infer a great deal about the nature of public discourse by examining these aspects of its internal structure. We can do this even more effectively as sociologists when we take account of what is known about the social contexts in which public discourse occurs.

Sociologists and practitioners in adjacent disciplines have been paying increasing attention to these aspects of public discourse in recent years. If the glue holding together society is not entirely an implicit consensus, not exactly a set of taken-for-granted assumptions, but conscious discussion and activities aimed explicitly at shaping public debate, then symbolism, symbol production, and symbolic practices all become central to the study of public culture. They take on material form, as Michael Schudson (1989: 154) has recently emphasized, making them amenable to empirical observation: "Symbols appear to us embodied, institutionalized. Watching television, reading the newspaper, going to school, talking to the family at dinner, or participating in a church service or an election or a high school commencement ceremony are all 'rituals,' if you will, in which symbols are embedded and embodied. The symbols do not exist apart from how they are conveyed, and our own participation in them and with them constructs not only their power but their very meaning." Private culture, too, such as an individual's prayer life or the famed cleanliness rituals of the "Nacirema" can also be said to have material substance. But it has been especially the public rituals, the public utterances and objects, to which sociologists have been drawn.

Studies of public discourse about moral issues have been prominent in this literature. Specific issues, such as abortion (Luker 1984), alcoholism (Gusfield 1981), and pornography, have been studied, as have more general questions about the fate of moral reasoning under pluralistic conditions (Bellah *et al.* 1985) and the resurgence of conservative political ideologies that champion traditional moral claims (Himmelstein 1990). Research in this area continues to be heavily oriented toward substantive issues. But increasing attention is being paid to questions of discourse itself. Rather than conceiving of conservatism or liberalism, say, as a broad worldview or value-orientation, researchers have begun to treat it as a kind of language. Questions arise, therefore, about the internal contrasts that give structure to this language, about recurrent scripts that familiarize arguments to their listeners, and about the mechanisms that allow speakers to leap from one script to another and either integrate or compartmentalize their arguments.

Increasing attention has also been given to the idea of symbolic boundaries in public life. Although this work has often taken a broad macroscopic orientation, it has nevertheless signaled the importance of the categories and distinctions that give order to public life but at the same time generate conflict and result in inequality and exclusion. Richard Merelman (1984), a political scientist whose work has attracted a wide readership among sociologists, has taken the "loose boundedness" of American culture itself as a problematic feature of modern life that helps make sense of many of our more specific cultural products, from television to advertising to political arguments. Michèle Lamont, in a forthcoming book, treats the ways in which moral claims themselves serve as symbolic markers of social distinctions. Students of religion have become increasingly interested in the symbolic transformations that underlie changing categories of religious identity, such as denominational boundaries, and boundaries used to segment thinking into sacred and profane, churchly and political, public and private, and so on (e.g. Wuthnow 1988).

At a more microscopic level of analysis, some of the most important work has been conducted by sociologists of science. Paying close attention to the discourse and texts of scientists, they have asked how the consensual truth claims of modern science are influenced, not so much by factual discoveries, or even by institutional resources, but by the registers in which words are spoken and the ways in which doubts are shielded from view. The methods of analysis that sociologists of science have developed for these studies clearly have applications for research on other kinds of authoritative texts as well.

These examples illustrate the extent of vitality and new thinking currently taking place in sociological studies of public culture. They reveal the depth of interest being given to questions of language, not as a communication device alone, but as a rich, symbolic text. Regularities are being found in the relations among symbols that help us see more of what public discourse is actually composed and to understand how it adapts to its social circumstances. But the surface has as yet only been scratched. To say that an ideology seems "cohesive," for example, now opens up a Pandora's box of empirical questions: What do we mean by cohesion? How do we measure it? What is its relation to the variety of meanings that can be conveyed? Or to say, as students of propaganda often have in the past, that a public appeal works better if it employs a high degree of redundancy also raises more questions than we might have supposed: Is redundancy a unitary concept? Or are there types of redundancy? Can there be redundancies between form and substance? How about various levels of redundancy within a text? Similar

11

questions can be raised about other kinds of symbolism; for example, about music: Is there any way to measure the degree of innovation in music? Would we expect there to be more variations within a musical score under some social circumstances than others? If so, how would we know if such variation were present?

These questions point in new directions in the measurement, and thus in the conceptualization, of symbolic structure. Sociologists can advance in exploring these questions by borrowing from language studies that focus on the syntax of texts or from literary studies that highlight techniques of sequencing and localization. Other questions point less toward new measurement strategies than toward new substantive applications and theoretical implications. If, for example, individuals follow familiar scripts that give their utterances a formulaic quality, do organizations do the same thing? If so, what are the implications? Or, if symbolism is indeed embedded in and constitutive of social action, then how should we think about its relations to institutions or such traditional categories as social class, power, and the means of production?

The advances that are currently being made in understanding public life in its cultural dimensions are not occurring as a result of any single theoretical perspective or methodological breakthrough. They are coming about as a result of the work of scattered individual researchers and clusters or schools of researchers who define themselves more by agreement on a few underlying premises than by adhering to a single method or theory. The resulting research is often bewildering for its diversity and, at minimum, frustrating to its readers because it fails to make connections with, or pay homage, to their favorite writers. It is, nevertheless, contributing in small, piecemeal ways to a better understanding of how public life in our society functions.

Scope of this book

The essays in this book build on the studies just cited. What has remained lacking in much of the work thus far, it seems to me, is an explicit, self-conscious concern with methods of analyzing the internal structure of texts that make up public discourse. This is not to say that scholars have been unmindful of these methodological questions. A good beginning has been made, especially by ethnographers and ethnomethodologists, but it is only a beginning. Quantitative studies have remained limited for the most part to the straightforward coding of content categories that has characterized content analysis procedures for nearly half a century. And qualitative studies have often been preoccupied with substantive issues to the exclusion of questions about form and its interplay with content.

The other limitation of current work on public discourse, in my view, is that it has focused so much on political rhetoric and the messages of the mass media that we have lost sight of the fact that other vocabularies and genres may be equally important to the shaping of our collective values. Studies of religion, art, music, and science have been progressing at a rapid pace in recent years as well, but often in isolation from each other and from broader questions about the public sphere. We have in this volume intentionally brought together studies from these various arenas to emphasize both common methodological concerns and common substantive issues. If a sociology of culture is to emerge as a unified sub-field, this sort of boundary transgressing is a must. What is common to religion and science and art and law, among other things, is that they are all concerned at some level with the public expression of collective values.

Taking their cue from recent efforts to rethink the nature of culture, the present essays examine a number of the symbolic codes that dominate contemporary public life. Rather than treating public culture as a set of attitudes and opinions to be understood chiefly by thematizing their content and estimating their prevalence, these inquiries examine the complex relationships between form and content within symbolic codes themselves and the ways in which these codes relate to symbolic dimensions of the broader social environment. The lesson to be gained from these studies is that the public realm is infinitely richer and more complex than even students of the mass media and information industries have argued. It is richer because the vocabularies that surround us contain much more than meets the eye (or ear); more complex, because these vocabularies constitute not only a lexicon with which to convey sentiments and information, but also a subtle arrangement of boundaries and connections, contrasts and parallels. And yet, these patterns can also be unraveled, revealing the regularities on which meaning in public life depends.

The essays in Part I focus on what I have called "Vocabularies of Conviction" – the varieties of public discourse in which statements about truth and belief are presented. Religious and scientific discourse provide the clearest examples of the ways in which these vocabularies are constructed. As the essays in this section demonstrate, both depend on much more than simplistic assertions of dogma or fact. Indeed, something as seemingly simplistic as a fundamentalist sermon or a television preacher's appeal for money turns out to be a highly skilled performance rooted in sophisticated symbolic and rhetorical strategies. Similarly, something as seemingly remote from facticity as spiritualism depends much more than might be supposed on the language of science, while science itself requires strategies of authorization that go well beyond mere empirical assertions.

Part II – "Vocabularies of Expression" – takes up a similar set of issues for the expressive arts, paying special attention to the larger social order dramatized therein. Despite the high level of creativity involved in music, art, and dance, these essays illustrate the fruitful possibilities to be gained from bringing together insights from musicology or related fields concerned with artistic technique with insights from the social sciences. Why a particular kind of popular music gains popularity, or why a shift in artistic expression takes place, is shown to be the result of an intersection of variations in internal structure and dynamics in the wider society. Through close inspection of national anthems, popular music, contemporary art, and ballet, these essays help us understand why certain kinds of expressive discourse become prominent in public life.

The final set of essays (Part III) focuses on 'Vocabularies of Persuasion" – the way in which public life is shaped by the various ideologies of politics, economics, law, and bureaucratic organizations. Using methods similar to those in the previous two sections, these chapters also question whether our very theories of ideology need to be re-examined in light of what current case-studies are suggesting about the relations between ideas and social structure. To further this debate, these essays explore some of the neglected ways in which the content and context of public ideologies interact. They emphasize the importance of considering institutional contexts in which form and style are shaped, but also the extent to which institutional action is itself contingent on regularities of form and style.

Notes

1. Sociologists will of course think of the term "value-orientation," which served in the work of Talcott Parsons (e.g. 1951) as a kind of underlying standard (cognitive, expressive, or moral) that could be used to identify order in the actions of individuals or patterns in whole societies. Another well-known formulation reflecting this understanding suggested that culture consists of "whatever one has to know or believe in order to operate in a manner acceptable to [a society's] members, and to do so in any role that they accept for themselves" (Goodenough 1964: 36).
2. Nowhere has the collapse of distinctions between culture and social structure been more evident than in recent deconstructive efforts oriented toward a transformation of Marxist categories; for example, Baudrillard (1981: 113) writes: "The analysis of the production of signs and of culture thus does not impose itself as exterior, ulterior, and 'superstructural' in relation to that of material production; it imposes itself as *a revolution of political economy itself.*"
3. Austin (1962) is often cited because of his emphasis on the primacy of action, although his arguments have been extended well beyond their original intent.
4. The fluidity of meanings is amplified further when symbols are regarded not so much as fixed patterns but as malleable forms, repertoires, or tool-kits that individuals can simply select to accomplish their desired ends (Swidler 1986).
5. Although, as I indicate, cultural sociology should be distinguished from related sub-fields such as discourse analysis and conversation analysis, one of the valuable lessons that these sub-fields have taught is to look closely at symbol systems to see their internal structure, even the importance of such micro-mechanisms as "repetition of words and phrases, structural markers, fine synchronization in

14

time, and an underlying hierarchic structure relating sequences to discourse acts" (Stubbs 1983: 19).

6. Griswold (1987) has made a similar argument, calling for rigor primarily in conceptualizing the study of culture as a way of bridging the gap between scientific and humanistic approaches to culture. The limitation of her methodological framework, in my view, is that it pays too much attention to the relations between cultural objects and other actors or contexts (producers, audiences, analysts, and larger cultural schemes) and too little attention to the internal characteristics of cultural objects themselves.

7. Several exhaustive reviews of the recent literature in cultural sociology are available; see Peterson (1990) and Wuthnow and Witten (1988).

8. The observable character of culture is especially evident in those definitions of culture that identify "symbolic objects" as the proper focus of inquiry; for example, Schudson (1989: 153), who defines culture as "the symbolic dimension of human activity," conceives of its study as "the study of discrete symbolic objects (art, literature, sermons, ideologies, advertisements, maps, street signs) and how they function in social life."

9. The phrase "local knowledge" comes from Geertz (1983), but as Boden (1990) emphasizes has become an important assumption of ethnomethodologists as well (Garfinkel 1984, 1988; Heritage 1984).

References

Bakhtin, Mikhail. 1986. Methodology for the human sciences. In Caryl Emerson and Michael Holquist (eds), *Speech Genres and Other Late Essays*. Austin, Tex.: University of Texas Press.

Baudrillard, Jean. 1981. *For a Critique of the Political Economy of Signs*, trans. Charles Levin. Saint Louis, Missouri: Telos Press.

Bellah, Robert N. *et al.* 1985. *Habits of the Heart: Individualism and Commitment in American Life*. Berkeley, Calif.: University of California Press.

Boden, Deirdre. 1990. The world as it happens: Ethnomethodology and conversation analysis. In George Ritzer (ed.), *Frontiers of Social Theory: The New Synthesis*. New York: Columbia University Press.

Garfinkel, Harold. 1984. *Studies in Ethnomethodology*. [1967] Cambridge: Polity Press.

Garfinkel, Harold. 1988. Evidence for locally produced, naturally accountable phenomena of order. *Sociological Theory* 6: 131–58.

Geertz, Clifford. 1983. *Local Knowledge*. New York: Basic Books.

Goodenough, W. 1964. Cultural anthropology and linguistics. In D. Hymes (ed.), *Language in Culture and Society*. New York: Harper & Row.

Griswold, Wendy. 1987. A methodological framework for the sociology of culture. *Sociological Methodology* 15: 1–35.

Gusfield, Joseph R. 1981. *The Culture of Public Problems: Drinking-Driving and the Symbolic Order*. Chicago: University of Chicago Press.

Heritage, John. 1984. *Garfinkel and Ethnomethodology*. Cambridge: Polity Press.

Himmelstein, Jerome L. 1990. *To the Right: The Transformation of American Conservatism*. Berkeley, Calif.: University of California Press.

Luker, Kristin. 1984. *Abortion and the Politics of Motherhood*. Berkeley, Calif.: University of California Press.

Merelman, Richard M. 1984. *Making Something of Ourselves: On Culture and Politics in the United States*. Berkeley, Calif.: University of California Press.

Parsons, Talcott. 1951. *The Social System*. New York: Free Press.

Peterson, Richard A. 1990. The many facets of culture. *Contemporary Sociology* 19: 198–523.

Schudson, Michael. 1989. How culture works: Perspectives from media studies on the efficacy of symbols. *Theory and Society* 18: 153–80.

Stubbs, Michael. 1983. *Discourse Analysis: The Sociolinguistic Analysis of Natural Language*. Chicago: University of Chicago Press.

Swidler, Ann. 1986. Culture in action: Symbols and strategies. *American Sociological Review* 51: 273–86.

Wuthnow, Robert. 1988. *The Restructuring of American Religion*. Princeton, NJ: Princeton University Press.

Wuthnow, Robert and Witten, Marsha. 1988. New directions in the study of culture. *Annual Review of Sociology* 14: 49–67.

Part I

Vocabularies of Conviction:
The Symbolic Construction
of Religious and Scientific Discourse

1

The restriction of meaning in religious discourse: centripetal devices in a fundamentalist Christian sermon

Marsha Witten

Sociologists of religion are criticizing meaning-centered approaches to culture (for example, symbolic analysis (Bellah 1970; Berger 1969) and thick description (Geertz 1973)) as overly subjective and are calling for more systematic methods for analyzing religious practices, doctrines, and discourse (see, for example, Wuthnow 1987).[1] Instead of attempting to pin down the meaning of worship practices, or of religious talk, for participants – a nearly impossible task because meaning can vary so widely among people, depending on their situations, prior experiences, competence in the communicative code, and so forth – the analyst is urged to discover the conditions that make behaviors meaningful. This can be done by exploring the context and form of the practices and discourse. On the broad environmental level, the conditions of meaningfulness may be sought by examining, for example, the institutional contexts within which people act; on the microscopic level, by studying the internal structure or the practice of discourse itself (Wuthnow 1987).

In this paper, I illustrate how such an examination of the internal formal properties of a text may be a useful tool in the study of religious discourse, by the in-depth analysis of the narratives used in a fundamentalist Christian sermon. My concern here is not with what the sermon means, but with the way in which the structure of the information it presents makes its messages meaningful, delimiting and disambiguating the messages it communicates. In other words, I explore how the text exploits what Northrop Frye (1982) would term its "centripetal tendency": structures of information that turn in on themselves, close meaning down, license or authorize a particular set of messages, discourage plural readings. To do so, I examine features in and among the narratives in the text that create a tight structural coherence, a relatively "airless" textual space, that present the sermon as a hermetic entity, a self-reinforcing utterance. Although this paper is devoted to the analysis of one sermon in depth, the method I display here would seem to offer much promise for the systematic, comparative study of the degree of disambiguation in religious texts in general.[2]

The restriction of meaning

On a Sunday morning in February 1986, in an affluent East coast town, a young minister preached to his congregants at a fundamentalist church on "The Meaning of Life." By all indications, the sermon was not an extraordinary one for clergyman or congregation, in content or in form. As Christian sermons have traditionally done (Brilioth 1965; Owst 1933), it concerned a religious topic, cited Scripture, and offered congregants guidance on spiritual issues; in the fashion of contemporary Protestant preaching (Ahlstrom 1972), it lasted about twenty minutes, was delivered from written notes, and was received uninterruptedly by congregants except for two occasions of laughter in appreciation of a comic statement. In other words, in terms of subject-matter, structure, and performance, the sermon delivered at that church on that day was an appropriate and rightful member of its genre, not obviously uncharacteristic of what a fundamentalist Christian sermon is "supposed" to be.

"The Meaning of Life" will serve as a useful case for identifying centripetal devices operating through the structure of the text. As I mentioned earlier, the rhetorical features that play a centripetal role are those that create a tight textual texture, in which a message may be presented "simply" and "clearly" while at the same time lessening gaps through which heterodox or unlicensed readings can creep. I will focus here on three such mechanisms – coherence, compactness, and redundancy of communicative structures – that are enabled by the prevalence of narratives in the sermon. After describing the overall structure of the text, I discuss these centripetal mechanisms in depth and demonstrate how they operate within and among the narratives in the first sections of the text.

Text as data: "The Meaning of Life"

The text analyzed here was transcribed from a tape of the worship service at a small fundamentalist church in a New Jersey town on February 6, 1986.[3] Before proceeding to the analysis, a brief description of the first sections of the sermon will be helpful. (A summary of this description appears below as Table 1.1.) The sermon begins with a short question series that inquires in general about the purpose of life. These queries are followed by a series of specific questions about how life should be conducted and problems managed (ranging from concerns about how to handle death to how to be successful in one's career) that are said to represent "top questions of life by a national survey" (paragraph 1). The opening segment is bounded from subsequent text as the speaker reiterates the general questions about the meaning of life that were posed at the sermon's start (paragraph 2).

The next paragraphs of the sermon (paragraphs 3–7) consist of a set of narratives[4] containing stories and examples[5] in which questing characters – including the speaker – fail to obtain sought-after answers in a variety of secular contexts. The first narrative describes the confused life of a friend – a financial planner – whom the speaker has counseled; even though he has a successful career, the financial planner fails to understand the "real answers." In the second, the speaker recounts how he and his wife became lost while en route by car to a hotel in downtown Boston and could not find their way, even after phoning hotel staff for directions. This narrative passes immediately into the third, in which two unnamed characters pull out a road map, and instead of choosing a destination, drive at random. Again with no transition, the fourth narrative is presented, in which a campus minister presses a college student to define his ultimate goal in life. Shown through Socratic questioning that his answers are absurd, the student finally flees the scene. The question, "So if we're facing real life, what are the real answers?", closes the first quarter of the sermon and provides a transition to the second section.

Paragraphs 8–16 supply a second series of narratives which demonstrate how characters who have attempted to find the answers to life through action in both secular and religious contexts have met tragic ends. Each narrative follows immediately on the heels of the one before it with no transitions. The fifth narrative describes the explosion of the space shuttle *Challenger* as the outcome to "our quest in technology." The sixth recounts the suicide of the Roman philosopher Seneca, whose quest for and achievement of knowledge resulted only in immorality and violence. The seventh narrative tells the tale of the Roman emperor Nero's meaningless and cowardly life, based on a quest for power. The eighth and ninth narratives debunk the putative stability of both marriage and secular success (the illustration given for the latter is the life and end of Marilyn Monroe). In the tenth, a comic strip character tells an ironic tale of his struggle for success that turned out to be utterly misplaced. This is immediately followed by the eleventh, in which the role of traditions in making sense out of life is assailed. The series ends with the twelfth narrative, a story about the people who were part of the People's Temple, "the Jim Jones group"; their quest for answers through religion is shown to have turned out meaninglessly. A transition to the third section of the sermon is again provided by a short question series: "So where's the answer? Where's the answer to life?"

The third quarter of the sermon (paragraphs 17–24) begins with the sermon's climax or turning point as a thirteenth narrative is told whose story supplies the answer to life. The speaker describes how he one day found the words "Jesus is the answer" inscribed on a billboard on the highway. "That," the speaker comments, is "where the answer lies. It's in a person. It's in a relationship with a person. And the person is Jesus."

The last few paragraphs have described the general organization and contents of the sections of "The Meaning of Life" to be discussed here. How may we now begin to search for and analyze centripetal devices in the text? I suggested earlier that the mechanisms of coherence, compactness, and redundancy of structures, operating through narratives, are important means through which meaning is closed down. There are three separate, but related, levels on which narrative may close down meaning: on the level of the individual story or example embedded in a larger narrative structure; on the level of the relationship among stories and examples or among the narrative discourse that embeds them; and on the level of the relationship between the story or example and the surrounding narrative discourse.

I turn first to an analysis of the ways in which an individual story or example itself, taken in isolation, can aid the suppression of interpretive alternatives by virtue of its form. The story form, I argue, gives discourse the possibility of radical compactness while at the same time maintaining a high degree of coherence; both qualities are important in interpretive closure. The examination of one particular story text, representative of others in the series in which it appears, will serve as a useful illustration.

The function of stories in meaning–reduction

The "Seneca" story, which appears in the second quarter of the sermon text, is recounted in full below. (I have numbered the sentences for ease of reference.)

Narrative 6: The "Seneca" story

(1) Maybe it's knowledge [that is the answer to the question of life]. (2) Maybe that why we go to college is because we need more answers. (3) We go to seminars in our jobs all the time to gain more knowledge because that's going to fulfill life. (4) Seneca, a great philosopher and scholar, believed that. (5) He believed that if you

gained enough knowledge that all the immoral things of life would go away, that peace would be attained on earth, that fulfillment would be found. (6) And he quested for knowledge and he gained knowledge and he found that his life became more immoral, that there became more violence, and he ended up committing suicide because he didn't have any answers. (7) Because knowledge does not contain answers to the real life questions.

The "Seneca" story is one of the tales recounted in the sermon about the failure of characters in the secular world to find answers to their quest for meaning. The story proper, in sentences 4–6, comprises the narrative content embedded within the wider narrative discourse; in addition to the story, this discourse includes a narrative frame – the story's "set-up," which here consists of sentences 1–3, and a commentary, an interpretation by the narrator of the story content (Genette 1980) (here consisting of sentence 7). The relationship between narrative discourse and story will concern me in a subsequent section of the paper; for now, I wish to explore the structure of the "Seneca" story itself, that is, sentences 4–6 of the text presented above. Here, I address two features of the story form that can help effect interpretive closure: compactness and coherence.

The story form allows a "story-world" to be created in a highly compact manner. Through the device of compactness, interpretive closure is enabled by lessening the possibility of digressive gaps through which alternative readings could enter. The empirical and logical standards of evidence and proof applicable to other forms of talk – such as exposition or argument – that make implicit or explicit claims to "truth" are suspended in the case of stories, for which literal correspondence to "the real world" is not the issue (Searle 1979). The stories in this sermon, of which the "Seneca" story is representative (see Table 1.2 below), exploit this capacity of stories to build worlds in compact and non-digressive ways. The entire saga of the Stoic philosopher Seneca's lifelong pursuit of truth is encapsulated here in three brief sentences (72 words). There is only one character in this tale: the Roman, Seneca. The complexity of his character is reduced to two closely related attributes that are explicitly stated, that of scholar and philosopher. Both his goal and his action – a desire and search for knowledge to supply the meaning of life – are redundant with these attributes, since these actions are normally those of a philosopher. We have learned nothing new here (the use of redundancy as a reductive device is explained in detail in the next section). Further, the action elements of the plot – Seneca's search for knowledge – and the outcome of his search – the worsening of conditions and his suicide – are narrated in sentences whose very syntax supplies a momentum toward closure. The few details of the quest we are given are sped through in short, linked clauses in order that the outcome – Seneca's suicide – be related as quickly as possible. Another possible story element, that of setting, is not mentioned. It is difficult to imagine a more economical way in which the story could be articulated; both in terms of its reduced plot and characterization, the story is almost completely non-digressive. The character and his actions lead simply and without narrative complexity to the story's outcome (and to its interpretation by the narrator; I discuss this point in a subsequent section).

A description of the story elements of the other six stories in the first half of the sermon text appears in Table 1.2. The story elements of these tend to be as constricted in their construction as the "Seneca" story. Only two of them assign explicit attributes to characters, and they are not only quite limited but also redundant with plot or character (for example, members of the People's Temple, in narrative 12, are "steeped in religion"). Only one narrative explicitly mentions a setting: in the second story, the minister becomes lost in downtown Boston. Other stories lack explicit placement in time or space. Finally, in terms of the momentum of plot structures toward closure, in four of the six stories the outcome of the action is not even given a separate sentence, but rather is narrated in a short clause tacked on to the final plot sentence.

A second centripetal quality enabled by the story form is coherence. Stories are complete and "competent," in the face of their omission of the kinds of evidential support necessary in other forms of talk, because of the coherence that stories normatively present: linkages among story elements such as characters, actions, and outcomes. Textual coherence may be measured by the text's degree of connectedness among words of sentences or paragraphs, or, in other words, the extent to which elements in the text "stick together," rely on one another for their meaning, create an "airless" textual structure. Like compactness, coherence helps to create unity out of textual elements and to discourage alternative readings.

Textual items may be linked to one another through either lexical or grammatical connections.[6] Lexical linkages occur when synonyms, word repetitions, or collocations (words related either by membership in the same class or through opposition) are used.[7] Grammatical connections occur when personal or demonstrative pronouns are used to refer textual items to previously used nouns (for example, "Joe" – "he"; "Joe" – "that boy"); when comparative references are made (for example, "it was even more violent"); when conjunctions are used to show additive, contrastive, or causal relationships (for example, "in addition"; "however"; "if . . . then"); and when ellipsis occurs (ellipsis is the omission of a previously articulated utterance, which the text then presupposes, for example, "Do you have a pencil?" "No, but John does [have a pencil].").[8] To use this scheme in order to measure the relative degree of connectedness in texts, one takes a ratio of the number of actually linked items to the number of possibly linked items in the text. Possibly linked items are those textual items that might satisfy conditions for lexical or grammatical connectedness. In the former case, they are "substantively important" parts of speech; in the latter case, they are personal or demonstrative pronouns, or comparatives, or conjunctions, or seem to indicate ellipsis. Whether they actually are links depends on the way in which they function in the text.

Fifty-three possibly linked items were located in the "Seneca" story. The text was then coded for the presence of actual links; 41 were found, making the text 77 percent connected (see Appendices 1 and 2 for the coded text and explanation of the procedure). While it is expected that stories will tend to be more connected than other forms of talk, 77 percent is high. To give a comparison, a story selected from a sermon delivered at about the same time at a liberal Protestant church, similar in length, is 60 percent connected; Jesus' parable of the Lost Sheep in Luke 15: 4–7 (New International Version), also similar in length to the "Seneca" story, is 63 percent connected; a version of Acts 3: 1–10 in a child's Methodist Sunday school text, which one would expect to be highly connected because it has been rendered to suit elementary school students' limited vocabulary and syntax, is also 63 percent connected (United Methodist Church 1984). Now it may be that shorter stories tend to be more connected than longer ones; digressions might be more likely to creep in given the longer duration of text. To test this possibility, the story embedded in narrative 2 in the sermon text (the "Lost in Boston" story), consisting of 210 words, was searched and coded. Out of 146 possible links, 107 were located, making the story 73 percent connected.[9]

In this section, I have discussed some of the uses of the story form in aiding in the creation of interpretive closure. But if, as we have seen, a single story can create a compact, coherent, and meaning-restricted story world, the effect is heightened by the redundancy of story forms. I turn to this topic in the next section.

Redundancy of stories and narratives that embed them

Insofar as a text is redundant, it places limits on the amount of total information it communicates, thus heightening its interpretive predictability; redundancy constitutes a "surplus of communication" regarding the same information, augmenting the probability that its message will be transmitted unambiguously (Suleiman 1983: 55). The goal of redundant communication is thus to reduce interpretive "space" – the possibility of gaps appearing in the text that might enable a plural reading. Redundancy is a quality of every communication; some redundancies are built into, obligatory within, the linguistic structure of particular tongues; others occur as part of a language's semantic constraints.[10] However, I am in search of something else: those structural redundancies which are not a property of the conventions of particular languages, but which a text presents as a matter of style or rhetoric: as a matter of choice and for particular effects. It follows from what I have said above that I view these structural redundancies as devices for the reduction of meaning, for closing up gaps that would make ambiguity likely.

The literary critic Susan Suleiman (1983), following Greimas (1966) and Genette (1980), has devised a typology of redundancies based on structural story and narrative elements that can occur in the realist novel; with some omissions and additions, this list is quite useful for my purposes in looking for redundancies among stories or examples and the narratives embedding them. Let us first turn to possible redundancies among elements on the level of the story:

(1)   Several characters have the same qualities (or a single character displays the same qualities throughout the story).
(2)   Goals of several characters' actions are the same (or a single character displays the same goals throughout the story).
(3)   Actions of several characters are the same (or single character displays same actions throughout etc.).
(4)   Means of actions of several characters are the same.
(5)   Outcomes of several characters' actions are the same.
(6)   The context is metonymically redundant with the character.
(7)   Several characters pronounce the same interpretive commentary (or a single character repeatedly does so).
(8)   An event is redundant with the interpretive commentary made by a character concerning it.

To see how many of these possible redundancies are displayed in the stories and examples of the sermon text, and how frequently they occur, an analysis was done of the possible elements in each text. Table 1.3 displays the results for stories and examples in the first quarter of the sermon text.

Redundancy types 1, 2, 3, 4, and 5 are present for each story or example, while 6, 7, and 8 are absent for all: these three latter items are missing not because the stories differ with respect to these elements, but because only one story even includes a context, and no characters within stories pronounce interpretive commentaries. (In this sense, the stories or examples are alike with respect even to the missing elements.)

We turn first to redundancies concerning characters' qualities. Each story or example presents two characters, one of whom is in the structural position of being "lost" *vis-à-vis* the other character. The financial planner obtains advice from the minister about his failing marriage and disturbed children in narrative 1; the minister himself is lost in the labyrinthine roadways of downtown Boston, and seeks directions from a hotel receptionist, in the second story; unnamed speaker 1, in narrative 3, neither knows nor cares about a destination for a car trip in his conversation with unnamed speaker 2; and the hapless student, in the fourth story, can only render a series of tentative answers which are rejected by the persistently inquiring campus minister. On the other hand, in each story, one of the characters is positioned as reasonably "settled": in the first narrative, the minister counsels the financial planner; in the second, the receptionist, sitting behind her desk in a Boston hotel, tells the minister that he "can't get there" from where he is; in the third narrative, unnamed speaker 2, while not suggesting a destination for their trip, at least desires to have one before setting off; and in the fourth narrative, the campus minister, the interrogator, is hoping to educe an overarching answer from the literal-minded student. Thus in all four narratives in this section of the sermon, there is redundancy on the level of qualities of character.

But there is a texture to this redundancy that goes beyond mere overlap. The two secular characters who are "settled" (the receptionist of the second narrative and the unnamed character of narrative 3) are given qualities that are similar to each other and dissimilar from the two ministers (characters who are "settled"in narratives 1 and 4). The secular characters do not actually know the answers to the questions that are being raised, while the minister-characters who are positioned as "settled" do know the answers (the minister in the first narrative is a counselor; the campus minister in the fourth narrative is using the Socratic method to show the student that his goals are mis-stated). Structural redundancy in this case is used to valorize particular characters in terms of their qualities: certain characters know the right answers. We will see in a subsequent section how these qualities are juxtaposed with those of characters in narratives in the second quarter of the sermon, who are positioned as failing in their quests for the answers to life.

As Table 1.3 shows, the stories in this section are also redundant on the level of characters' goals (again characters are divided between those who have the answers and those who don't), their actions (to ask and listen, or to answer), and means by which their actions take place. In every case, the content of the story concerns talk, a dialogue, either implicit, as in the case of narrative 1 (as the means through which counseling is conducted), or explicit, as in the other three. And in every case, the outcome of the dialogue is failure: the financial planner in the first story is left "not knowing the real answers"; the minister's attempt to get good directions from the receptionist is futile; the couple driving aimlessly can't reach a decision about a destination; and the college student must leave the scene in order to escape the probing of the campus minister. The story structures are completely parallel in the elements of goals, actions, means of action, and outcomes; the redundancy closes down alternative readings of the debunking of talk, of dialogue, as a means to finding the answer to life.

Table 1.4 shows a similar analysis of stories and examples in the second quarter of the sermon text. Each story is peopled by a single character or group, whose qualities in all cases but one (narrative 9) are limited to the desire for some resource that may hold the answer to life; redundant structures of action in the world for the purpose of gaining this resource (conducting scientific experiments, questing for knowledge, striving for power, adhering to "false" religions) end in equally redundant structures of failure (the space shuttle exploding, the suicide of Seneca, the city of Rome burning down, the "meaningless" lives of the People's Temple members). In their repeated positioning of characters as meeting a violent or tragic end, these stories and examples debunk the efficacy of action as a means to the answer to life. With dialogue and action equally and emphatically removed as sources of "the answer," the twelve stories and examples in the first half of the sermon lead plausibly to the narrative "turning point": the thirteenth narrative in which the minister tells of finding the answer to life – "Jesus is the answer" – inscribed on a highway billboard. No dialogue; no action; just a monologic statement, a declaration, that has gained authority by the structure of the stories in the narratives preceding it.

Structural redundancies can also occur on the level of narrative discourse, that is, the narrator's telling of or commentary on the story content. This can include any "interference" with the story itself: indicating his feelings about the story, interpreting events, signalling the internal organization of the story, etc. (Suleiman 1983: 57). Let us look, therefore, for redundancies on the level of narrative discourse in the narrator's pronouncement or commentary about a character, event, or context.

Table 1.5 shows the analysis of elements of the narrator's interpretive commentary for narratives in the first two quarters of the sermon text. The most salient feature of the table is that all narratives but one do contain an explicit commentary, that is, the narrator's voice is markedly present as an authoritative commentator on the stories that are told. In terms of the sentence structure of interpretive statements, three sets of redundant structures can be seen: narratives 5–8, clustered in the middle of the narrative series, contain interpretive statements in the form of a dependent clause (for example, narrative 5: "'Cause there isn't an answer there".); the first and last narratives (1 and 12) contain dependent statements in complex sentences (for example, narrative 12: "And these people found that religion really had no answers, as they found it".); and narratives 2 and 7 contain complex sentences with conditional statements (for example, narrative 2: "It doesn't do any good to have a roadmap, it doesn't do any good to have directions, if you don't know where you're going".).

But given the limited number of syntactic structures available in English, perhaps we should not make much of observing syntactic overlaps in commentaries among twelve narratives. Nor perhaps should it surprise us much that all narrative commentaries occupy the last position or sets of positions in the narratives, literally giving the narrator the final word; commentaries usually follow the material upon which they are commenting. The more important redundancy occurs among the commentaries' lexical formulations: every single one contains a declarative statement or group of statements that comments negatively on the action or outcome of the story, creating a parallel structure. The function of these interpretive commentaries when seen in relationship to the narratives' embedded stories and examples is discussed in the next section.

Redundancies between the story
and the narrative discourse

Finally, I turn to an examination of redundancies bridging story and narrative discourse, that is, structural parallels between the story content and the narrator's interpretive commentary. Redundancies on this level are particularly potent in aiding centripetal tendencies in text because of the nature of the communicative relationship between story and interpretation. In narrative commentary, the speaker of the story embedded in the narrative discourse steps outside the "story-world" he has just created to remark on the message he has communicated within it. This is the meta-communicative level of discourse, that is, "talk about talk," the level on which the speaker indicates "how to take" the message that has just been communicated in the story: how it should be interpreted. Narrative commentary can create tension between its utterances and those on the level of the story, negating or problematizing the story's message, by commenting ironically upon it, expressing caveats about its "veracity," or flatly denying its plausibility. Alternatively, it can take a neutral stance toward the story, merely asserting that it has "reported" it. Or it can affirm the story's content, asserting that it should be taken "seriously," bolstering its message through repetition, parallelism, and structural redundancy.

Table 1.6 shows elements of the relationship between the level of story or example and that of narrative interpretation in the first two quarters of the sermon text (I have also included narrative 13, the account of the minister finding the answer on a billboard, for contrast).

In every case in which there is a commentary, that is, in all narratives except for the tenth, the interpretation is redundant with the outcome. For the first twelve narratives (omitting the tenth), this means that the speaker's interpretation (shown in summary on this table) affirms the futility of dialogue or of action that has been indicated by the outcome of the story. In the thirteenth narrative, the outcome of the minister's reception of the answer to life from an inscription on a signboard – the only positive action yet recounted in a story – is reiterated, reinforced, by his own interpretive commentary that affirms, positively, that "that is where the answer lies. It's in a person. It's in a relationship with a person. And that person is Jesus." By means of the qualities of compactness and coherence of the narrative form, and by multiple layers of redundancy in narrative structures, "Jesus is the answer" has been confirmed on the three levels of narrative communication –

that of the level of the story, the level of narrative discourse, and the level of the relationship between the two – as the single, "correct," authorized answer to the problems of life.

Conclusion

This paper demonstrates a method for the formal, internal analysis of the conditions of meaningfulnness of a religious text. I have illustrated the method through a close study of a fundamentalist Christian sermon. The analysis indicates in particular how the patterns within and among the narratives embedded in the text function centripetally, that is, aid in the achievement of interpretive closure. Key centripetal elements, I have argued, are qualities of coherence and compactness, and redundancies of story and narrative structure. In isolating these features and demonstrating how they may work, this paper suggests several directions for future research in religious discourse. First, it makes it possible to conduct systematic comparisons of the degree of meaning-restriction in sermons or other authoritative religious utterances, and the types of discursive devices used to close down meaning, among churches of different religions and denominations, and differing with respect to economic resources, gender, class and race of membership and of the preacher, and theological positions (along a continuum of liberal to conservative theologies). For example, one might hypothesize that sermons preached by women would be more disambiguated, regardless of denomination, than those preached by men; as relative newcomers to the ministerial role, female ministers may rely more than male preachers on interpretive closure of sermons to help establish their authority. On a somewhat subtler issue, one might study the link between theological position and the variety of the discursive repertoires used to disambiguate meaning. One intriguing, and somewhat paradoxical, feature of the fundamentalist sermon analyzed in this paper is the complexity of the discursive devices it uses in order to communicate simplicity. In the sermons of other religious groups, on the other hand, centripetal devices may be largely limited to redundancies based on simple lexical repetition. Findings of these studies could be suggestive for further work on the social structural characteristics of groups and the relative complexity of their language use; we might find, for example, that communicative codes that are "restricted" in the sense of being highly disambiguated nevertheless are stylistically quite elaborate.

Appendix 1

Potentially linked items in the "Seneca" story and the conditions for their linkage:

(1) Seneca, a (2) great (3) philosopher (4) and (5) scholar, (6) believed (7) that. (8) He (9) believed that (10) if (11) you (12) gained (13) enough (14) knowledge that all (15) the (16) immoral things of (17) life (18) *would go away* (19) [possible ellipsis], that (20) peace (21) *would be attained* on (22) earth, (23) [possible ellipsis], that (24) fulfillment (25) *would be found*. (26) And (27) he (28) quested for (29) knowledge, (30) and (31) he (32) gained (33) knowledge (34) and (35) he (36) found that (37) his (38) life (39) became (40) more (41) immoral, (42) [possible ellipsis] that there (43) became (44) more (45) violence, (46) and (47) he (48) ended up (49) *committing suicide* (50) because (51) he (52) *did[n't] have* (53) answers.

(Italicized phrases – auxiliary verbs and their main verbs, and the two lexical items in the expression "committing suicide" – are treated as one unit.)

Items potentially linked to others by *lexical tie* with another texual item:

(1, (2), (3), (5), (6), (9), (12), (14), (16), (17), (18), (20), (21), (22), (24), (25), (28), (29), (32), (33), (36), (38), (39), (41), (43), (45), (46), (49), (52), (53).

Items potentially linked to others by *comparative reference* to another item:

(13), (40), (44).

Items potentially linked to others by *pronoun reference* to another item:

(8), (11), (27), (31), (35), (37), (47), (51).

Items potentially linked to others by *demonstrative reference* to another item:

(7), (15).

Items potentially linked to others by *conjunctive tie* with another item:

(4), (10), (26), (30), (34), (46), (50).

Items potentially linked to others by *ellipsis* of another item or items:

(19), (23), (42).

Appendix 2

Actually linked items and their ties:

(1) Seneca, a (2) great (3) philosopher (4) and (5) scholar, (6) believed (7) that. (8) He (9) believed that (10) if (11) you (12) gained (13) enough (14) knowledge that all (15) the (16) immoral things of (17) life (18) *would go away,* (19) [possible ellipsis], that (20) peace (21) *would be attained* on (22) earth, (23) [possible ellipsis], that (24) fulfillment (25) *would be found.* (26) And (27) he (28) quested for (29) knowledge, (30) and (31) he (32) gained (33) knowledge (34) and (35) he (36) found that (37) his (38) life (39) became (40) more (41) immoral, (42) [possible ellipsis] that there (43) became (44) more (45) violence, (46) and (47) he (48) ended up (49) *committing suicide* (50) because (51) he (52) *did[n't] have* (53) answers.

(Only one link is shown per item, even though some items may be linked to more than one other word (for example, (5) scholar is linked both to (3) philosopher and to (1) Seneca).)

Items linked to others though *lexical ties*:

(3)–(1); (5)–(1); (9)–(6); (14)–(5); (20)–(3); (21)–(12); (22)–(17); (24)–(12); (25)–(12); (28)–(12); (29)–(14); (32)–(12); (33)–(29); (36)–(25); (38)–(17); (41)–(16); (43)–(39); (45)–(20); (46)–(24); (49)–(45); (52)–(21); (53)–(28).

Items linked to others through *pronoun reference*:

(8)–(1); (27)–(1); (31)–(1); (35)–(1); (37)–(1); (47)–(1); (51)–(1).

Items linked to others through *demonstrative reference*:

(7)–(story frame: lines 1–3 of "Seneca" narrative).

Items linked to others through *conjunctive ties*:

(10)–("that" after item 14, which functions as "then", supplying rest of conditional statement); (26)–(prior sentence); (30)–(prior clause); (34)–(prior clause); (46)–(prior clause); (50)–(prior clause).

Items linked to others through *comparative reference*:

(40)–(10); (44)–(20).

Items linked to others through *ellipsis*:

(19, omission of "he believed that if you gained enough knowledge")–(clause formed by 8–14); (23, omission of "he believed that if you gained enough knowledge"–(clause formed by 8–14); (42, omission of "he found that"–(clause formed by 35–36 and "that").

Notes

1. Thanks go to Robert Wuthnow, Wendy Griswold, Michèle Lamont, Joan Morris, Charles Slater, and Larry Wu for their helpful criticism. An earlier version of this chapter was presented at the 1988 meeting of the International Communication Association in New Orleans, La.
2. I am currently working on a comparative analysis of contemporary American liberal and conservative sermons for centripetal aspects of text.
3. Since some of the analysis to follow depends on the structure of sentences, it is important to note that punctuation was added to the transcript based on delivery. Periods are used to indicate full stops (these are clearly audible on the tape as falling intonations), commas to show pauses, colons to indicate introduction of explanations or summaries, question marks for queries (marked by question words and rising intonation), and quotation marks to show direct quotations (marked by preceding indicators such as "he said", by placement in sections of text with previously defined speakers, or by biblical citations). The transcribed version of the sermon contains 3,692 words and 583 marks of punctuation. Paragraphing was added to the transcribed text following standard written English conventions of separating utterances when topic shifts occur; this was done for ease of reading and reference, but bears no role in the analysis.
4. A narrative is a discursive form that contains a story or an example (Genette 1980). It often also contains a frame – the story's "set-up," and a commentary – an interpretation by the narrator of the narrative content.
5. A story is a discursive form in which events are presented that follow upon each other logically and chronologically, and that are experienced or accomplished by characters in a context. An example is a discursive form in which an illustration, comparison, or analogy is presented that, while usually involving characters, may lack contexts or clearly stated sequences of events (Suleiman 1983).
6. This discussion of connectedness draws upon the discussion of cohesion in Halliday and Hasan (1976). Connectedness is related to, but is more inclusive than, their notion of cohesion. Cohesion is an idea centered in the reader. That is, it deals with relationships within texts that allow the reader to interpret some elements of text by virtue of other elements of the text: cohesive devices supply the reader with the ability to decode certain items through recourse to other items that are presupposed. By definition, cohesion occurs only between, and not within, sentences. The term connectedness is used to refer to a larger set of textual relationships. It is centered in the text, not in the (hypothetical) reader, so that it includes any lexical or grammatical linkage (with the exception discussed in note 7 below). For this reason, it includes relationships within, not just between, sentences.
7. Although theoretically one could count as a lexical linkage two usages of any word – such as the indefinite article ("a") or a preposition (e.g. "on"), to do so would run the risk of trivializing the measure. Instead, I have counted as links only those repetitions, synonyms, collocations, etc. among "substantively important" semantic or grammatical categories ("parts of speech"): in the terms of traditional grammar, nouns, adjectives, "important" adverbs, and verbs.
8. Definitions of all of these categories are given in Halliday and Hasan (1976).
9. Details of the coding of these texts are available from the author.
10. As an example of an obligatory redundancy, third-person subjects and their verbs agree in number in the present tense verb system of English; the singular unmarked noun ending and its marked verb ending ("the boy walks") are in this

33

sense redundant. As an example of a redundancy based on semantic constraints, adjectives are partially redundant with the substantives they modify, since the relationship of modification can exist only if the two elements share some qualities.

References

Ahlstrom, Sydney. 1972. *A Religious History of the American People*. New Haven, Conn.: Yale University Press.

Bellah, Robert. 1970. *Beyond Belief.* New York: Harper & Row.

Berger, Peter. 1969. *The Sacred Canopy*. Garden City, NY: Doubleday.

Brilioth, Yngve. 1965. *A Brief History of Preaching*. Philadelphia, Penn.: Fortress Press.

Frye, Northrop. 1982. *The Great Code*. San Diego, Calif.: Harcourt, Brace, Jovanovich.

Geertz, Clifford. 1973. *The Interpretation of Cultures*. New York: Basic Books.

Genette, Gerard. 1980. *Narrative Discourse*. Ithaca, NY: Cornell University Press.

Greimas, A. J. 1966. *Semantique Structurale*. Paris: Larousse.

Halliday, M. A. K. and Hasan, Ruqaiya. 1976. *Cohesion in English*. London: Longmans.

Owst, G. R. 1933. *Literature and Pulpit in Medieval England*. Cambridge: Cambridge University Press.

Searle, John. 1979. *Expression and Meaning*. Cambridge: Cambridge University Press.

Suleiman, Susan, 1983. *Authoritarian Fictions*. New York: Columbia University Press.

United Methodist Church. 1985. *Elementary B Student Book, Children's Bible Studies*. Nashville, Tenn.: Graded Press.

Wuthnow, Robert. 1987. *Meaning and the Moral Order*. Berkeley, Calif.: University of California Press.

TABLE 1.1
Structure of sermon text

Section	Paragraph	Text type	Narrative type	Theme
1st quarter	1–2	Question series		What's the meaning of life?
	3	Narrative 1	Example	Businessman in trouble
	4	Transition		
	5	Narrative 2	Story	Minister lost in Boston
	6	Narrative 3	Example	Couple drives aimlessly
	7	Narrative 4	Story	Campus minister fruitlessly questions student
2nd quarter	8	Narrative 5	Story	We seek answers in science
	9	Narrative 6	Story	Seneca looks for knowledge
	10	Narrative 7	Story	Nero seeks power
	11	Narrative 8	Example	We seek fulfillment in relationships
	12	Narrative 9	Example	Marilyn Monroe as icon of success
	13	Narrative 10	Story	Comic strip man tells ironic tale
	14	Narrative 11	Example	We seek fulfillment in traditions
	15	Narrative 12	Story	People's Temple members look for answers in religion
	16	Transition		
3rd quarter	17	Narrative 13	Story	Jesus is the answer

TABLE 1.2
Compactness of story elements, first half of sermon text

Narrative	Characters	Attributes	Setting	Separate outcome sentence
2	Minister Receptionist	None	Boston	No
4	Campus minister Student	None	None	Yes
5	Space shuttle	None	None	Yes
6	Seneca	Philosopher Scholar	None	No
7	Nero	Cowardly	None	No
10	Comic strip man	None	None	No
12	Jim Jones people	Steeped in religion	None	No

TABLE 1.3
Story or example elements, first quarter of sermon text

| | | Redundancy type: | | | | |
		(1)	(2)	(3)	(4)	(5)
Narrative	Characters	Qualities	Goals	Actions	Means of action	Outcomes
1	Minister	Counselor	To give right answers	Counseling	Talk	Dialogic failure (Status quo)
	Businessman	Advisee	To get answers	Asking, listening	Talk	
2	Minister	Lost	To get answers	Asking, listening	Talk	(Getting lost)
	Receptionist	Settled	To say there is no answer	Answering wrongly	Talk	Dialogic failure
3	Speaker 1	Wants to move anywhere	To go anywhere	Answering	Talk	Dialogic failure
	Speaker 2	Wants to know destination	To determine goal	Asking	Talk	(Driving aimlessly)
4	Student	Doesn't know answer	To give any answer	Answering wrongly	Talk	Dialogic failure (Exit)
	Campus minister	Full of questions	To elicit right answer	Asking	Talk	

TABLE 1.4
Story–example elements, second quarter of sermon text

Narrative	Characters	Qualities	Goals	Actions	Means of action	Outcome
5	We	Want solutions	Scientific knowledge	Get into laboratories	Science	Explosion
6	Seneca	Wants fulfillment	Philosophical knowledge	Quested for knowledge	Learning	Suicide
7	Nero	Wants power	Power	Strove for power	Striving	Burned Rome down
8	I, we	Want relationships	Relationship	Marriage (implied)	Marriage (implied)	Divorce
9	Marilyn Monroe	Nothing to live for	Not stated	Not stated	Not stated	Died tragically
10	Comic strip man	Wants success	Success	Climbing ladder	Climbing	Wasted effort
11	We	Want traditions	Comfort	Running, going	Keeping busy	Irrelevance
12	Jim Jones group	Want religion	Love	Sitting in pews	Joining cults	Meaningless lives

TABLE 1.5
Structure of narrative discourse, first half of sermon text

Narrative	Narrator's commentary	Syntax	Position in narrative
1	And I guarantee you that [ ] doesn't know real answers.	Complex	Last
2	It doesn't do any good to have a roadmap, it doesn't do any good to have directions, if you don't know where you're going.	Complex	Last
3	And that's how many of us live our lives. We don't have any idea where we're going. We're just kind of on these little roads. And they deadend and we find another way and kind of drive on that for awhile. We find ourselves never getting anywhere in our lives.	4 Simple 1 Compound	Last
4	And that's how many of us think. We don't have answers to the whys of our lives. We don't know why we're doing the things we're doing.	Simple	Last
5	'Cause there isn't an answer there.	Simple (clause)	Last
6	Because knowledge does not contain answers to the real life questions.	Simple (clause)	Last
7	Because there are no answers in power.	Simple (clause)	Last
8	That there is no fulfillment of all our answers and all our questions in marriage.	Simple (clause)	Last
9	'Cause you can have everything in the world and if you don't have any reason for it, it becomes meaningless.	Complex	Last
10	None	None	None
11	Traditions can try to bring me some answers, but I always find that traditions become irrelevant. At some point, our traditions become irrelevant and we hold on to things that don't make sense anymore.	Compound	Last
12	And these people found that religion really had no answers, as they found it.	Complex	Last

TABLE 1.6
Relationship between stories–examples and interpretation in sermon text

	Narrative Characters	Actions	Outcomes	Interpretation
1	Minister Businessman	Counseling Asking, listening	Dialogic failure (Status quo)	Planners don't have answers
2	Minister Receptionist	Asking, listening Answering wrongly	Dialogic failure (Getting lost)	Nothing helps except knowing where you're going
3	Speaker 1 Speaker 2	Answering Asking	Dialogic failure (Driving aimlessly)	Aimless movement is useless
4	Campus minister Student	Asking Answering wrongly	Dialogic failure (Exit)	We don't know answers
5	We	Get into laboratories	Explosion	Isn't an answer there
6	Seneca	Quested for knowledge	Suicide	Knowledge has no answers
7	Nero	Strove for power	Burned Rome down	No answers in power
8	I, we	Marriage	Divorce	No answers in marriage
9	Marilyn Monroe	Not stated	Died tragically	Success is meaningless
10	Comic strip man	Climbing ladder of success	Wasted effort	None
11	We	Running, going	Aimless busyness	Traditions are irrelevant
12	Jim Jones group	Sitting in pews	Meaningless lives	Religion has no answers
13	Minister Roadsign	Reading Signifying	Reception of the Answer	Jesus is the Answer

2

The gospel of giving:
the narrative construction of
a sacrificial economy

Susan Harding

"Mom cried," Jerry Falwell wrote in his 1987 autobiography, *Strength for the Journey*, "when she heard that 2,500 students and the faculty of our growing college met in the freezing snow on Candler's Mountain in a 'miracle rally' to pray that one day a great Christian university would stand upon that place" (p. 273). A few weeks before the rally, in January 1977, the furnace broke down at Timberlake Middle School, a condemned building where Falwell's "growing college" had been meeting for several years. The furnace could be fixed, but the school was scheduled to be torn down that summer. Falwell would have to move his campusless college again, yet "God seemed to slam every door shut in the effort to provide a temporary campus for Liberty Baptist College. It became clear to Jerry that God was driving him back to a very special mountain" (Strober and Tomczak 1979: 73). Those who braved the winter elements and so moved Falwell's mother that day on Candler's (renamed "Liberty" by Falwell) Mountain were praying specifically for a financial miracle, one that would enable them to build a permanent campus on that special mountain.

> They sang the victory song, "I Want This Mountain," prayed, and claimed Liberty Mountain by faith. They asked God to enable them to eliminate all unsecured indebtedness by February 28, 1977, so that contractors could begin buildings for LBC's 1977–78 academic year. (Strober and Tomczak 1979: 76)

The "unsecured indebtedness" amounted to $2.3 million. By the end of February Thomas Road Baptist Church (TRBC) had received $2.5 million over operating expenses, just what they had prayed for and then some. "It was evidently the miraculous working of God" (Strober and Tomczak 1979: 76).[1]

By fall of 1977 two buildings were completed and others were in progress. Building continued through the year, but not fast enough to suit Falwell or to accommodate the 1,000 entering freshmen who arrived in August 1978. At the college's first chapel service that year, held outdoors for want of space, Falwell delivered another miracle appeal, one that doubled his grasp (asking for $5 million in a little over a month) and cast an exceptionally big biblical mantle on his shoulders. Gerald Strober and Ruth Tomczak quoted the sermon at length in their 1979 authorized biography, *Jerry Falwell: A flame for God*:

Jerry Falwell explained the seriousness of the situation to the thousands of students. "Our world is in trouble today. That is why you are here to train and prepare to minister in a world of more than four billion people who desperately need Jesus Christ. This summer we have experienced the constant threat of postal strikes, which has affected our offerings. The cost of our Clean Up America Campaign has been tremendous, but we could not, nor can we ever, stop proclaiming righteousness in our nation. Thus you see unfinished buildings that you desperately need. We serve a prayer-answering God. We have gathered on this mountain today for a prayer meeting. We desperately need $5 million and have come to ask God to supply that need by September 24, which I have set aside as 'Miracle Day'."

Then Jerry stood in the August sun and preached a message from the Book of Joshua. He described the people of Israel and their situation as they faced the high strong walls of Jericho. The Thomas Road Baptist Church was facing similar obstacles.

"The Jews had come through four hundred years of bondage. God delivered them from the Red Sea by the hand of Moses, and after forty years of wandering in the wilderness, delivered them from the river Jordan by the hand of Joshua. They had come far by faith, but now, having arrived in the Promised Land, they found the walls of Jericho immovable. The inhabitants of Jericho had been reported to Joshua to be 'giants.' Everything seemed lost to the children of God. Defeat seemed imminent."

Jerry drew a parallel: "Liberty Mountain is our Promised Land. For many years we have prayed for this thirty-five hundred acres of sanctified property. After twenty-two years of miracles, we have arrived on Liberty Mountain. But now we find ourselves looking up at the high walls of bills and unfinished buildings. A miracle is needed."

The students listened attentively as their chancellor told how Joshua met the unseen Captain. The Lord assured Joshua of victory and gave him the plan for it. The Jews were told to march around the walls once a day for six days. Then, on the seventh day, they were to march around seven times. The men of war were to march up front. The seven priests with trumpets of rams' horns were to march directly behind them each day, sounding the trumpets all the way. The ark of the covenant would be carried in their midst. The congregation was to follow the ark.

Drawing an analogy between men of war and prayer warriors, Jerry called for thousands of local prayer warriors to "walk point," symbolic of those who go first into battle. He asked millions who were watching by television to do the same. He assured the prayer warriors that, as they circled the walls of impossibility, the preachers at Thomas Road would keep preaching and sounding forth the message of the gospel. He asked Christians of North America to join with him on this trek of faith and pray with them for a miracle.

On each of the six days preceding the September 24 "Miracle Day," Jerry drove along the circumference road of Liberty Mountain, an 11.3 mile trip. He began at the main entrance of the college and prayed continually as he drove. On Sunday, September 24, Jerry rose early and encircled the mountain seven times – 79.1 miles – before the early church service at Thomas Road. The offering that day and from the previous six weeks totaled more than $7 million. $2 million more than what had been prayed for. People stood and wept and praised God who loves to answer the prayers of his people. (pp. 79–81)

Of course, it is impossible to know for certain that Jerry's circling the mountain those mornings, along with the prayer warriors praying, actually moved God to bless the ministry with $7 million. And it would be naive to think that his sermon on the mountain, in and of itself, moved millions who were watching to send in all that money. The sermon was one piece of a much larger campaign that included other sermons, television and radio spots, and direct mail. Moreover, it is a time-honored practice among fund-raisers to manipulate the figures, not necessarily by lying, but, say, by including money promised, or borrowed, or raised by some other means, or at an earlier date, in the total.

We do know two things, however. First, Falwell's ministry raised large amounts of money, surely many millions, on behalf of Liberty Baptist College (LBC) throughout the 1970s, especially during the period 1973–8, when his total ministry income first began to leap forward quite incredibly. The annual intake appears to have increased about five-fold during that five-year period, from approximately $4 to $20 million.[2] Second, a good deal of that money did indeed come from the audiences reached by the LBC fund-raising campaigns. Falwell's appeals, including the Jericho maneuver, yielded money – lots of it. The question is, what, more precisely, was the relationship between those rhetorical campaigns and the money raised?

Immediately, we have a choice. We can look through the language of Falwell's appeals at all the other factors at work, or we can tune into his language and consider its appeal, its constitutive and motivating force, from the point of view of the faithful. By pursuing the latter course I do not mean to suggest that the other factors were irrelevant or inefficacious.

For example, Falwell's appeals most certainly tapped into pre-existing "interests" among his constituents, interests he and his co-pastors had a hand in constituting. He told them things they wanted to hear about Liberty – that hem-lines and hair-lines were carefully monitored there, and that, unlike other colleges, Liberty was a place where students learned to love America and respect authority. At the same time, while Liberty was not of this world, it was in it; it would give its students access to credentialed degrees, better jobs, still higher education. And then, too, Falwell's pitches followed surefire fund-raising formulas. Crisis-talk ("your dollars will make the difference between total disaster and great success") always works better than upbeat-talk ("everything is going fine, send in your two cents today"). Finally, Falwell was most certainly for those who listened to him faithfully a figure of authority; when he said, "send money," they were at least more inclined to obey, rather than ignore or mock or defy, him.

Much more could be said about these and other "factors" behind the success of Falwell's fund-raising appeals. The problem with attending only to them, with not taking seriously what Falwell actually said, is that the world of fundamentalists, the discursive one in which they live, is thereby erased and infilled with purely secular meanings and figures and forces. If we listen instead to Falwell's words as his faithful followers might, gradually it becomes clear that there is more going on than the secular ear can hear. Fund-raising is not just a matter of "pushing the right buttons," or of effectively leading people to believe they are getting something instead of nothing. What looks like fund-raising (or, even, fleecing) to unbelievers is "sacrificial giving" among fundamentalist Baptists. The money raised has more in common with the biblical blood of lambs than it has in common with what gets spent on a shopping spree. In a way the whole point of giving to a God-led ministry is to vacate the commercial economy and to enter another realm, a Christ-centered "gospel," or "sacrificial," economy in which material expectations are transformed. If we attend to what Falwell said, as incredible as it seems, and as tortuous as the path may be, we may, ultimately, glimpse that other realm.

Everything is true

Fundamentalist Baptist interpretation rests on a hermeneutic of faith, absolute faith, not suspicion, and biblical inerrancy is the first and founding rule of the discourse. The Bible is entirely "true" in the ordinary sense of accurately depicting historical events. Biblical stories are "referential," their meanings by and large "literal," that is, somehow obvious, straightforward and commonsense, not allegorical or symbolic. (From a literary critical point of view, there is no such thing as "literal meaning." Meaning emerges from interactions between text and interpreters constrained by conventions, knowledge, contexts, and so forth. But we are investigating a community whose conventions mark certain interpretations and interpretive strategies as "literal," therefore, for our purposes, there is such a thing as "literal meaning.") The rule of inerrancy extends, not explicitly and by no means irrevocably (as in the case of the Bible) to preachers and other "men of God." Specifically, everything Jerry Falwell, or someone authorized to speak for him, says is "true."

On the mountainside, under the August sun, Jerry Falwell recounted to the entering class of 1978, and later to his Old–Time Gospel Hour audience, the story of Joshua and Jericho as history, not legend, or myth, or parable. God parted the waters of the Red Sea for Moses and of the River Jordan for Joshua. The Lord (the "unseen Captain") visited Joshua and gave him a victory plan which he and his warriors and priests carried out to the letter, circling the city once each morning for six days and seven times on the seventh day. Strober and Tomczak did not complete the story in their retelling, nor perhaps did Falwell in his telling, but their audiences knew the walls of Jericho fell down flat when the people shouted and the priests blew the trumpets, and the Israelites took the city and utterly destroyed all that was in it. God kept his promise to Joshua, who had faithfully carried out his plan.

From the beginning, Falwell interlaced Joshua's tale with a second, contemporary, story that reiterated with exquisite precision and updated details the same tests of faith and imagination evoked by the first. "Liberty Mountain is our Promised Land," Falwell told his gathered church. On the brink of conquest, they faced great obstacles, "high walls of bills and unfinished buildings." A miracle was needed. Falwell mimicked the plan that God gave Joshua when he confronted the walls of Jericho. He asked his local and television "prayer warriors" to go into battle and circle the walls of impossibility, praying for a miracle. Falwell drove around the mountain (11.3 miles), praying, each day before "Miracle Day" for six days, and on the seventh day, he compassed it seven times (79.1 miles). And the offering that day and from the previous weeks totaled $7 million. God had once again answered the prayers of his people.

Both these stories are entirely true. Indeed, they are not simply "true stories," they are "storied events." Event and story in fundamentalist discourse have not been torn asunder. Biblical narrators, past and present, are literally historians. They tell histories, the way things actually happened. Their stories do not represent history, they are history. Likewise, the connections that appointed narrators propose between one story, such as Joshua's, and another, such as Jerry's, are not mere filaments of interpretation tying tales together in some folk Imaginary. They are historical tissues, sinews of divine purpose, design, and will that join concrete events across millennia.

Everything is according to purpose

The people gathered on Liberty Mountain in August, those who heard Falwell's sermon broadcast a few weeks later on the Old-Time Gospel Hour (OTGH), and those who read its rendering in Strober and Tomczak's biography, filtered his appeal through an endless mesh of traces and presuppositions: other tellings of Joshua's tale, including the biblical text, and a variety of commentaries on the story; a set of side texts and contexts – other stories and storied situations in Falwell's discursive church which framed and infilled his appeal that sunny afternoon; and a characteristically fundamentalist Baptist set of preconceptions about how juxtaposed stories, their characters, and their outcomes are related as divinely designed events. Here are a few intimations of what those who listened and read might have brought to bear upon Falwell's appeal.

Fundamentalist Baptists read the story of Joshua and Jericho as a tale of God's omniscience and of the victorious life and blessings which await those who are faithful and obedient to God. God told Joshua before the final battle, "I have given into thine hand Jericho." In announcing this certainty before the fact, God, according to the Liberty Bible Commentary, showed himself to be "above time, and that which is yet future for us is present for Him. What was for Joshua yet to happen in the capturing of Jericho, was for God already an accomplished fact" (Falwell, Hindson, and Kroll 1982: 404). Still, the accomplishment of that fact depended on Joshua and Israel's blind obedience:

> God's mysterious methods are not always understandable to us. But God does not ask us to understand them; rather, He asks us to obey them. Israel at the fall of Jericho is a good example of this truth. Although God's methods were mysterious, nevertheless Israel trusted them explicitly . . . followed them exactly . . . employed them enthusiastically . . . continued them expectantly . . . and accomplished them entirely . . . God's work, done in God's way, always has God's blessing. (Falwell, Hindson, and Kroll 1982: 406)

The Old Testament tale of tumbling walls is also simultaneously read as prefiguration ("typification") of Christ's victory and of Christians' victory through Christ (Willmington 1981: 921). Paul told the Corinthians (I Corinthians 6: 11) that the wilderness experiences of the Israelites "happened unto them for examples: and they are written for our admonition" (Habershon 1974: 11). Joshua, specifically, is a "type," or "shadow," of Christ. "The types are but a 'shadow of good things to come and not the very image of the things' [Hebrews 10: 1]; and therefore, like all shadows, they give but an imperfect representation" (Habershon 1974: 22). Also, like a shadow, the relation between it and that which casts it is metonymic: "A type is a sort of a model of the thing it refers to. It has certain characteristics of the real thing" (Harris 1977: 6). The authors of the *Liberty Commentary on the*

New Testament compare a type to the mark or imprint left by an engraving tool. A type is "a copy of the original" and the perfect master original, which came after (yet came before) all the Old Testament figures who anticipated him imperfectly, is Christ. Moses foreshadowed ("typified") Christ as the one who delivered his people from bondage (sin), and Joshua, as the one who gave entrance to the Promised Land (earthly blessings and Heaven itself) (Falwell, Hindson, and Kroll 1977: 659).

As fundamentalist Baptist preachers invariably make plain when they witness to the lost, both the Old and New Testaments foreshadow the persons, events and things in the world in much the same way the Old Testament foreshadows (provides "the very alphabet of the language" to inscribe) the New Testament (Habershon 1974: 11). The similarity in interpretive strategy is, however, usually not stated explicitly. Instead of "foreshadow" and "typify," "fulfill" and "complete," contemporary Bible readers are advised to "apply" the Bible to their daily lives. In his 1978 appeal, Falwell drew "parallels" and pointed out "analogies" between the story of Joshua and his own, financial, Jericho, but, as we shall see, his reasoning, as in other (but by no means all) fundamentalist Baptist applications of the Bible, was as figural as if he were reading the Old Testament through the New. One of the few of Falwell's early sermons that is available shows that Joshua's tale was fully typologized in Falwell's preaching store and capable of other "applications."

Falwell delivered "Ministers and Marchers" at Thomas Road Baptist Church in March 1965, and widely disseminated it in the form of a booklet, so widely that it resurfaced to haunt him after 1979 when he formed the Moral Majority. It is in fact his only publicly extant sermon from the 1960s. In it, Falwell marshalled the fundamentalist Baptist battery of arguments against preachers engaging in politics, and his targets were the preachers, black and white, who led the Civil Rights Movement. After asserting that the proper Christian ministry is one of transformation not reformation, Falwell objected to the pro-civil rights preachers' effort "to prove" Christians should "lead people out of bondage in situations where they are being discriminated against" by "lifting out" of the Bible such instances as Moses leading the Jews out of Egypt. Such an application is not acceptable, because Christians, according to type, have already crossed over the Jordan into the Promised Land.

The 400 years of Egyptian bondage is a type of the sinner's experience before he is converted. We all live in bondage to sin until we know the truth of the new birth. When the Jews came out of Egypt, they immediately came into 40 years of wilderness wandering. This is a parallel of our infant and carnal Christian life as we struggle before learning the lessons of faith and rest in God. If church leaders are going to use Moses and the Jews in Egypt as a justification for what they are doing today with the negro in the South, they should also go on and tell the Jews [blacks?]

that they are going to lead them in 40 years of wandering in which everyone of them will die. That is exactly what happened to all of the Jews. Only Caleb and Joshua lived through that experience. Then, a new generation went into the Promised Land. The Promised Land is a parallel to the victorious Christian life on the earthly level, and our eventual Heaven on the eternal plain. To try to force any other meaning than this is simply making the Bible say what you want it to say. (Falwell 1965: 6)

Because the Falwell early sermon corpus is so thin, it is impossible to know how often he reiterated this application of Joshua's story or how else he applied it, but we may be fairly certain that Falwell's audience listened to his 1978 appeal not only through a knowledge of Joshua as a "type" of Christ, but also as it was framed through multiple "applications" of the story.

The mountain was another type and application tucked between the lines of Falwell's sermon and of Strober and Tomczak's account. The phrases "a very special place" and "thirty-five hundred acres of sanctified property" cued the associations, which had probably been elaborated since Falwell first announced his purchase of the Candler's Mountain land around 1970, and were apparently heavily deployed during the mid-1970s.

In February 1976, a promotion appeared in the church publication *Faith Aflame* entitled "THERE'S SOMETHING ABOUT A MOUNTAIN that makes it hold such an important place in Scripture . . ." The title ran across two pages against an equally expansive backdrop of a mountain with the sun, presumably rising, behind its peak. A side column listed the Scriptural mountains:

- Noah's ark came to rest on a mountain
- Abraham took Isaac to a mountain to be offered as a sacrifice
- God gave the 10 Commandments to Moses on a mountain
- Moses viewed the Promised Land from a mountain
- Elijah challenged the priests of Baal on a mountain
- Jesus gave us the great "sermon on the mount" on a mountain
- Jesus was transfigured on a mountain
- Jesus was crucified on a mountain
- Jesus ascended on a mountain
- Jesus is coming again to a mountain

The text, five columns of it, began:

WHAT GREAT SIGNIFICANCE DOES A MOUNTAIN HAVE TODAY? In 1972 God made available to Liberty Baptist College a beautiful tract of mountain land near Lynchburg which could become our world headquarters if Christians everywhere catch this vision. Since the humble beginning of our ministries in 1956, God has always moved in miraculous ways to bless and expand this work far· beyond our expectations.

The text then identified Jerry Falwell as the man God called to lead his people to his mountain, described "the sacrificial giving of wonderful people from all walks of life" that built this ministry thus far, and revealed the "new vision" – "to 'claim the mountain' in 1976."

Just before it veered off into an unusually intense typological appeal for money, the promotion indulged in some language barely distinguishable from the "health and wealth theology" which Falwell would find himself attacking during the PTL scandal ten years down the road.

> Yes, we want that mountain; we want to claim it for God in 1976 and we're going to ask you to "stake a claim" for the land . . . Be much in prayer for us in this step of faith. Remember, LUKE 6: 38 [Give, and it shall be given unto you . . .] really does work. Stake your claim now. God just might give you a gold mine of blessings – materially and spiritually.

Next Dr Harold Willmington, Dean of Thomas Road Bible Institute, was quoted as pointing out that "we are in a parallel situation to the Jews in the days of Haggai the prophet." God had brought poverty on the Jews then because they provided for themselves "while the house of God was lying on the mountain in waste":

> God commanded them to "GO UP TO THE MOUNTAIN, and bring wood, and build the house; AND I WILL TAKE PLEASURE IN IT, AND I WILL BE GLORIFIED, saith the Lord." This is what God wants on Liberty Mountain today and He promised to bless those who obey his words . . .
>
> These are solemn words by the God of heaven. If Pastor Jerry Falwell and the ministries need a "house of God" that will enable many thousands to worship the Lord together on the mountain, IT MUST BE BUILT . . .
>
> We believe Christians everywhere WILL FOLLOW THIS EXAMPLE: for in chapter 2, verse 9 [of Haggai] we read: "The glory of this latter house shall be greater than the former . . ." Isn't that fantastic? The present progress we have made will seem small compared to what God will do in "His new house" which must be built. For we can expect, as did the people of Haggai's day, that God will bless us. Here's the promise – Haggai 2: 19: ". . . from this day will I bless you." Get in on this blessing! Stake a claim on God's Mountain.

So, two years later, when Jerry Falwell fashioned himself as Joshua on the verge of the Promised Land, the scene was already heavily saturated with mountainous biblical innuendos. Jerry was not only Joshua, but a touch (at least) of Noah, Abraham, Moses, Elijah, Haggai, and Christ himself. His gathered church resembled their gatherings, their peoples. His and his church's trials, persecutions, sacrifices, and triumphs fulfilled theirs. As their prayers were answered, so would his church's be, "for we can expect, as did the people of Haggai's day, that God will bless us."

The valley of the shadow of death

One more rather monumental and still unfolding storied situation informed Falwell's audience that afternoon on the grassy slope, one that had pitched him into the big leagues as a persecuted figure. The $2.3 million "unsecured indebtedness" which Falwell finally absolved himself of in February 1977 was the remnant of the "most traumatic" crisis his ministry had ever faced (D'Souza 1984: 87). In the summer of 1973, the Securities and Exchange Commission (SEC) sued Thomas Road Baptist Church for "fraud and deceit" in the sale of bonds and declared it "insolvent" and unable to redeem the bonds. The church had sold $6.5 million worth of bonds to 1,632 "investors" in 25 states in 1971–3 with an "inaccurate prospectus," and the church's ledgers "had not been kept up to date" (Strober and Tomczak 1979: 54). " Nobody could tell exactly how much had been raised by the church [in 1973] or where the money had come from and where it was going" (D'Souza 1984: 87). The worst accusations were cleared up fairly quickly, however, in August 1973, when a federal judge dropped the "fraud and deceit" charge, cleared TRBC and Falwell of any willful wrongdoing, and placed the church's financial operations under the supervision of five local businessmen until all its "unsecured indebtedness" (totalling $16 million) was eliminated.

Liberty Baptist College was very much implicated in all this trouble. The Candler's Mountain property was a big financial leap for Falwell when he bought it around 1970, committing him to a $1.25 million mortgage (Falwell 1987: 310). Building LBC into an accredited fundamentalist Baptist college, as well as launching a national television and radio ministry, the Old–Time Gospel Hour, were even bigger commitments, and it was they that inspired the bond sale as a quick means of raising millions of dollars. Although LBC figured from the beginning in a panoply of appeals, almost all the money went into building the OTGH network. The idea was that the increased catchment of contributors created by the OTGH would eventually fund the college (Falwell 1987: 312). And it did, but not substantially until 1977 when the last of the $16 million debt was retired.

Later, Falwell could say that the SEC scandal was "an educational period for Thomas Road because 'it forced us to move from a one-horse church to a corporate position' " (D'Souza 1984: 87). His ministry cut overhead costs, hired professional accountants, public relations experts, and an advertising agency to coordinate fund-raising, and they adopted cost-efficient procedures for buying radio and television time (D'Souza 1984: 88). Falwell also considered it a kind of spiritual turning point:

> Looking back, Jerry says this was the church's most crucial period. The SEC crisis was a time not only of testing but also preparation for greater service and accomplishment. The church learned never to fear any opponent . . .
> Jerry comments now [1979], "These ministries have been down through the

valley of the shadow of death. Christ had to bring me to the place where I relinquished control of my total ministry and offered it to Him . . . Financially and legally, we were beaten upon every side. We learned how to call upon God, for He alone is able . . . I can honestly say that . . . valley was the turning point in our ministry. It has been a miracle. Spiritually, it has been a transforming time, for God has taught us how to conquer through prayer. I am so glad there is no problem so big, so overwhelming, but what God is up to the task." (Strober and Tomczak 1979: 58)

The spiritual transformation was also, more evidently, a rhetorical trans-formation. It appears that it was on this journey through "the valley of the shadow of death" that Falwell acquired ever-larger biblical prefigurations, or "shadows."

Falwell's evangelist friend and mentor, B. R. Lakin, was attending a conference when the SEC announced its charges in April 1973. He was driving from Lynchburg to West Virginia when, as he related to Jerry, "God told me to come back here to help you."

Old Dr. Lakin spent the week. There was nothing he could do legally to end our troubles. But he ministered personally to my own tired spirit. He retold the Old Testament stories about ancient clashes between the government and the prophets. He reminded me of the New Testament stand the apostles and first-century Christians had to take against kings, governors, courts, and ruling bodies. He dragged out all his best dramatic accounts of the prophets and the priests, the martyrs and the saints. And he inspired me through the telling. (Falwell 1987: 322)

"Take a fearless stand, Jerry," Lakin said, and Jerry did. Probably not for the first time, but certainly with more conviction than ever, Falwell early on claimed, "the devil is after us," and he cast himself as under siege by "big guns" on the SEC and by a hostile national press. A humble and thoroughly innocent servant of God, broken-hearted and contrite, Jerry interceded ceaselessly for his church. "After hours of prayer, Jerry would rise and smile peacefully, more convinced than ever that God had placed His hand on Thomas Road Baptist Church in a very special way" (Strober and Tomczak 1979: 55).

Over the following years, Falwell clearly took to heart Lakin's examples from the Bible, as we have already seen some evidence of in his college fund-raising pitches. In 1975, Falwell led a seven-month anti-debt road-show with the LBC chorale for his OTGH audience scattered across the country. It further enlarged the image of his self-sacrifice.

Jerry was away from his family for days at a time, [a student on the tour reported] and got very little sleep; yet he never complained . . . Some criticized Jerry in those days for asking for money. But we who knew him knew that he never asked for a dime for himself. He asked for us, for LBC students, who needed a Christian education. (Strober and Tomczak 1979: 65)

Right after one rally, in Seattle, Falwell and a few students reportedly went to an adjacent hall to see the tail-end of a Led Zepplin concert that had earlier disturbed their own meeting (Strober and Tomczak 1979: 66).

> There they witnessed a horrifying scene. Thousands of young men and women were lying on the floor, engaged in every filthy act imaginable. The discordant sounds were deafening. On the stage the rock star hero of thousands of American young people stood with outstretched arms in front of a cross, with psychedelic, florescent lights twirling around him. (Strober and Tomczak 1979: 66)

Jerry "felt in a small measure the tremendous weight of sin that was placed on Jesus Christ at the cross, and his heart ached." He resolved anew to help young Christians "turn this country upside down for Christ" (Strober and Tomczak 1979: 66).

The following year, the nation's bicentennial, Falwell organized another massive tour, this one called "I Love America." They were hugely successful rallies, at once ballooning his audience, reputation, and income. It was in his main sermon on that tour, "America Back to God," that Falwell began to assume the political mantle and voice of the Old Testament prophets.

> What has gone wrong? What has happened to this great republic? We have forsaken the God of our fathers. The prophet Isaiah said that our sins separate us from God. The Bible is replete with stories of nations that forgot God and paid the eternal consequences . . .
>
> Our country needs healing. Will you be one of a consecrated few who will bear the burden for revival and pray, 'O, God, save our nation. O, God, give us a revival. O, God, speak to our leaders?' The destiny of our nation awaits your answer. (Strober and Tomczak 1979: 70–1)

The SEC scandal, in other words, was one means by which God was leading and preparing Jerry Falwell for a political role.

When the SEC barred Falwell from "borrowing money from friends," he felt he had two alternatives: disband the college and the OTGH or ask God for a miracle (Strober and Tomczak 1979: 66). Of course, he asked God for a miracle, and Falwell's side of the bargain, evidently, was to expand his place in biblical rhetoric and narrative immensely – as a man of action, and ultimately of politics, as well as a man of words. The Old–Time Gospel Hour tour became the "I Love America" rallies became the "Clean Up America" campaign became the "America, You're Too Young To Die!" extravaganza became the Moral Majority. In 1987 Falwell wrote that God had used "the entire ugly event" of the SEC suit "to teach us important lessons that we desperately need to learn if we [are] to be ready for the even greater future he [is] planning."

By then Falwell was presenting himself and his followers at some length as Paul and the early church ("facing their own investigation and persecution by the Roman emperor" (Falwell 1987: 333)) and Christ himself ("Jesus, too, had suffered from similar headlines . . . With every triumph there is crucifixion" (Falwell 1987: 315)). What Falwell mastered during the mid-1970s was the biblical language to convert defeat into victory, death into life – and debt into wealth.

> Sometimes it pleases God for us to fail . . . What seems to be defeat at the moment becomes ultimate victory, because in that defeat we learn what we need to know in order to win the whole contest, the ball game, this thing called life. (Falwell 1987: 331)

A sacrifice is due

So there was a lot more happening than met the eye on that mountainside in August 1978 when Jerry Falwell preached from the Book of Joshua. He and his prayer meeting were informed, infilled, like a palimpsest, by other Joshuas, other prophets, other mountains, other Jerichos. All of that which came before, in some measure, prefigured him that afternoon, and his story completed and fulfilled them.

More specifically, Falwell's circling Liberty Mountain in prayer and in his car completed Joshua's victory. God spoke to Jerry through the story of Jericho as plainly as he (the unseen Captain) had spoken to Joshua that night thousands of years before. He gave them each a plan of victory and God's plans never fail, because their outcomes are, from God's vantage, already "an accomplished fact." God always "looks back," he always speaks from the point of view of the end of history, when everything has indeed already happened. Jerry's encompassing was not magical, it did not induce God to act on his ministry's behalf. His circling was submissive, an act of obedience and sacrifice. It was Jerry enacting God's plan for him, Jerry, in that moment of crisis, and "God's work, done in God's way, always had God's blessing." If God told Jerry to build a house of God on Liberty Mountain, "it must be built."

All this translates into money rather elegantly and, under the influence of a master preacher such as Falwell, amply. The pitch, no matter how it is dressed up biblically, sounds to the unborn-again ear like mere fund-raising ("Send us money so we can build a college"). But the biblical attire is everything to the faithful. An appeal for sacrificial giving catches them up in a sacred enactment of core gospel meanings. Just as Joshua obeyed God and was, necessarily, blessed, so was Jerry, and so will they be. They too will complete Joshua's story, not only through prayer but through sacrificial giving. We may be certain that Jerry explicitly asked for money from his television and radio audience after his Joshua exegesis, and even had he not, everyone would have understood that obedience to God in this instance included sending in money.

Faithful Christians (and fundamentalist Baptists are among the most "faithful" in this respect) sacrifice themselves narratively, in their conduct, and financially *to God*. Their gifts of money, like their gifts of words and habits, do not go to any man or ministry, but go directly to God and represent obedience to him. As Ed Dobson, one of Falwell's top co-pastors, explained,

> Giving is worshipping God. We're not giving to a church or person or ministry when we give, but to God. God has a ledger with a debit column and a credit column, and God credits every gift. God does miracles because people give sacrificially.

God, for his part, always blesses those who obey him, and blesses them abundantly.

> The whole of Christianity is giving. One year the Thomas Road Baptist Church adopted as their theme verse Luke 6: 38, "Give, and it shall be given unto you; good measure, pressed down, and shaken together, and running over, shall men give into your bosom. For with the same measure that ye mete withal it shall be measured to you again." As thousands of members gave sacrificially, they learned that God will be no man's debtor. Each found that God gave back to them far more than they had given. (Strober and Tomczak 1979: 51)

Here then are the central terms of gospel economics. Money (like the blood of Old Testament animals or the blood of Christ) is a sacrifice given to God and represents obedience to him. God, in turn, blesses, financially and in other ways, those who obey. Again, the gifts do not induce God to give back; they are not efficacious.[3] Men are not getting God to act for them; God is getting men to act for him. And God blesses those who fulfill his plan. The $7 million in Jerry's coffers on February 28, 1978, had not effectively come from his people but from God, who blessed his ministry because he and his people had done God's work in God's way.

Falwell's empire – virtually all that radiated out from his local church – was built out of these sacrificial rites of offering. The church itself was built on and sustained by tithes, 10 percent of the annual income of members, money which already belonged to God and was not considered a gift. Everything else, the entire contributed income of the OTGH, represented sacrificial giving, and, as Falwell has said, "no one has given sacrificially until he has gone beyond ten percent" (Strober and Tomczak 1979: 151). The $1 million Thomas Road budget in 1970 was mostly made up of tithes. A good deal of the $3.5 to $7 million budget for 1973 probably came from the bond sale. Most of the total revenue for 1977 (about $20 million), on the other hand, came from sacrificial offerings, which fired the ministry's phenomenal growth after 1973. The budget in 1980 was $51 million; in 1987, it was nearly $100 million (FitzGerald 1986: 153; Falwell 1987: 332).

From the beginning, Jerry Falwell curried and lured big financial backers, but, until the late 1980s at least, most of his OTGH income came from "small contributors," people living on earned incomes for whom a gift to Falwell meant a sacrifice materially as well as symbolically. When Falwell asked for $5 million in August 1978, he had a good idea that he would get that much, given receipts from previous months, and because many of his contributors, as members of a variety of "clubs," were committed to giving a fixed sum each month. In the 1970s, these clubs included Faith Partners, Founders, Doorkeepers, the Pastor's Team, Station Sponsors, and members of the "I Love America" Club and Ten Thousand Club. And then there were special appeals – for emergency relief, missionary work, on behalf of patriotism, and against pornography and homosexuality. There were banquets and rallies and tours, and many opportunities for "Christian stewardship," such as a "Christian will," a "life income agreement," a "transfer of life insurance policies to the Lord," or a "living memorial to a departed loved one" (FitzGerald 1986: 152 ff.; *The Old-Time Gospel Hour News* 1971–3).

Money from all these sources was lumped together when Falwell announced the success of a fund-raising appeal, and, indeed, in the ministry's spending practices as well. Most of the money from all appeals, of necessity, fed the machinery that raised the money to begin with. But this kind of boundary blurring does not bother contributors. Sacrificial giving involves a "relinquishing of control" to God, "for He alone is able." It is precisely good not to know exactly where the money goes, so that it goes into a void of sorts, seemingly out of human hands.[4] If a contributor is financially strapped, the gift is so much more the meaningful. It is more of a literal sacrifice and the sense of escape from irksome budgetary constraints is heightened. Fundamentalist Baptists, the middling and wealthy as well as the poor, are customarily tight financial managers, routinely treating themselves to seminars and tapes and manuals that peak their consciousness about the finite flow of money in and out of their hands. Giving sacrificially breaks them out of those cycles, and the sweet release must give them a taste of divine things to come, and at the same time it allies them with God in his concrete miraculous work on earth.

A people gives its church many gifts, of course – sociability, services, creativity, loyalty, prayers, and more – and all of them, insofar as they are free gifts, function, like tithes and sacrificial offerings, "outside" the market economy, according to noncommercial logic. They generate an invisible world, a "kingdom of the spirit," in which God is worshiped continuously through all sorts of sacrificial giving and God blesses people with "good measure, pressed down, and shaken together, and running over." Born-again believers want very much to "get in on this blessing," and for Falwell's electronic church, the only tangible free gift they can give to "get in on" the blessing is money.

That Falwell's empire and its financing have been surrounded by skeptics – a hermeneutic of suspicion – from the beginning is actually part of what makes it all work so well. The outside, worldly, cynical voice says his fund-raising is gimmickry, fleecing, hucksterism, nothing but a con-game, and the only thing that distinguishes it from selling cars or Coca-Cola is that the product is intangible, some would say non-existent. Even among believers, among Falwell's faithful followers, his image as a "man of God" is shadowed by misgivings, and by a secondary image of him as a small-time southern merchant who struck it rich by indulging in dubious, often reckless, occasionally sub-legal, business practices.

As long as Falwell is able to juggle his double image, the tension works for him by creating the grounds for a leap of faith, for it is precisely the transfiguration from the worldly image into the divine that believers effect when they give to his ministry. "God does miracles because people give sacrificially," because they obey God and act on faith, because they step out on a limb for God, and the bigger the limb, the bigger the faith, the bigger the blessing (Falwell and Towns 1984). In the mid-1970s Falwell turned the most skeptical moment his ministry had ever faced, or would ever face to his escalating advantage by harnessing the generative power of his oppositional other, his critical twin, which overnight ballooned from local and state journalists and clergy into the SEC ("the government") and the nation's press corps (later cast as the leading voices of "secular humanism"). And the harness was the figural rhetoric which cast him as a prophet-apostle-martyr-saint, sacrificing himself and speaking for God, and whose people *must* respond with sacrificial gifts according to God's plan.

There is something significantly non-literal about this figural (or typo-logical) rhetoric. Falwell's Jericho in August 1978 was a mountain, not city. Its "high walls" were made of bills and unfinished buildings. His "warriors" "walked point" in their prayers, and, unlike Joshua who led his grand procession on foot, Falwell circled the mountain alone in his car. Falwell might have said he was just updating God's plan, making it relevant to today's world, not changing its true (literal) meaning. Fair enough, but that obscures the wonderful irony of fundamentalist Baptist discourse revealed here. Their own doctrine and daily self-descriptions, as well as their worldly reputation, would cast fundamentalists as rigid interpreters of a closed canon. Falwell's rendering of Joshua and Jericho conformed to this flattening image. But between that story and one next to it, the story of Falwell's Jericho, the canon opened up dramatically. Fundamentalists are still writing the Bible, inscribing it in their lives, endlessly generating a third Testament in their speech and action. Their Bible is alive, its narrative shape enacts reality, infills it with form and meaning. It is, we might say, miraculous, this discourse which effects the world it speaks by constituting subjects who bring it about.

54

Notes

Extracts from *Jerry Falwell: Aflame for God*, by Ruth Tomczak and Gerald Strober are reproduced by permission of Thomas Nelson Publishers, © Jerry Falwell and Gerald Strober.

1. Strober and Tomczak (1979: 76) stated that $2.5 million was raised, and the same figure appeared in a story about LBC in *Faith Aflame* (July–August 1977), a church publication. I consider this figure and many of the other figures on church finances in this essay "soft." In this case, two publications happened to report the same figure, but figures often vary wildly between accounts. Fund-raisers, of course, are generally under pressure to overestimate, and, it seems, some fundamentalists feel special pressure in the name of witnessing for Christ. In a chapel service for college students in the mid-1980s, Jerry Falwell recounted that his old friend and mentor, B. R. Lakin, once advised him to say he was well-fed even if he were starving, lest he suggest to an unbeliever that God did not in fact provide.

    On the other hand, Falwell in his autobiography said that "Lying, half-truths, and exaggerations should be off limits for everybody in public life, especially for those who follow the One who said, 'I am the truth . . .'," and that church finance statistics were "close to accurate" (1987: 328).

    Fortunately, for my purposes accuracy is not paramount. Figures and statistics quoted and culled from fundamentalist accounts should be read as figments of a story, of a construction of reality, not literally, not as "facts."

2. These figures are "extra-soft" because sources vary so much. My estimate triangulates four accounts: Church publications reported that in 1971 income was $2 million (*World of Life*, February 1972) and $23 million in fiscal year 1976/7 (*Faith Aflame*, July–August 1977); Falwell reported in 1987 that his ministry's income increased from $3.5 million to $12 million between 1973 and 1976 (1987: 332); and D'Souza reported that ministry revenue rose from $7 million in 1973 to $22 million in 1977 (1984: 88).

3. The Pentecostal "gospel of giving," known as prosperity or health and wealth theology, does seem to be efficacious – gifts to God do induce him to give back blessings to those who give.

4. I am grateful to Peter Brown for this formulation.

References

Dobson, Edward. 1981. Giving. Lynchburg Va.: Old-Time Gospel Hour Cassette Ministry.

D'Souza, Dinesh. 1984. *Falwell: Before the Millennium*. Chicago: Regnery Gateway.

Faith Aflame. Lynchburg, Va.: Thomas Road Baptist Church.

Falwell, Jerry. 1965. Ministers and marchers. Lynchburg, Va.: Thomas Road Baptist Church.

Falwell, Jerry. 1987. *Strength for the Journey*. New York: Simon & Shuster.

Falwell, Jerry, Hindson, Edward E., and Kroll, Woodrow Michael. 1977. *Liberty Commentary on the New Testament*. Lynchburg, Va.: Liberty Press.

Falwell, Jerry, Hindson, Edward E. and Kroll, Woodrow Michael. 1982. *Liberty Bible Commentary: Old Testament*. Lynchburg, Va.: Old-Time Gospel Hour.

Falwell, Jerry and Towns, Elmer. 1984. *Stepping Out on Faith*. Wheaton, Ill.: Tyndale House Publishers.

FitzGerald, Frances. 1986. *Cities on a Hill*. New York: Simon & Shuster.

Habershon, Ada. 1974. *The Study of the Types*. Grand Rapids, Mich.: Kregel Publications.

Harris, Ralph W. 1977. *Pictures of Truth*. Springfield, Mo.: Gospel Publishing House.

The Old-Time Gospel Hour News. Lynchburg, Va.: Thomas Road Baptist Church.

Strober, Gerald and Tomczak, Ruth. 1979. *Jerry Falwell: Aflame for God*. Nashville: Thomas Nelson Publishers.

Willmington, Harold. 1981. *Willmington's Guide to the Bible*. Wheaton, Ill.: Tyndale House Publishers.

World of Life. Lynchburg, Va.: Thomas Road Baptist Church.

3

When scientists saw ghosts and why they stopped: American spiritualism in history

Eva Marie Garroutte

Shadowy presences, blobs of ectoplasm, spectral voices: these are the stuff of spiritualist records from America's nineteenth century. Many are the stories, moreover, of possession, of visits to other worlds, of mysterious spirit lovers, or even supernatural "pregnancy."[1] But the significance of American spiritualism is hardly exhausted by the provision of entertaining examples of human foibles. In fact, it offers sociology an excellent opportunity to set practical limits around one of its central generalizations.

Sociology takes for granted that ideas about the world are social in origin, and therefore that ideas which might come to be accepted in any given circumstances are virtually limitless. At the same time, it cannot fail to recognize that some ideas are more likely than others to be widely accepted in particular times and places. At present, however, sociology does not know nearly enough about those factors that facilitate the establishment of an idea system, those that restrict it, and how they do so. Spiritualism, as a movement which passed through its entire boom-and-bust life cycle within half a century, lets us seek generalizable answers to these questions.

American spiritualism: history

Before going further, we must take a brief look at the biography of spiritualism. Most historians of this curious movement pinpoint its origin in

57

the activities of Margaret and Kate Fox, two little girls who, in 1848, purported to have established communication with the disembodied personage of "Mr. Splitfoot" (Nelson 1969: 4). By 1850 they had become renowned public figures and had opened the floodgate of a movement that would surge across the nation. As Moore writes (assuredly with no pun intended), "important men of business, politics, the arts, and journalism discussed the implication of spiritualism's claim with dead earnestness" (1977: 38).

Even in an age of burgeoning fanaticisms, spiritualism as a religious movement stood out. Ministers made passionate arguments for and against, the denominations buzzed with the debates, and spiritualist "circles" sprang up everywhere: "[n]ever before, or since, has any religion spread so rapidly or become so popular within such a short period" (Nelson 1969: 68; similarly, Podmore 1902: 226).

It did not, however, limit itself to religious claims, but ventured into the domain of science as well, where it met with some interesting reactions. Scientists, in fact, began seeing ghosts. The eminent chemist Robert Hare, and the chemist and inventor John Jay Mapes, for example, made investigations and ended up converted (Isaacs 1975: 203, 294). John Fairbanks, editor of *Scientific American*, announced in the 1856 *New York Times* that he was "in sweet converse with his departed sister's spirit" (Brown 1972: 276). The issue was discussed in scientific journals, and distinguished committees from the University of Buffalo, the University of Pennsylvania, from Harvard, and from the New York Philosophical Society, set out to try to make the spirits' acquaintance as well. Complete unbelievers there were, of course. But even those who refused to try to see the ghosts in a literal sense paid considerable attention to them just the same: they took care to censure spiritualism with a vigor not visited upon the irrelevant or trivial.

This article assumes that, in order for spiritualism to cause such a tidal wave of interest, it had to be able to mobilize two types of resources – both tangible and what I have called "discursive" resources – and to do so within several contexts or "markets." It attempts to determine how specific characteristics of spiritualism articulated with particular features of changing markets, so as to affect its fortunes as a mass movement.

The "religion" of spiritualism and its tangible resource needs

Spiritualism interwove religious and scientific themes in such a way that to describe it, as is customary, as a "scientific religion" is misleading; in its self-proclaimed goals it also styled itself a thoroughly "religious science." As a religious movement, it attempted to establish spirituality upon the firm foundation of reason and empirical evidence (Isaacs 1975: 166; Moore 1977:

7, 49). As a scientific movement, it purposed, through the critical observation of intersubjectively-verifiable events, and through the use of controlled experimentation, to extend the domain of natural law so as to comprehend everything in heaven and earth (Bednarowski 1973: 79). The duality of spiritualism's goals meant that it had to compete in two different markets for tangible resources: markets comprised not only of the resources themselves, but also of the interlocking actions of many social units in relation to them.

In the religious market, spiritualism sought, in company with other religious movements, such tangible resources as money, clergy, theologians and other professional personnel, worship facilities, and converts. In the mid-nineteenth century, this market exhibited several distinguishing characteristics. The first was its extraordinarily large number of competitors: from the early years of the century, the full complement of traditional American denominations had been augmented by new groups which sprang up, it seemed, almost overnight (Cross 1950; Ahlstrom 1972: 473–511). Recommending spiritualism most highly in the resultant intense competition was its knack of economizing on resources and "making do." Its start-up costs, for example, were almost nonexistent: unlike other religious groups, it demanded no cathedrals, no vestments, no ceremonial accoutrements, but could be practiced in the first dark room one stumbled into. The need to acquire leadership resources was similarly addressed. Even in a period when other religions found clergy in pitiably short supply (Johnson 1989: 27), spiritualism was never at a loss because it drew its mediums from a pool of laborers other groups often rejected: the uneducated, women, children, and blacks (Podmore 1902: 265; Moore 1977: 105).

Similarly, in the heated competition for the services of professional personnel other than clergy, spiritualism flourished by practicing thrift – and theft. As a principle, it resolutely rejected all creeds and shared moral programs, and the resultant flexibility granted the movement unlimited license to plunder other religious encampments (Moore 1977: 61, 68). Thus, instead of having to cultivate its own hymn writers, theologians, liturgists, and the like, spiritualism often simply appropriated the songs, the traditional practices, the theologies, the central themes and concepts which the personnel of many other groups had labored to create (Bednarowski 1973: 22; Cross 1950: 344).

Spiritualism's flexibility gave it an advantage, too, in obtaining "consumer resources." It had little difficulty in gathering a following even in a market which presented such a vast array of religious offerings as the nineteenth century. One reason was that its highly adaptable teachings did not require converts to abandon former beliefs and commitments; they could combine with almost any set of convictions. Spiritualism could therefore get at least partial use even of membership resources already allocated elsewhere.

Besides its overcrowding, a second characteristic of the market which affected spiritualism's ability to mobilize tangible resources had to do with its composition, or the typical competitors which made it up. The religious movements with which spiritualism contended, even the seemingly bizarre, often represented little more than traditional Christianity with a twist.[2] They added to their basic Christocentrism a tendency to traffic in absolutes (biblical literalism, categorical moral proscriptions, dogmatic doctrinal beliefs), and the result was their confinement to marginal differentiation, at best.[3]

Spiritualism, by contrast, threw off any necessary affiliation with Christianity (although one wing of the group chose to recognize many of its teachings). Moreover, it carried the rejection of absolutes to its extreme: each believer tailored a religion to his own specifications, and none could gainsay him. As a result, it unlocked religious possibilities that ran the gamut from the extravagant to the traditional. Those who wanted ectoplasm, levitation, healings, free love, glossolalia, or ghosts of all description could have them; those who would settle merely for absolution or consolation in bereavement would not be turned away either.

Spiritualism retailed its measureless selection of religious goods, too, at prices no competing group could match: it did not sentence its converts to a lifetime of tithing, missionary endeavor, church attendance, moral observance, or anything else. The cheapness and diversity of spiritualism's religious goods probably would not have permitted it to outstrip competitors in the struggle for consumer resources, however, had it not been for one important characteristic of those resources. Although I have indicated that spiritualism could get partial use of adherents who were allocated elsewhere, the fact is that a large part of the available people were not *formally* so allocated: most mid-century Americans were religious, but by their own lights alone. Only a minority held church membership (Cross 1950: 41; Johnson 1989: 26–7). This typical non-affiliation meant that most consumer resources were not bound to formal creeds, which typically forbade forays into spiritualism (Moore 1977: 40); rather, they were free to be diverted to spiritualism's doorstep.

The "science" of spiritualism and its tangible resource needs

I have noted that spiritualism strove to produce not only a scientific religion, but also a thoroughly religious science. Its scientific yearnings placed it, along with other scientific movements, into a market for resources such as laboratories, equipment, funds, research centers and researchers, and media of communication.

The first feature of this market which augured well for spiritualism was its composition: the typical scientific competitor was small and weak. Even a scientific claimant as widely popular as geology enjoyed only a newly-acquired and precarious respectability (Daniels 1971: 221). Their weakness prevented any of the resource-rivals from establishing a monopoly; none had acquired the power to exclude upstart claimants, such as spiritualism, from the competition.

Allowing spiritualism to make the most of the foothold thus established was another market feature, namely, the serious limitation of certain resources. Conditions had certainly improved from those of the piteously-underequipped 1830s and early 1840s, when there was, almost literally, nothing to work with (Struik 1962: 257). Yet the remaining shortages of basic equipment and laboratory facilities still severely limited investigations in many of the sciences. Not so, however, with spiritualism. Here one did not need to travel about the country (like geologists) or acquire elaborate implements (like the mesmerists). Each investigation, even the most casual, not only created an opportunity for the conversion of an individual investigator, but also gave spiritualists an opportunity to crow about scientific interest.

Another way in which the resource shortage contributed to the success spiritualism enjoyed in mobilizing the resource of researchers concerned scientific reputations. The deficits in basic scientific equipment and facilities meant that, throughout the first half of the nineteenth century, European investigators were forever stealing a march on Americans in publishing findings (Daniels 1971: 134). Spiritualism, as a new, exciting field not yet monopolized by the Europeans, would have offered American investigators something of a fresh start.

Additionally important to the emergence of spiritualism as a scientific contender was the market's state of flux. Some scientific claimants were clearly in the ascendancy, while others were dying. In this market, spiritualism – largely because its claims were various enough to allow it to be grouped with a number of different sciences – managed to capitalize on effort already expended and resources already amassed by representatives of both types of groups. On the one hand, it got financial and consumer resources by associating itself with the prestige and popular approbation which the up-and-coming sciences such as geology had been cultivating so painstakingly for decades. It also picked up on a forum already made popular largely by their efforts – the lyceum lecture. On the other hand, it stepped into a ready-made communication network, when the trained personnel of mesmerism's sinking ship transferred their interests and resources directly to the promotion of this newer science (Podmore 1902: 203).

The last characteristic of the mid-nineteenth century resource market important to spiritualism's success concerned the structure of the monetary resources within it: money frequently came from private individuals (Struik 1962: 239, 432–3). In years past, many people's pursuit of science as a hobby kept private interest – and the potential for loosened purse strings – high. Professional science encouraged this interest further by accepting contributions, such as botanical and mineralogical collections, or meteorological and ethnographic observations, from these sources (Daniels 1971: 165–6).

By 1850, however, "chemistry, paleontology, geology, botany, and zoology had all adopted theoretical structures of such complexity that only a specially trained intellect could adequately comprehend them," and science had passed out of the stage where it either wanted or needed non-professional contributions (Daniels 1971: 167). In shutting out the hobbyist, however, it lost an important means of ensuring continued private interest. Hobbyists resented being shut out of science. Spiritualism, by contrast, represented the consummate do-at-home science. Its universal, first-hand accessibility to any and all kept private persons interested, and thus kept the channels of support open.

Such were spiritualism's competitive advantages in the market for monetary resources. On the other hand, it also suffered from a significant disadvantage which vitiated, but did not nullify, its competitive strengths. The problem related to the first tremors of a coming shift in market composition. While it is true that all the competitors in 1850 were small and weak, some groups exhibited movements toward professionalization and increasing power.[4] Feeble as these impulses were, they were accompanied by scientific chafing at the widespread sentiment that research was amenable to evaluation by the general public. Scuffles broke out between professionals and non-professionals over the question of who defined proper science (Daniels 1971: 165–73).

Into this tableau of developing professional interests had burst spiritualism, proclaiming itself Everyman's science. A central feature of spiritualist teaching was a radically democratic ideal: that unaided reason made knowledge available to all (Isaacs 1975: 166; Moore 1977: 22). This, of course, was precisely the message that professionalizing science wished most to discourage. Its deeply egalitarian urge may have hampered spiritualism's ability to mobilize researchers, at least from among those closest to the core of professionalizing science. On the other hand, even these professionals could do little except ignore the new claimant. They bided their time, not only because they had not yet attained a tangible-resource monopoly, but also because of conditions in the discursive resource market, which discouraged a direct attack on spiritualism's claims. We may turn now to a consideration of the latter.

The mobilization of discursive resources

Spiritualism, all things considered, was at least fairly well favored in terms of the characteristics which, given the relevant markets, suited it to competition for tangible resources. But in order to become a mass movement, spiritualism had also to mobilize discursive resources.[5]

I suggest thinking of the mobilization of discursive resources as largely similar to the mobilization of tangible resources: we may imagine movements of varying goals seeking claims within particular market contexts. This suggestion assumes that there exist:

(a)   many movements and potential movements, differentiated by self-defined, constitutive goals, that is, by goals so central that the abandonment of them implies that the movement has become a different movement;
(b)   an almost-infinite pool of lexically- and syntactically-possible claims;
(c)   markets for these claims, constituted in part by interaction, and in part by a substructure of very basic, pre-theoretical assumptions about the nature and ordering of the world.

The pre-theoretical assumptions, I suggest, comprise a schema, or model, for claims. The schema enables those claims which are consistent with it to be accepted as legitimate by large numbers of people. On the other hand, it negates the legitimacy of claims which are inconsistent with it; these are not likely to be accepted as legitimate by large numbers of people. Clearly, movements that would be successful on a mass scale tend to need access to legitimate claims. Yet their own constitutive goals may stand in the way: these goals will be consistent only with some *subset* of all possible claims, which may or may not include legitimate claims.

Consider an example. First, imagine one possible schema which includes a pre-theoretical assumption about the divine as possessing a dual nature, which is a consummate expression of both evil and good. Next, imagine a second schema which includes an assumption about the divine as possessing a single nature, which is the consummate expression only of good.

Given either schema, the possibility exists for the birth of a Movement X, characterized by the constitutive goal of furthering members' religious development through their imitation of the evil aspect of God's nature. Also given either schema, the goals of Movement X restrict the selection of claims it can adopt: it may not adopt a claim stating, for instance, "we must selflessly serve others," without becoming a different movement.

There is, however, one important difference between the Movement X's appearance within Schema One and its appearance within Schema Two, as illustrated by Figures 3.1 and 3.2. Given Schema One, at least part of the subset of claims A from which Movement X may select are legitimate: they are consistent with the pre-theoretical assumptions. Given Schema Two, Movement X chooses from the *identical* subset of claims, but that entire subset is illegitimate. Whereas it is quite possible that the claims Movement X selects could form the basis of a mass movement given Schema One, this is much less likely given Schema Two. Having thus sketched the particulars implied in the concept of "the mobilization of discursive resources" generally, we may turn to this task as it concerns spiritualism.

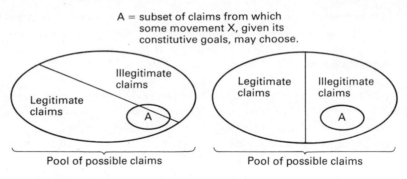

A = subset of claims from which some movement X, given its constitutive goals, may choose.

Figure 3.1   *Figure 3.2*

Spiritualism and discursive resources

In 1850, the dominant schema from within which both scientific and religious movements drew their claims had been substantially influenced, through informal channels, by Scottish Common Sense Realism (Bozeman 1977: 3–32). Salient among its assumptions was the comparability of facts drawn from Scripture with those drawn from nature (ibid.: 61, 128; Hovencamp 1978: 11); the complementary, absolutely non-contradictory nature of these two kinds of facts (Bozeman 1977: 96); and the possibility of certain and complete knowledge, of statements that accounted for *all* the facts, whether derived from reason or revelation (ibid.: 109; Moore 1979: 214). Together, these assumptions contributed to a schema enabling the legitimacy of claims that crossed freely back and forth between religion and science: it was proper and customary for both sciences and religions to make claims which hopelessly – in our view – mixed the two domains. The typical geology textbooks, for example, combined discussions of research findings with illustrations and discussions of the way in which the very rocks cried out to confirm biblical teachings (Daniels 1971: 219).

Given such a schema, spiritualism in 1850, a movement with the constitutive goal of creating a scientific religion and a religious science, was free to choose its claims from the subset of legitimate ones. Other religions and other sciences drew on much the same pool of claims, which explains why even those early scientists who disapproved of spiritualism could not challenge the legitimacy of its claims head-on.

Later resource mobilization: difficulties and decline

To understand how spiritualism's viability as a mass movement was compromised after 1850, we must move twenty years ahead, to a second stage in spiritualism's life cycle. This second stage consisted in a revival, after the Civil War had disrupted the flood tide movement of the 1850s (Brown 1972: 124–5; Moore 1977: 64). Although the reawakening of interest was substantial, it did not match spiritualism's original popularity (Brown 1972: 152).

The diminishing success was related, in part, to changes in the tangible resource markets. Spiritualism, of course, retained the ability to thrive on very few monetary resources. It also continued to put to good use personnel resources that no one else wanted. But by the 1870s its array of remarkably various and bargain-priced religious goods that had attracted consumers earlier had become less distinguishable from those of the denominations. The churches had been turning from heavy-handedness toward congregational conciliation ever since mid-century, and they had now had twenty years to develop the trend. They increasingly asked less of their members in terms of sacrifice and commitment, and granted greater latitude for people to find their own way to salvation (Johnson 1989: 137–58). Some were also gravitating strongly towards new strains of biblical criticism that wandered far from literalist understandings, thus expanding the religious possibilities available within them (Hovencamp 1978: 59–60). Spiritualism simply stood out less in the 1870s in what it could offer to attract religious consumers. In addition, many more people had become church members, thus formally affiliating themselves with bodies which generally did not look kindly on spiritualism.

By the 1870s the tangible resource market for scientific competitors was also transformed. Equipment and facility resources were more abundant (Struik 1962: 7). Science had professionalized and institutionalized considerably, meaning there were now relatively fewer self-made scientific men. There were more people, that is, with clear, vested interests in the professionalization of science; there were also fewer of those who, being unattached to scientific institutions, were most likely to have found the scientific resource economies spiritualism offered a considerable advantage. Finally, orthodox science was increasingly coming into its own in terms of government support, Civil War legislation such as the Morrill (land-grant) Act having marked "a genuine turning point for science in the government" (Daniels 1971: 269; similarly, Struik 1962: 442–4); consequently, spiritualism's ability to tap private sources had become less of an advantage.

Along with a crippling inability to evolve organizational structures to prevent the dissipation of such tangible resources as it had once mustered, such factors rendered the spiritualist movement of 1870 a weaker competitor than it had been in 1850. In time, the problems would only intensify. But they alone did not destroy spiritualism: there were much more threatening changes afoot in the markets for discursive resources. Whereas in 1850 spiritualism enjoyed a largely unproblematic access to legitimate claims, by 1870 there began to appear indications that the dominant schema was in transition in such a way as to shift the division between legitimate and illegitimate claims and imperil spiritualism's access to the former. By 1900 these trends would have solidified in a triumph for the new schema and a rout for spiritualism.

It is possible to trace the schematic transistion, and to show that the degree of its completion is correlated with indicators of spiritualism's decreasing ability to mobilize legitimate claims. In the attempt to do so, I have used the textual analysis of a scientific periodical at two points in time. The periodical is the *Popular Science Monthly (PSM)*, a high-quality publication and "one of the major sources of popular scientific influence in the late 19th century" (Walker 1956: ii). Given that its contributors were ordinarily among the most prestigious of their day, it may also be considered to reflect more scholarly opinion as well. The first time period selected for analysis is from May 1872 to December 1877, the first five and a half years of the periodical's publication. The comparison period is exactly 30 years later, covering issues published from May 1902 through December 1907.

In the following analysis I present evidence for these points, related to the transformation of the discursive resource market:

(a)   that in 1872, the dominant schema was in transition, such that claims drawing on both old assumptions, which discouraged separation of religion and science, and on new assumptions, which demanded this separation, enjoyed some legitimacy;

(b)   that by 1900, the new schema had come to dominance;

(c)   that the ability of spiritualism to make legitimate claims is correlated with this transition.

Figures 3.1 and 3.2 summarize these changes, with Figure 3.1 representing schematic conditions in 1870 and Figure 3.2 representing schematic conditions in 1900. Subset A represents those claims from which spiritualism, given its constitutive goals, could choose at any time.

The *Popular Science Monthly*: textual analysis

Points (a) and (b) may be argued by examining the treatment of religious material in *PSM*. If the dominant schema is indeed in transition in 1872, we will expect to find its contributors making more religio-scientific claims in this period than in the 1902 period. In addition, we will anticipate a greater frequency of discursive practices (strategies and styles of argumentation and choice of subject matter) which, like religio-scientific claims, assume the old schema. Some significant number of claims and discursive practices which assume the emerging schema will also be expected in the early period, but even more in the later.

Turning to the early issues of *PSM*, the frequent appearance of religious themes is certainly striking. In 20 randomly-sampled issues from the 1872–7 period, there appear no less than 61 items relating to religious subjects (not including spiritualism). These range between brief mentions of less than one page to extended articles of up to 27 pages, with 19 of the items (over 70 percent) being five or more pages in length. The subject of these pieces is illuminating: while concerns range over questions such as whether Christianity encourages or discourages patriotism, or whether a decline of religion necessarily implies a decline in morality, fully 30 items deal entirely with the question of the "conflict" between religion and science, or the proper relationship between the two. A few more (five articles) deal with this issue to a substantial degree, although not exclusively.[6]

The "conflict" articles leave the reader in no doubt as to which schema they prefer coming to dominance. There appear frequent excoriations of religion for interfering in science, and a broad consensus that religion and science must be kept quite separate. The former, it is stipulated, will discover truths by "looking within upon the soul," the latter by "looking without upon the world" (White 1876: 385). None of these claims is consistent with the old schema, but all are perfectly consistent with the new.

For all their enthusiasm to discuss the conflict between religion and science, contributors to *PSM* betray an anxiety that their suggestions for its resolution may fail to convince. They resort alternately to threatening and conciliating Christianity. There are, first, reminders that science and religion, when intermingled, only imperil religion (for example, Youmans 1874: 499). These are followed by more substantial threats: that religion which refuses to mind its own business represents, by definition, something other than "true" religion (for example, Dawson 1876: 73).

At other times, the scientific writers may tender various blandishments. Fashionable among these are assurances that science could not disprove religion even if it wanted to; promises that science, for its part, intends to remain strictly within the domain now staked out for it, and not to trespass on religion's allotment; and kudos for the religious enterprise in general. Similarly, authors frequently avow Christian faithfulness for themselves and their discipline: science, records the editor, "is itself the promoter of the profoundest faith" (Youmans 1873: 119–20). Such sequential attempts, first to intimidate, then to appease, religion, suggest that science realizes that the schematic transformation it is engineering is a very delicate, political act, and one not yet completed. They suggest, that is, a recognition that the group at whose expense the transition is made may yet rebel.

The most significant indicator of unresolved schematic disturbance, however, is the combination of *PSM*'s ranting about the inappropriateness of combining science and religion with examples of its own inability to resist doing precisely that. For example, in describing the expectations the world should henceforth cherish for science, *PSM* articles may adopt distinctly ecclesiastical language. One article advises readers that "modern science has brought the world a fifth gospel" which will permit mankind to "work out . . . [its] own salvation" (*Christian Union* 1872: 218–19). Not content with such affirmations, articles also commonly mix claims by promoting science as a substitute source of religious goods. Science now proffers new religious revelation, inspiration, even messianic hopes. It represents, for instance,

> the pledge of an *unimaginable progress* in the future . . . which will furnish . . . the means of a more effulgent and glorious solution of the dark problems of life and destiny that it is possible to reach by unaided conjecture. (Godwin 1873: 105)

All these indicators suggest that claims assuming the old schema by mixing scientific and religious themes are still legitimate in 1872 – but only perilously so. The appearance of many claims and discursive practices assuming the new schema, in which science and religion occupy completely separate domains, portends changes to come.

The portents are apparently accurate: by 1902 *PSM* has changed its content markedly. Whereas the 20-issue sampling of the 1870s uncovered 61 religious items (an average of about 3 per issue), all 68 issues from the 1902–7 period produced only 7 treatments of religious themes (an average of slightly more than one item per every 10 issues). Six of these treatments, moreover, comprise only small subsections of articles on quite different topics.[7] Only a single article from this entire five and a half year period is entirely religious in focus.

The comparison of the 1872 period (wherein claims and discursive patterns drawing on both old and new schemata were frequent) with this later period (in which they are almost non-existent) is entirely consistent with the argument for a schematic transition which is resolved by 1900. Having thus argued the first proposed points, we may proceed to address point (c), which proposed a correlation between the degree to which the schematic transition had been completed and the failing legitimacy of spiritualism's claims.

If such a correlation exists, spiritualism's claims should still be legitimate in the transitional, 1872 period, and we should expect that *PSM* may find it an appropriate subject for discussion. We should expect, further, that it will be the subject of discursive practices which treat it as either a significant good or a serious threat. Once spiritualism's claims have become illegitimate, however, it should comprise a much less likely concern for science.

Beginning the analysis with the 74 issues of the 1872–7 period (this number includes the supplements *PSM* has recently added), we find 21 treatments of spiritualism. Of these, 9 are feature articles that deal with spiritualism exclusively or to a substantial degree, 4 are either appearances in columns devoted to miscellaneous short items or brief mentions in longer articles, 2 are book reviews, and 6 are appearances in a column entitled "Books

Received." Pieces range from 1 to 16 pages in length, with 8 items being 5 or more pages long.

Twenty-one appearances for spiritualism in 74 issues is not an unimpressive figure, particularly given the narrowness of the subject and the huge diversity of topics *PSM* habitually treats. The content of spiritualist items confirms the impression that science, in 1872, considered spiritualism a claimant enjoying at least precarious legitimacy. While the tendency in the discussions is negative, that is, the consensus is not complete. Of the 15 items possible to categorize, 4 adopt a positive position toward spiritualism, 4 a neutral or balanced position, and 7 a negative one: there actually are more items which at least give spiritualism the benefit of the doubt than there are negative items.

Not only the prevalence of positive and neutral views, however, suggests the legitimacy of spiritualism's claims. Even negative pieces underscore it by protesting rather too much. For example, one allusion styles "so-called spiritualism" as "intellectual whoredom" (Tyndall 1875: 148), and a book review jibes:

> [the author] tells us that he has been for twenty-five years an observer of modern Spiritualism. Had he not published this book, the world might never have known the extent of his gullibility. He has only himself to blame. (*Popular Science Monthly* 1876: 757)

Spiritualist items also sometimes betray the seriousness with which they take the offending movement in their anxiety to explain away (rather than ignore) the convictions of scientific persons who claim spiritualist beliefs. This defanging of the opposition may be accomplished by personal attack. A piece on the spiritualist investigations of the highly-reputed British chemist William Crookes exemplifies the strategy. Focusing on Crookes's spiritualist investigations, the article disparages "his conception of truthfulness and honor, his claims to belief as a witness and to respect as a man." It closes by declaring that he does not qualify for membership in "the brotherhood of science" (*Engineering and Mining Journal* 1872: 127). The illustration is all the more instructive when compared to a second article about Crookes devoted to a discussion of his career as a whole; this unqualifiedly celebrates him as "foremost" of all "the active and successful scientific workers of England at the present time" (*PSM* 1877: 739). The startling contrast between two articles on the same person, one focused on his spiritualist researches, and the other not, strongly suggests that science could not yet dismiss spiritualism's claims as illegitimate.

Negative articles on spiritualism do not just sling mud, however, but go as far as to refute its factual claims one by one. Thus there appears a notice for a performance in which a Professor Pepper "announces himself as ready to give all the 'manifestations' usual at 'spirit seances' through non-supernatural means" (*PSM* 1872: 383). In a related vein is a piece in which table-turning is explained by the involuntary ("ideo-motor") action of those whose hands rest on the table, and supposed spirit revelations by the unconscious thoughts of the inquirer (Carpenter 1872: 30). A book review refers to its object's explanation of "mediomania" as "produced generally by derangement of the sexual organs" (*PSM* 1874: 752).

In spite of all the attention science bestows on spiritualism in 1872, a comparison of negative articles with positive and neutral ones suggests it will not have to do so much longer. Somewhat surprisingly, both types of articles assume the same criteria for the legitimacy of claims. Derogatory pieces mockingly assert that spiritualists make explanations based on the existence of ghosts, thus discrediting spiritualism as a science largely by remarking its linkages to aspects of spiritual reality: they assume, apparently, that if spiritualism is a religion it cannot be a science, too. Pro-spiritualist and neutral articles, however, defend themselves, or allow the benefit of the doubt, by the exactly opposite tactic. Avoiding religious references, they speak, instead, of "psychic" or "odylic" force, about the operation of as-yet-unknown natural laws, or about the exercise of hidden human capabilities such as clairvoyance. That both spiritualists and non-spiritualists are by now assuming the same schema, and trying to formulate claims that do not mix science and religion, suggest that the final triumph of the new schema cannot be too far hence.

Indeed, when we inspect the evidence for the legitimacy of spiritualism's claims in 1902, we find virtually nothing. In all the 74 issues of *PSM* from this period, there are no mentions of spiritualism, save for a single, dismissive allusion in an article about hypnotism. This finding is also consistent with the argument that a readjusted schema negated the legitimacy of spiritualism's claims such that science needed no longer to pay any attention to it.

Summarily, the substantial amount of space devoted to spiritualism in the early *PSM*, along with the qualities of the reception it meets there, are consistent with the argument that its claims were still legitimate in 1872. By the same token, the later abandonment of spiritualism as a topic suggests that, by 1900, it no longer presented the threat of a movement bearing legitimate claims.

The collapse of original spiritualism

Spiritualism, then, gradually lost the ability to mobilize legitimate claims in the market for discursive resources. Along with this disability came a reduced capacity to sustain itself as a mass movement: researchers agree that renewals of interest after the 1870s grew smaller and smaller (for example, Ahlstrom 1972: 490; Kerr 1972: 118–20; Moore 1977: xv). By 1900 the original spiritualist movement was no more. To this last, it may be objected that spiritualism revived after both World Wars, and still exists today as a modest-sized movement. However, such later movements present a significant difference from that of the last century. Later followers surrendered their intention to build up a new religious science, forswearing their earlier pleading for rigorous, empirical investigation of their claims. Instead, they moved toward the "proofs" of individual experience. As Brandon summarizes:

> the outstanding feature of . . . [the] Spiritualist mass-movement of the early twentieth century was that, unlike that of seventy years before, the so-called "physical phenomena" were nowhere in evidence. Where they had once been such an important element of popular appeal . . . [later believers] . . . were not interested in ectoplasm. (1983: 222)

Confronted, in other words, with the illegitimacy of the claims available to it, by virtue of its constitutive goal, spiritualism abandoned that goal, and became simply a religious movement. As such, it can still survive, for it has access to legitimate claims as much as any other religion. It no longer thrives, however, probably because of an exacerbation of inauspicious trends in the tangible resource market, the roots of which require an investigation in themselves.

Logically enough, given a readjusted schema which divided religion and science as a matter of course, twentieth-century spiritualism made a second, opposite adaptation as well. This second adaptation emphasized the scientific elements of spiritualism and "tried to avoid the religious and reform controversies that had helped produce the public visibility of spiritualism" (Moore 1977: 170). Like the reformed religion of spiritualism, this new science of parapsychology survived by endorsing a goal (the exploration of extraordinary powers of the human mind and of hypnotism) that enabled it to select from among legitimate claims. Today, it toils along, held back mainly by difficulties in tangible resource mobilization. The division of original spiritualism into separate movements, one religious and one scientific, adds confirmation to the argument for a schematic transition which compromised the legitimacy of religio-scientific claims.

Conclusion

In this paper, I used the example of spiritualism to explore the possibility of setting practical limits on a central sociological generalization: that, since ideas are social in origin, any movement might appear in any given circumstances. I related spiritualism's changing success as a mass movement to changes in its tangible resource market, and especially in its discursive resource market. In the latter case, I used a textual analysis of a nineteenth-century scientific magazine to argue that the relevant change involved a transition in the dominant schema: a shift in the boundary between legitimate and illegitimate claims which was correlated with the declining ability of spiritualism to make legitimate claims. I concluded by noting that its success as a mass, religio-scientific movement declined at the same time as its ability to make legitimate claims, and that its later differentiation into separate religious and scientific movements constitutes further evidence for a schematic transition that crippled groups endorsing religio-scientific claims.

Notes

1. In 1854, "a respectable married lady" of High Rock, Massachusetts, received word from the spirits that she was to be "the Mary of the New Dispensation." After suitable birth agonies, she produced a spiritual principle which indwelt a (putatively) perpetual-motion machine. Her tender "nursing" of the "new-born child" for weeks after, however, came to naught: the New Motor was destroyed by frightened townspeople (Podmore 1902: 298–9).

2. Cross observes of Adventism, for example, that for all its spectacular prophecies about the end of the world and the strange actions it incited, its "most distinctive feature was in fact its extreme closeness to orthodoxy" (1950: 297). Similarly, Ahlstrom remarks the Shakers' intense biblicism, and notes that their emphasis on celibacy was "the only moral precept which they did not share with standard Protestant statements of Christian virtue" (1972: 494). The same observation of general orthodoxy holds for revivalism: for all the behavioral irregularities that might occur at their meetings, the important revivalists such as Charles Finney and Jedediah Burchard added little to traditional doctrine (Cross 1950: 160, 188).

3. I am grateful to Jane Munzer (Princeton University) for pointing out the limiting effect of introducing absolutes into religious systems.

4. Signs of things to come included the opening of New England's first scientific schools at Yale and Harvard in 1847, and the formation of the first general professional society, the American Association for the Advancement of Science, in 1848.

5. I am greatly indebted to Marsha Witten (Temple University) for her thoughtful and fruitful comments on this section of the article.

6. Given justifiable concerns about the reliability of content analysis when performed by a single investigator, I have invoked a mechanical, rather than an interpretive standard for the categorization of material. This mechanical standard categorizes the content of articles and other items as "religious" or "spiritualist" on the basis of an enumeration of specific words (for example, "God," "religion," "soul," etc.). A similar standard determines whether the item deals with its theme exclusively, substantially, or briefly.

7. For example, two articles describe Galileo's experiences with the Inquisition, one discusses rites of folk medicine (some of which involve religious incantation, etc.), one reprints an address on the League of Nations which includes scriptural allusions, and so on.

References

Ahlstrom, Sidney. 1972. *A Religious History of the American People.* New Haven: Yale University Press.

Bednarowski, Mary Farrell. 1973. Nineteenth-century American spiritualism: An attempt at a scientific religion. PhD diss., University of Minnesota.

Bozeman, Theodore Dwight. 1977. *Protestants in an Age of Science: The Baconian Ideal and Antebellum American Religious Thought.* Chapel Hill, NC: University of North Carolina Press.

Brandon, Ruth. 1983. *The Spiritualists: the Passion for the Occult in the Nineteenth and Twentieth Centuries.* New York: Knopf.

Brown, Burton Gates, Jr. 1972. Spiritualism in nineteenth-century America. PhD diss., Boston University.

Carpenter, [William B.]. 1872. Epidemic delusions. *Popular Science Monthly* 2 (Nov.): 15–36.

Christian Union. 1872. Scrutable providences. Reprinted in *Popular Science Monthly* 1 (June): 217–19.

Cross, Whitney R. 1950. *The Burned-over District: the Social and Intellectual History of Enthusiastic Religion in Western New York, 1800–1850.* Ithaca, NY: Cornell University Press.

Daniels, George H. 1971. *Science in American Society: A Social History.* New York: Knopf.

Dawson, J. W. 1876. The so-called "conflict of science and religion." *Popular Science Monthly* 10 (Nov.): 72–4.

Engineering and Mining Journal. 1872. No title. Reprinted in *Popular Science Monthly* 1 (May): 126–7.

Godwin, Parke. 1873. The sphere and limits of science. *Popular Science Monthly* 3 (May): 105–10.

Hovencamp, Herbert. 1978. *Science and Religion in America: 1800–1860.* No place of publication: University of Pennsylvania Press.

Isaacs, Ernest Joseph. 1975. *A History of Nineteenth Century American Spiritualism as a Religious and Social Movement.* PhD diss., University of Wisconsin, Madison.

Johnson, Curtis D. 1989. *Islands of Holiness: Rural Religion in Upstate New York, 1790–1860.* Ithaca and London: Cornell University Press.

Kerr, Howard. 1972. *Mediums, and Spirit-Rappers, and Roaring Radicals: Spiritualism in American Literature, 1850–1900.* Urbana, Ill.: University of Illinois Press.

Moore, James R. 1979. *The Post-Darwinian Controversies.* Cambridge: Cambridge University Press.

Moore, R. Laurence. 1977. *In Search of White Crows: Spiritualism, Parapsychology, and American Culture.* New York: Oxford University Press.

Nelson, Geoffrey K. 1969. *Spiritualism and Society.* London: Routledge & Kegan Paul.

Podmore, Frank. 1902. *Modern Spiritualism: A History and a Criticism*, Vol. 1. London: Methuen.

Popular Science Monthly (PSM). 1872. Notes. Vol. 1 (June): 383–4.

Popular Science Monthly. 1874. Review of *The Philosophy of Spiritualism, and the Treatment of Mediomania* by Frederic R. Marvin. Vol. 5 (Oct.): 751.

Popular Science Monthly. 1876. Review of *Startling Facts of Modern Spiritualism* by N. B. Wolfe. Vol. 8 (April): 757.

Popular Science Monthly. 1877. The scientific labors of William Crookes. Vol. 10 (April): 739–41.

Struik, Dirk J. 1962. *Yankee Science in the Making.* [1948] New York: Collier.

Tyndall, John. 1875. Martineu and materialism. *Popular Science Monthly* 8 (Dec.): 129–48.

Walker, Don D. 1956. The Popular Science Monthly, 1872–1878: A study in the dissemination of scientific ideas in America. PhD diss., University of Minnesota.

White, Andrew D. 1876. The warfare of science. *Popular Science Monthly* 8 (Feb.): 385–409.

Youmans, E. L. 1873. Mr Godwin's letter. *Popular Science Monthly* 3 (May): 115–20.

Youmans, E. L. 1874. Agassiz. *Popular Science Monthly* 4 (Feb.): 495–9.

4

Reading science as text

David E. Woolwine

Introduction

Some decades ago Robert K. Merton wrote that the sub-field of the sociology of science was largely neglected within the larger discipline (1973a). At the same time he expressed the hope that sociology would witness a reversal of this pattern. A similar hope was expressed in Merton's seminal article, "Paradigm for the sociology of knowledge" (1973c). In that essay, using notions derived from Karl Mannheim, he hypothesized the social conditions under which a full-fledged sociology of knowledge might come into being. The conditions ideal for the development of the sociology of knowledge are described as those in which increasing social conflict brings about incompatible differences in the modes of thought of groups within society. Merton goes on to note that distinct "universes of discourse" then come into being, each of which challenges the validity and legitimacy of the others. Finally, under such conditions, thought begins to be traced back to sociological, psychological, and economic bases, and reciprocal analyses of discourses as "ideological" develop.

Conditions such as these are precisely those recognized and commented upon by Richard Rorty in *Contingency, Irony, and Solidarity* (1989) and by Jean-François Lyotard in *The Postmodern Condition: A Report on Knowledge* (1984) as those most characteristic of the 1980s, a period which they call the postmodern. In other words, the conditions that Merton saw as necessary for the development of the sociology of knowledge have not only come to pass but presently flourish, both in Western societies as collectivities and in their academic subsectors. There has, therefore, been a concomitant reversal of the trend Merton bemoaned in the early 1950s. The sociology of knowledge, the sociologies of religion, culture, and science, have become increasingly central and formative to the discipline. They have become the porous boundaries through which ideas, approaches, and theories from other disciplines have entered sociology and are places where the most exciting theoretical and empirical work is presently being done.

This chapter will concentrate on the state of affairs existing in the sociology of science. I argue that the sociology of science may be seen as having had a unique place within the discipline of sociology. This is one in which it has been open to, and borrowed from, other disciplines, and from other sub-fields in sociology, but a core set of problems, especially in a sense one problem, has driven it, produced its boundaries, and set it off from other, related sub-fields. I argue that the sociology of science has been organized around the dichotomy sameness/difference, specifically around ways of saying how scientific knowledge and scientific practice are "different from," and how they are the "same as," other forms of knowledge and practice. Finally, I argue that the sociology of science has reached a point in its development where it has begun to bring self-reflexively into its core notions and tactics derived from literary theory. It has begun to explore what would come of treating "science," "scientific tests," and scientists' (and others') discourse about science as texts, explicitly emphasizing both the textuality of science and sociology's study of science.

This structurally, and sociologically, generated move within the sociology of science is in line with the larger trend within sociology away from the study of values and beliefs held "internally" by actors and toward the analysis of observable structures of symbol systems (Wuthnow 1987). As the following account will demonstrate, the sociology of science has been impelled away from a Mertonian concern with values and norms and toward the study of the structures and strategies of writing implicit in scientific texts and texts about science. This has not, however, entailed an entire rejection of the "social world" separate from the text, for the most recent students of science (Latour 1987; Haraway 1989; Mukerji 1989) have also attempted to link up texts, the practices generating texts, and the particular structures and images embedded in particular texts, to concentrations and distributions of power in the "world."

Merton and structural-functionalism

Both structuralism in the work of Ferdinand de Saussure (1983) and deconstruction in the writings of Jacques Derrida (1976; 1978) have suggested that the use of paired opposites is a necessary strategy for writing and thought. Such categorical opposites, in their deployment, draw boundaries around the incessant flow of particulars, of the unique, providing a limit that allows for the coming into existence of writing, speech, and thought. One such pair, perhaps the most elementary, is that of sameness/difference, and in the case of the sociology of science it has been the necessary, unlimited, and impossible attempt to write the boundaries of the sameness and difference of science that has set it upon its task of generating ever more diverse and complex texts.

Merton's sociology of science (1973b) clearly exhibits this concern with establishing sameness/difference. Ostensibly the goal of Mertonian sociology of science is to uncover and make explicit the ways in which scientific institutions and the normative structures of science are both like, and different from, other institutions in society. On the one hand, science is similar to, or the same as, other human activities in that it is a social activity and therefore, according to the structural-functionalist theory developed by Merton, must be accompanied by institutions in which its goals are established and carried out, and in which each subsequent generation of scientists is socialized and trained. Part of this "institutionalization" is the establishment of normative structures by which it is determined which behaviors, and types of behaviors, are to be encouraged and permitted and which punished and forbidden. On the other hand, Merton also argues that science is "different" from other human activities by his treatment of the *content* of scientific knowledge. For here Merton argues that the sociology of science would more fruitfully proceed if it left this area alone. Here is an area so unlike other areas of human activity and production that sociology does not easily proceed therein.

This choice on Merton's part has had two, perhaps unintentional, outcomes or consequences. The first outcome is that those norms which Merton proposed as supportive, or even necessary for, science – "universalism," "communism," "disinterestedness," and "organized skepticism," as well as certain organizational characteristics of science as a sub-system (for example, the supposed relative isolation of science from political influence) – are then taken as supporting the production of a certain type of knowledge, that is, "correct" scientific knowledge. ("Correct" here understood as uniquely functional, rational, or true.) In other words, by looking at institutions and norms, and away from scientific knowledge *per se*, the structural-functionalist sociology of science was able to return to a discussion of the content of scientific knowledge.

Of course Merton's analysis of the norms and institutions of science does not alone explain its structural-functionalist ability to produce what is thought to be uniquely rational, true, or powerful knowledge. Usually some philosophy of science is incorporated, or felt to be needed, as part of an account that would produce a more complete explanation. Usually the philosophical element in the synthesis is derived from the thought of Karl Popper (1968) or some variant thereof which holds that science possesses a unique set of methods or procedures for experimentation and verification or falsification.

A second, clearly unintentional, but perhaps to be expected, outcome (Zloczower 1960; Ben-David and Zloczower 1972; Turner *et al.* 1984) has been the *direct* engagement by some sociologists, excluded from or uninterested in Merton's research agenda, with the content of scientific knowledge. In fact the next stage in the history of the sociology of science was an outflanking of the structural-functionalists by means of directly addressing the issue of the social influences on the production of scientific knowledge. This stage, existing to today, has been largely dominated by what has come to be known as "constructionism." Constructionism is not, however, a unity. Rather it is a collection of approaches and perspectives, of which the following are the most notable: the Strong Programme (the chief spokespersons for which have been Barry Barnes and David Bloor), ethnomethodology and laboratory studies (for which Steve Woolgar has emerged as a spokesperson), and what, in this treatment, will be called textual studies of science (for which Michael Mulkay remains representative).

The Strong Programme

The Strong Programme is usually taken as involving the following four tenets: (a) The sociology of science should be concerned with the causes of scientific knowledge, that is, it should concern itself with the conditions which bring about belief or knowledge. (b) Both "truth" and "falsity," "rationality" and "irrationality," "success" and "failure" require socio-logical explanation (that is, in Derridian language, one term in the pair is not privileged over the other). (c) The same type of explanation, or the same type of cause, should be employed in explaining both "true" and "false" beliefs. (d) The pattern or type of explanation developed within the Strong Programme should be applicable to sociological knowledge as well (that is, reflexivity is required) (Bloor 1976: 4–5).

In its tenets, and in the types of causal explanations given for the development of scientific knowledge, the Strong Programme clearly emphasizes the ways in which science can be seen as the same as other social activities. In fact, in this perspective, scientific knowledge, specifically the content of scientific knowledge, becomes indistinguishable from what in a Mannheimian system would be seen as ideology. The immediate effect of the Strong Programme was to inspire, generate, or collect and organize, a large number of empirically based studies which showed, or purported to show, that scientific knowledge, and in particular conflicts about scientific dis-coveries and models, are often influenced by "social interests." ("Social interests" here means the desire of a scientist, or group of scientists, to win recognition, or power, or to advance a particular model or research agenda.)

Another way in which we have been brought by this school to see scientific knowledge as ideological is by its presentation of scientific models and theories as reflections of images or metaphors drawn from the "culture" in which scientists reside. These models are argued to reflect or support powerful cultural or political biases about the nature of social structure (that is, they reflect, or image, the "interests" of the ruling classes, or of a ruling class).

Beyond causing us to see the ways in which scientific knowledge can be taken as ideological, the Strong Programme, in the works of Barry Barnes (1974), also performed another task. Here, by specifically addressing the difference of science, by attempting to say what distinguished scientific activities from other types of human activity, the Strong Programme has also developed a consistent, and largely integrated, way of looking at science. This perspective, furthermore, has been able to stand as an alternative to the Mertonian–Popperian synthesis.

Barnes says that "sciences" share many characteristics but that it is impossible to say a priori or, more simply, without empirical investigation, which of these characteristics are shared by which science, or even to know when we have produced an exhaustive list. "Science" is a set of activities, organized around disciplines, subdisciplines, and research programs, all varying over time and place, which share certain family resemblances (to use Wittgenstein's well-known phrase). One such characteristic, *almost* universal in "successful" sciences, is a trend toward mathematization and quantification. There is also a tendency toward theorizing and abstractness that sets scientific knowledge off from other practical and often "powerful" commonsense and concrete forms of knowledge (for example, that of chefs and builders). But, Barnes argues, it would be a mistake to attempt to identify, in the Popperian sense, one scientific method or one set of procedures that is the source of the strength (the "difference") of science. Here empirical research into local scientific cultures is thought to reveal a rich diversity of practices. Scientists cannot, or have not, been shown to possess a unique shared set of conventions for procedure and evaluation. What characterizes specific sciences (their "difference" from other activities – beyond a tendency toward abstraction and quantification) are, in Barnes' view, "special linguistic forms," "special esoteric clusters of activity," and "characteristic artifacts." What is actually at work, functioning as scientific culture in a localized area, Barnes would argue, is the job of historically informed sociologists, or sociologically informed historians, to find out and make explicit. He also goes on to outline other characteristics of science as a whole which he believes empirical research has, in fact, uncovered and which are entirely in line with Merton's views (differentiation into specialties, relative autonomy *vis-à-vis* the larger society, and the possession of some internal system of social control, that is, rewards and punishments). Barnes also argues for several characteristics that do not fit neatly into the

Mertonian–Popperian synthesis. These are, first, ideas derived largely from the work of Mary Hesse (1963), namely, the use of "metaphor" by scientists in constructing models and, secondly, the largely inductive nature of scientific procedures.

As stated above, "metaphors," "images," and "models" become central to this sociology of science and it then becomes a matter of empirical investigation to uncover to what extent such ways of thinking are related to social bases or social interests. The emphasis on social and personal interests as playing a role in the construction of scientific knowledge, or in the resolution of conflicts within science over competing models, is the strong hypothesis offered by the Strong Programme. It is not necessitated by the Barnes–Hesse synthesis, nor by the four tenets, but neither is it contradicted by them and it is a place to begin research. It has, however, generated interesting, contentious, and somewhat enduring historiography and sociology which I, for one, value. This point is also made by Steve Shapin (1983) in his review of the empirical accomplishments of the Strong Programme.

There have been two major responses within constructionism to the Strong Programme. One, on the part of ethnomethodologists, has been to criticize it for taking as unproblematic the ability of its investigators to identify the "models or metaphors" and "interests" of the scientists whom they study. This criticism, although pertinent, has not generated of itself a body of empirical research. What has generated empirical work among ethnomethodologically informed sociologists of science has been a selective use of ethnomethodological notions and other, ethnographic, research practices. This will be discussed immediately below. The second response can also be briefly discussed at this point, and that has been the adoption by Michael Mulkay and others (Mulkay *et al.* 1983; Gilbert and Mulkay 1984; Mulkay 1985) of the Strong Programme's concerns with conflict resolution and interests. However, in taking up these issues Mulkay, at least, has turned to an analysis of strategies of writing, structures of scientific texts, and rhetorical practice, as places to look for "explanations" for why some scientific claims get accepted as "true." In other words, Mulkay has increasingly textualized the concerns of the Strong Programme.

Ethnomethodology and laboratory studies

Ethnomethodology is the study of how individuals and groups construct either consensus or the necessary illusion of consensus (that is, in a sense construct "reality") by means of linguistic practices, behavioral rules, interpretation of rules, record keeping, and classification (Garfinkel 1967). Much of this can be classified under the rubric "accounting" or the producing of "accounts," which structure reality and give it facticity or objectivity.

What Woolgar (1981a; 1981b) as an ethnomethodologist points out, in his critique of the Strong Programme, is that although it has focused on the way knowledge is constructed in the interaction of producers who are largely limited in their choice of metaphors and influenced in their actions and choices by social interests, the Programme itself is asymmetrical in its own procedures. Woolgar argues that Barnes and others take scientific knowledge as constructed but take as unproblematic their own ability to identify metaphors and, especially, interests. He would ask: Are not the practitioners of the Strong Programme under the same cognitive constraints as the scientists they study? This unproblematic unreflexivity of the Strong Programme, Woolgar feels, reveals an ultimate "realist" position on its part and one that is at odds not only with its own fourth tenet but with constructionism in general. Woolgar argues that the only way out of this dilemma is a full-fledged constructionism, the way to which has already been revealed by ethnomethodology, namely, an acceptance of the view that "accounts are the reality." One reasonable consequence of these criticisms of the Strong Programme would be, therefore, to adopt the full ethnomethodological program, to view scientific reality and knowledge as "accounts" and to study how such accounts are built up and maintained in linguistic and other practices.

This is, in fact, the *ethnomethodological* point in Latour and Woolgar's (1987) *Laboratory Life: The Social Construction of Scientific Facts*. Here scientific knowledge is presented as the consequence of accounting practices and "facts" are constructed in speech, activity, and writing. In this book Latour and Woolgar are presented as anthropologists of science first closely observing and recording scientists' behavior in the laboratory. Scientists are shown engaging in a series of "activities" (doing experiments on animals which involve cutting, shaking, marking, etc., handling equipment, reading, writing, talking). It becomes apparent to the anthropologists that the outcome of such activities is various literary products, usually scientific articles. From this they reason that the ultimate goal of laboratory practice, and by extension all science, is the production of "literary inscriptions." Science is these activities, its goal is to produce literary inscription. The inscriptions themselves are then used by scientists to convince others that something is a "fact" – in the case of *Laboratory Life*, that a substance called "TRF(H)" exists and that it has specific physiological effects. Furthermore, along with the production of "facts," and as a necessary basis for their production, is the production of "facticity," namely, the belief that facts actually exist and that their history has nothing to do with their truth-value. Here scientific articles come into the picture in a big way since it is the inclusion of facts in scientific articles that produces facticity. For scientists, articles are the devices by which a consensus about the world is constructed and maintained on two levels: articles build consensus about the facticity of certain specific "facts" and they maintain the belief in "facticity" itself.

Literary practice and devices, for example, inscriptions, the scientific article, become the central notions in this sociology of science.

However, the strength of this type of constructionism has been less the dogmatic uncovering of the rules "discovered" by ethnomethodologists such as Garfinkel (the "ad hoc rule," "indexicality," the "etc. rule") than a synthesis of the general ethnomethodological attitude of taking reality as accounts with elements derived from a more general ethnographic tradition. This synthesis has been fortuitously combined with the selection of the laboratory site as the locus at which to investigate the production of reality as accounts. The major element drawn from more general ethnographic traditions (although also present in standard ethnomethodology) has consisted in the methodological practice of an initial distancing of the socio-logical observer from the "culture" of the subject. In the case of science this has meant treating a subsector of our "common" culture (that is, scientific practice, behaviors, and institutions) as something foreign to the sociologist or anthropologist of science. This approach has also involved a further move away from the Mertonian attempt to get at the internalized norms of scientists, as well as a partial solution to the problem of identifying "interests" faced by the Strong Programme. It does this by requiring that the observer pretend that even the most elementary statements and behaviors of scientists can only be understood by a hermeneutic which employs close observation and recording in the whole context of the laboratory.

However, two immediate objections can be raised to ethnomethodo-logically informed constructionism and ethnographic laboratory studies. First, it too is not reflexive enough, it too does not reflect upon its own base assumptions, it too presents its findings as "real," not "constructed." Latour and Woolgar admit as much in the postscript of their book, *Laboratory Life*. There, in a section on reflexivity, they claim that although their account was meant to be "the construction of fictions about fiction construction" other laboratory studies have unreflexively attempted to record science *"as it happens"* (1987: 282). Secondly, this is not the only tradition dealing with reality as accounts; others also present reality in this manner but draw upon a more literary notion of "account making," namely, that of the production and reading of texts. Once, therefore, the sociology of science has reached this stage of reflexivity, and has brought to view all reality as accounts, it has not been unreasonable for it to begin an incorporation of other forms of textual analysis into the subdiscipline.

Textuality: textual studies of science

To recognize the textuality of a work (for example, documents, literary works, science, sociological discourse about science) is, as Dominick

LaCapra has put it, to pay attention to it as a work, as a thing produced by language, grammar, interpretation, and practice. As LaCapra has written,

> More generally, the notion of textuality serves to render less dogmatic the concept of reality by pointing to the fact that one is "always already" implicated in the problems of language use as one attempts to gain critical perspective on these problems, and it raises the question of both the possibilities and limits of meaning. (1982: 50)

Now, programmatic statements, and paradigms for future sociological work, even though explicitly presented as initial and temporary, have a way of hardening, limiting options, and becoming straitjackets for research, as well as focusing debate on the programme or paradigm itself rather than on the work generated by it. I will, therefore, in this section, instead of offering a paradigm for the textual studies of science, give several examples where such an approach has already been adopted, briefly discussing the strategies employed in each. In the next section I will then point to recent works where sociologists and historians of science have connected "text" to the "world," and will speculate on what the next stage of development in the social studies of science might be.

I have selected three responses in the literature to the problems posed by reading science as text and by the occasional reflexive application of this insight, or view, to the sociology of science itself. I will first discuss the use of deconstructivist notions in the sociology of science. Here I will look at Michael Mulkay's essay "Conversation and texts" in *The Word and the World* (1985), and will show how deconstructivist strategies can be detected at work in this particular text. Secondly, I will discuss the use of ironic distancing as a response to the problems of reflexivity. Again the example will be drawn from Mulkay's *The Word and the World*, in this case from "Introductions." Finally, drawing on both Mulkay, and on Donna Haraway's *Primate Visions* (1989), I will discuss the weakening of the distinction between fiction and other more "objective" forms of writing, such as sociology and history.

By analyzing, in "Conversations and texts," an exchange of letters between two scientists concerning a conflict in stoichiometry, Mulkay is able to argue that paired opposites such as "fact/opinion," "fact/meaning," "fact/fiction," and "observation/interpretation" are used by scientists in a specifiable manner. He argues that one term of the pair is always offered as preferred and that an attempt is always made to appropriate that term to oneself in the exchange. The use of paired opposites in this manner generates the body of letters which Mulkay analyzes, since each move on the part of the two scientists, each use of such a set of terms, necessitates interpretive work in the attempt to appropriate the preferred term of the set. This interpretive work itself generates other texts utilizing paired opposites, leading to yet further attempts at mastery and appropriation. This, when combined with the fact that neither scientist is compelled, by difference in power, or by the rules of the game, to admit defeat (since this is an exchange of letters between supposed equals and there is no third party to whom they may appeal), leads to a series of letters which is, in principle, infinite. All of this is in line with deconstructivist, especially Derridian, notions concerning the deployment of dichotomous pairs in speech and writing, namely, that each term in a debate necessarily implies its "opposite," that writing and speech are forms of struggle for mastery, that the primary tactic for achieving such mastery is the appropriation to oneself of a "preferred" term by means of the suppression of the relationship between it and its pair, and that arguments are only "won" – the debate is only brought to an end – by a combination of such tactics of suppression and forgetting, and by exercises of power.

When we apply the need to do interpretation work to the activity of doing sociology itself another effect is achieved – ironic distancing. This is accomplished in parts of *The Word and the World* where Mulkay highlights the constructed nature of his own text. For example, in "Introductions," The Book first speaks for itself – in a standard monologic style, informing us, without question, of what it is about. Reader, however, and then Author, break into the text and engage in a dialogue with each other in which Author ultimately distances himself from The Book, claiming that he cannot accept full, intentional, responsibility for it. But Author as well soon falls into monologic form, attempting to establish a final truth about the text and demonstrating the difficulty of maintaining dialogue within the genre of book introductions.

By raising in the text itself the possibility of applying his own "discovered" forms of monologic discourse (which hides its origins in seeking to establish an authoritative voice) and dialogue (which is more patently literary and invites multiple interpretations) Mulkay achieves a distancing from his own text. In the face of this artful self-reflexivity we are forced to ask how seriously Mulkay takes what he is doing, and since this question is raised in the introductory section we are alerted and put on guard as to what Mulkay might be up to in the remaining sections of the book. Mulkay is, at the least, pointing to the fact that he, as an author, is caught in the same rules of writing and discourse he seeks to "uncover" and points to the limits of his power. The ultimate limit, in this case, seems to be the ironic questioning, by means of the self-reflexive distancing, of whether this is a serious or playful text (or whether that is a distinction which matters), whether the categories of monologue and dialogue are "objectively there" in the text or "created," and just how free, or constrained, Mulkay as a writer-sociologist is. Finally, we are led to ask if the ironic stance of simultaneous discovery and making, of reading naively and archly, is not the only way of being "already implicated" in the text as one seeks critically to analyze, and create, other, more localized, texts.

Another response to the textualization of reality, and of one's own practices, is to highlight the "fact" that all texts are makings by refusing to distinguish in any ultimate sense "fact" from "fiction." Again, Mulkay does this especially well in the chapter of the *The Word and the World* entitled "The Scientist talks back: A one-act play." In this essay Mulkay playfully constructs a one-act play in which Scientist and Sociologists 1, 2 and 3 discuss replication. Since this play serves the same purpose as a philosophical treatise on, or sociological study of, replication, it is a replication of other analytic discourses on the subject and, since it is a "fiction," it leads us to question the distinction between fiction writing and objective knowledge. The text is a self-commenting and ironic accomplishment.

Donna Haraway in *Primate Visions* is more straightforward. Nonetheless, she achieves the same effect – a questioning, by means of the text, of the distinction between the genres of historiography and science fiction. Haraway's task is to show us that primatology has functioned as a uniquely fruitful locus for constructing nature, gender, and species. Borrowing explicitly from feminist perspectives, and employing a largely "Strong Programme" reading of *Laboratory Life*, a main part of her work is concerned with exhibiting the connections between gender notions and societal "interests" (maintaining particular notions of gender as an exercise of power, or changing them as a way of restructuring power relations) and the scientific "discoveries" of primatology. However, alongside her historical account of primatology Haraway places a reflexive running commentary on her own writing of history. The commentary does not allow us to forget for a moment that Haraway's work is as much a construction as those of the modern discipline she studies, and one also caught in structures of gender–power relations. She writes

> By history I mean a corrosive sense of the contradictions and multiple material-semiotic practices at the heart of scientific knowledge. History is not a completed past simply waiting to be applied to deepen a time probe or to give a perspective. It is a discipline reworked by postmodern insights about always split, fragmented, and multiple subjects, identities, and collectivities. All units and actors cohere partially and provisionally, held together by complex material-semiotic-social practices. In the space opened up by such contradictions and multiplicities lies the possibility for reflexive responsibility for the shape of narrative fields. (1989: 172)

One effect of this sort of textual self-commentary, by emphasizing the constructed and deconstructing nature of all texts, is to allow us, in the last chapter of *Primate Visions*, "Reprise: Science fiction, fictions of science, and primatology" to see as reasonable the claim that we can "read" primatology as science fiction and science fiction as primatology.

Summary

If the sociology of science has been generated by means of the dichotomy sameness/difference, then, since the ethnomethodological deconstruction of the Strong Programme, "sameness" has been the dominant term. It may also be the case that with the textualization of the world we have argued ourselves into an impasse of sameness out of which we will not come. I think this view, however, greatly underestimates the resourcefulness of writers. What I, rather, would predict for the sociology of science is the following: (a) a continued use of insights and strategies drawn from literary theory and discourse analysis, and (b) eclectic attempts to link the "texts" of science to the "world" – to write both the sameness and the difference of science in a more modest and localized fashion.

I argue for (a) because I take it for granted that the problems of interpretation, of writing, of being already present in the text, are ones of which many sociologists are at least aware. Once raised such issues are not easily ignored. Furthermore, the responses discussed in the previous section (direct application of deconstructivist strategies to the reading of scientific texts, ironic distancing from one's own text, the refusal to admit an ultimate distinction between fact and fiction) do not exhaust possible ploys that can be developed in the textual studies of science. Textuality remains, therefore, both a problem and a promise. One cannot predict what future textual studies of science will look like, but I suspect that they will continue within the present trend in the sociology of culture of looking for observable structures in discourse, but will emphasize fewer conflicts in science and investigate to a greater extent scientists' own descriptions of scientific activities. This would be in line with Mulkay's call for greater dialogue between sociologist and scientist in constructing the texts of the sociology of science (1985: 102). Questions remaining to be explored in this area include: How do scientists talk about fraud? What strategies of writing and rhetoric exist around the identification, management and control of fraud? How do scientists talk about, and explain, citation use? How are citations used, or said to be used, in the construction of scientific articles? What "philosophies of science" exist among scientists? By what strategies of writing and rhetoric are these philosophies constructed and what role do they play in scientific practice? How do scientists talk about technique? How do scientists describe the role of technique in their own practice?

Linking up the texts of science to the world will also be a response because sociologists, including those engaged in textual studies, continue to be interested in the differential distribution of power, status, and economic resources that are traditionally taken as constituting the "social world." It is the world which resists what we say or write about it and it is the limit, the final "difference," to any of our texts (Derrida and McDonald 1981). On the other hand, it has become impossible to speak and write directly, or naively, about this radical difference. Because of the problems raised in textual studies sociologists are becoming aware that one can only attempt such discourse if one is careful not to speak in a totalizing fashion, if one accepts the fragmented manner of speaking and writing which characterizes our postmodern period, if one rejects as hopeless any attempt to "solve" the problem of the relationship of the text to the world. What one then produces are localized, insightful, and detailed, empirical accounts. This need to produce only localized studies may be seen as a weakness, as a retreat from sociology's goal of generalizing. But localization, and concrete empirical studies, do not mean lack of generalization, although they will probably mean lower level generalizations more tentatively offered. Moreover, other trends in sociology are unqualifiedly hopeful, such as recent indications that sociological theory is becoming decentralized (Ritzer 1990). This should free sociologists to draw upon the rich variety of texts and theories present in sociology in order to make their own individual texts about the connection of the text to the world. Furthermore, sociologists will be able to do so without too great a concern for remaining within paradigm, programme, or school, or even within "sociology" itself. The result of the convergence of these two trends should, therefore, be more "creative," eccentric, or eclectic, accounts.

Examples of such increasingly eclectic attempts at relating text to the world can be found in recent work in the sociology and history of science. One such example is Chandra Mukerji's sociological history of oceanography, *A Fragile Power: Scientists and the State* (1989). Mukerji's account consists of a concrete detailing of the structuring effects soft governmental money has had on scientific careers, institutions, and research, in the discipline of oceanography. She argues that soft money is an ideal form of funding from the perspective of the American state apparatus in that it both allows scientists to believe they exercise autonomy, while at the same time it directs research and maintains a reserve labor force of scientists which can be brought into use by the state when necessary. In subtle ways state power in its distribution of economic resources influences the content of science, or in Mukerji's terms, "directs the discourse of science." Donna Haraway's *Primate Visions*, discussed above, is another example of an eclectic use of notions drawn from a variety of sources. Haraway does not seek to "theoretically integrate" ideas from materialism, semiotics, feminist theory, and the ideas of the Strong Programme. Rather she uses them in telling her politically informed story of primatology.

Bruno Latour's *Science In Action* (1987) is a detailed treatment, on a largely non-empirical level, of the problems of linking text to the world. Many of his points in this book are a working out of those made in the earlier *Laboratory Life*. For example, he discusses the ability of literature (specifically collections of scientific articles) to define and redefine certain articles as "objectively" true or false. Latour argues that in writing an article by citing other articles a scientist is restating and redefining the content of the articles cited as an act of appropriation. There exists no fixed meaning to articles used as citations; in fact stronger articles may be those which possess sufficient ambiguity, or margin, for them to be greatly redefined in context and thereby more easily appropriated and used. It can also be pointed out that a focus on "meaning" in this sense, as the difference which exists between various texts (the "original" article and the one which seeks to use it) is in accord both with newer sociological notions of objectivity (the ability to find, or produce, observable structural differences in texts) and with Derridian definitions of meaning as difference and absence. "Meaning" lies in difference – not in some mental state of the author of the cited, or the author of the citing, article, nor in either article taken separately. Latour deals with a great number of issues in *Science In Action*, and it is impossible to go into them all here. Suffice it to say that the book represents a treatment of the interaction of textual practices (often cast in Derridian terminology) and such worldly factors as machine use, laboratories, scientific networks, mobilization and access to resources, and the development of specialized roles in science. *Science In Action* may be the most thorough attempt to date at linking textual studies and traditional sociological concerns, and stands as a refutation of the criticism that this particular brand of sociology of science ignores power and resource issues or is incapable of contributing to more "mainline" debates in the discipline as a whole.

Finally, as a specific empirical locus at which to produce attempts to link text to the world I would propose the politics of the body. By "politics of the body" I mean the interaction of science, citizens, the media, and the state, in the areas of (a) reproduction rights, (b) AIDS research and treatment, (c) the medical treatment of the dying, (d) issues of national health insurance, medical treatment as a "right," and local medical policies in regard to the poor. This is not the only area of empirical research which could be fruitful. Others also come to mind, environmental science and policy making being one example, but what this, along with the other areas, offers is a specific place at which to investigate the power of government, science, citizens' groups, and the media in the making of political and policy decisions in which scientific knowledge plays a central role. Ideally what would be produced is a richly articulated set of connections between the textual structures of the various types of statements issued (internal bureaucratic, public media, "scientific," public policy), and the economic, status, and power resources mobilized by the players. Such a description would then give us some indication as to how, at the present time, the interaction of various groups with varying degrees and types of resources, and structures exhibited by various types of texts, produce scientific or political outcomes. These types of studies would, furthermore, work against the opinion, presently held in some quarters, that sociology has become a mandarin discipline, that is, one focusing largely on itself and its own texts as opposed to issues of public life.

What has been offered here is a narrative, a history as story, of the (largely) American and British side of the sociology of science. It is, of course, one among an infinite number of possible narratives, and one told from a particular perspective. Its point has been to convince others that the sociology of science has been impelled, both by its goal of stating the sameness/difference of science and by sociological factors associated with discipline building, toward the incorporation of insights from literary theory and discourse analysis in its own texts about science. It is suggested that the issues associated with textuality, and interpretation, once brought to the attention of a discipline, cannot be ignored or wished away. How they are dealt with, however, is another matter. Here no strict rules can be laid down in advance, nor any specific predictions made. Furthermore, it has been argued that even with the development of "textual studies of science," there is no need to abandon the useful insights of past work in the field – Mertonian, Strong Programme, ethnomethodology and laboratory studies. This is especially the case if one's goal is to give a detailed and convincing account of a specific development, or a specific area of interaction between science and scientific texts, and society and societal texts. The decentering which seems to be accompanying the maturity of sociology should also allow for the inclusion of the insights of past sociologies along with those of the present. Inclusion and excess of theory and explanans rather than exclusion and the narrow use of one theory's set of ideas is probably best – whatever tells a story convincingly (Cixous 1975). Finally it should also be pointed out again that the sociology of science holds the continued promise of exciting and relevant work. As stated above, in our late twentieth-century postmodern culture, where science, technology, the media, the state, and citizen's groups, become ever more interactive in creating public discourse about power and policy issues, sociologists of science, by producing socially engaged accounts, can enter debates where they can make a difference.

References

Barnes, Barry. 1974. *Scientific Knowledge and Sociological Theory*. London: Routledge & Kegan Paul.

Ben-David, Joseph and Zloczower, Avraham. 1972. Universities and academic systems in modern societies. *European Journal of Sociology* 23: 45–84.

Bloor, David. 1976. *Knowledge and Social Imagery*. London: Routledge & Kegan Paul.

Cixous, Hélène. 1975. Sorties: out and out: Attacks/ways out/forays. In *The Newly Born Woman*. Minneapolis, Minn.: University of Minnesota Press.

Derrida, Jacques. 1976. *Of Grammatology*. Baltimore, Md.: Johns Hopkins University Press.

Derrida, Jacques. 1978. *Writing and Difference*. Chicago: University of Chicago Press.

Derrida, Jacques and McDonald, Christine V. 1981. Interviews: Choreographies. *Diacritics* 2: 66–76.

Garfinkel, Harold. 1967. *Studies in Ethnomethodology*. Englewood Cliffs, NJ: Prentice Hall.

Gilbert, G. N. and Mulkay, Michael. 1984. *Opening Pandora's Box: A Sociological Analysis of Scientists' Discourse*. Cambridge: Cambridge University Press.

Haraway, Donna. 1989. *Primate Visions: Race, Gender, and Nature in the World of Modern Science*. London: Routledge & Kegan Paul.

Hesse, Mary. 1963. *Models and Analogies in Science*. London: Sheed & Ward.

LaCapra, Dominick. 1982. Rethinking intellectual history and reading texts. In D. LaCapra and S. L. Kaplan (eds), *Modern European Intellectual History: Reappraisals and New Perspectives*. Ithaca, NY: Cornell University Press.

Latour, Bruno. 1987. *Science In Action*. Cambridge, Mass.: Harvard University Press.

Latour, Bruno and Woolgar, Steve. 1987. *Laboratory Life: The Social Construction of Scientific Facts*. Princeton, NJ: Princeton University Press.

Lyotard, Jean-François. 1984. *The Postmodern Condition: A Report on Knowledge*. Minneapolis, Minn.: University of Minnesota Press.

Merton, Robert K. 1973a. The neglect of the sociology of science. In R. K. Merton, *The Sociology of Science: Theoretical and Empirical Investigations*. Chicago: University of Chicago Press.

Merton, Robert K. 1973b. The normative structure of science. In R. K. Merton, *The Sociology of Science: Theoretical and Empirical Investigations*. Chicago: University of Chicago Press.

Merton, Robert K. 1973c. Paradigm for the sociology of science. In R. K. Merton, *The Sociology of Science: Theoretical and Empirical Investigations*. Chicago: University of Chicago Press.

Mukerji, Chandra. 1989. *A Fragile Power: Scientists and the State*. Princeton, NJ: Princeton University Press.

Mulkay, Michael. 1985. *The Word and the World: Explorations in the Form of Sociological Analysis*. London: George Allen & Unwin.

Mulkay, Michael, Potter, J., and Yearly, S. 1983. Why an analysis of scientists' discourse is needed. In K. Knorr-Cetina and M. Mulkay (eds), *Science Observed: Perspectives on the Social Studies of Science*. Beverly Hills, Calif.: Sage.

Popper, Karl. 1968. *The Logic of Scientific Discovery*. New York: Harper & Row.

Ritzer, George (ed.) 1990. *Frontiers of Social Theory: The New Syntheses*. New York: Columbia University Press.

Rorty, Richard. 1989. *Contingency, Irony, and Solidarity*. Cambridge: Cambridge University Press.

Saussure, Ferdinand de. 1983. *A Course in General Linguistics*. London: Duckworth.

Shapin, Steven. 1983. History of science and its sociological reconstructions. *History of Science* 20: 157–211.

Turner, Steven, Kerwin, Edward, and Woolwine, David. 1984. Careers and creativity in nineteenth century physiology: Zloczower *Redux*. *Isis* 75: 523–9.

Woolgar, Steve. 1981a. Interests and explanations in the social studies of science. *Social Studies of Science* 11: 365–94.

Woolgar, Steve. 1981b. Critique and criticism: Two readings of ethnomethodology. *Social Studies of Science* 11: 504–14.

Wuthnow, Robert. 1987. *Meaning and the Moral Order: Explorations in Cultural Analysis*. Berkeley, Calif.: University of California Press.

Zloczower, Avraham. 1960. Career opportunities and the growth of scientific discovery in nineteenth century Germany, with special references to physiology. MSc diss., Hebrew University, Jerusalem.

5

Paradox in the discourse of science

Joan M. Morris

Introduction

In this paper I will (a) discuss the concept of "interpretive community" as it applies to scientific communities; (b) explain why establishing new scientific journals presents a paradox in that it imposes a need for addressing aims which may be considered conflictual; and (c) present a discourse analysis using journals' opening editorial statements, providing examples which illustrate the ways in which this paradox is addressed in the founding of new scientific journals.[1]

New journal editorials are used because they offer the analyst a unique opportunity for investigating scientists' conceptions of the development of science. It is an appropriate place for reflections on recent histories and descriptions of the processes involved. The eventual success or failure of the venture represented in the new journal can only be borne out by time, but the editorials give us access to the hopes and expectations which were set out for the journal at its inception.

Establishing community in written discourse

Austin's original (1962) differentiation between "performatives" (speech acts aimed at getting something done) and "constatives" (descriptive statements) laid the groundwork for further discussion of speakers' intentions. Austin eventually gave up the performative–constative distinction, admitting that all language is actually performative. All language is aimed at getting something done and this includes both spoken and written language. In a discussion of literary works, Eagleton (1983: 118) says written discourse "can be seen as speech acts, or as an imitation of them . . . [it] may appear to be describing the world, and sometimes actually does so, but its real function is performative: it uses language . . . to bring about certain effects in the reader . . . discourse as social action."

Conversation, which is obviously interactive, is usually considered qualitatively different from written discourse. Face-to-face interaction as a form of communication is different from written discourse in key ways. The most obvious is that conversation allows exchange between participants; transactions are negotiated in ongoing fashion. It is this interactive dimension of discourse that is identified by ethnomethodologists as fundamental. Conversation analysis insists on the context-dependency of discourse. For the conversation analyst, the significance of a speaker's communicative action can only be adequately understood within the ongoing sequence of actions which constitute the present circumstance (Heritage 1984). This is related to Garfinkel's insistence that talk is both indexical and reflexive (1967).

Written discourse, on the other hand, not being produced in the physical presence of an actual conversational partner, is not transactional in the same way. Since written texts are usually produced by a solitary author, to claim that texts can be interactive entails a renegotiation of the term. This conception requires a more explicit dependence on the influence of community on language use. While ethnomethodology is based on the insistence that individuals both generate and make sense of social action through existent patterns (codes, orders), that emphasis is sometimes displaced by a focus on the contextual dependency and problematics of individual interaction. However, the basis of conversation analysis (similar to the method used herein) is the premise that language systems epitomize patterned social action. Language is functional as a communicative medium only within a community of competent language users. This requires knowledge of a language system which exists for individuals prior to and independent of specific interaction situations. The language system works for a community of users because of its structural properties, that is, as a set of implicit linguistic rules through which messages may be negotiated but the rules, themselves, are not subject to negotiation.

The reciprocal effect of the relationship between community and language has been studied from several perspectives. Sociolinguists' conceptions of "speech communities" have been described in terms of codes (Bernstein 1990), styles (Hymes 1974), or registers (Halliday 1978) and various taxonomies have been established for classifying particular linguistic communities (Cicourel 1985; Labov 1972; Coulthard and Montgomery 1981). In the field of literary criticism, the term, "interpretive community" has recently been used by reader–response critics from various perspectives (Bleich 1975; Fish 1980; Leenhardt 1980; Pratt 1988).

Community is more than a taxonomic device for subdividing language groups. An interpretive community provides a social context within which communication can occur.[2] Interpretive communities are social systems which provide intelligibility and "the meanings that constitute the social context are realized through selections in the meaning potential of language" (Halliday 1978: 189). Communicators are bound by the conventions of the communication system, in fact, by the "prejudices inherent in the very language [they] speak" (Waddell 1988: 112). However, it is only *within* a community that communication is possible. Language is thus inherently interactive, and is "indissociably [*sic*] interwoven with our practical forms of life" (Eagleton 1983: 147). In this sense, written and spoken language are meaningful only within socially interactive communities. Whether face-to-face or writer-to-reader, social relevance is a prerequisite to communication. Interpretive communities provide the context which both allows and limits understanding and as Fish warns us to keep in mind, "the understanding achieved by two or more persons is specific to that system and determinate only within its confines" (1980: 304). This is similar to Garfinkel's insistence on the determinacy of present contexts.

While it is true that communicators create community as they interact, there is also the requirement that some level of commonality exist before transactions can take place. One must have some basis for interpretation before messages can be attributed meaning. If we begin at a general level, we could say that a shared language is required if communication is to occur. But at an even more general level, it is possible to imagine communication without a common language, among individuals who do not share a common language (perhaps, as some researchers maintain, even among members of different species). In such cases, what is shared is difficult to quantify. The content of messages may be vague, but still be considered to communicate something (ardent pet owners, for example, fervently claim to communicate regularly with their animals).

If such "communication" can be said to occur at a very general level, at another extreme we might find an esoteric form of communication which is shared by only a few "insiders." For example, highly specialized scientists might use a technical language which is only comprehended by a few; in other words, most of us would find their lab talk incomprehensible, although we have a common language with them. Within the community which understands such messages, we can assume a great deal more is shared. A body of technical and specific scientific knowledge is shared by community members which makes their communication more efficient.

Ludwik Fleck's *Genesis and Development of a Scientific Fact* provides a sociological account of the development of knowledge within scientific communities.[3] His "thought collective" is based on the idea that communication of ideas is possible only within collectivities of individuals who share thought structures, that is, interpretive communities. Though Fleck was writing about the development of a specific research area, his model has general applicability. It is similar to the position stated above in that it views cognition, not as a strictly individual process but as the result of *social* activity, and language, not as a neutral medium of communication but as essentially constitutive in shaping commonsense versions of the world.

This view does not leave individual agency out, but sees individuals as components of a collectivity (the whole which is greater than the sum of its parts). Since individuals belong to a number of thought collectives, there is always overlap. When aspects of one thought collective are applied to another, unique combinations may be made, giving the impression that an individual has made a creative leap. But the major point is that the content of knowledge and communication is understandable to members of a collectivity only to the extent that similarities are shared. Fleck (in much the same way that Kuhn described later) held that scientific knowledge, as well as any other kind of knowledge, is socially constructed. This is a similar position to that of Fish who, as discussed above, maintains that communication can only occur within a community which shares a socially constructed worldview, that is interpretive communities both allow and limit communication.

Community, then, provides both the context and the foundation for interaction, whether written or face-to-face. Communicative aims, though embodied in individual communications, are provided and defined within the parameters of particular communities. Written forms of discourse, such as conversations, are both conceived and constrained within the boundaries of their communities and are thus subject to many of the same constraints.

Written discourse, as acknowledged above, differs from face-to-face interaction in that, unlike a living speech situation, it is not negotiated interactively (cooperatively between social actors) in an ongoing fashion. It would be a mistake, however, to assume that this implies a written text has some sort of static and inflexible meaning. Indeed, one might claim that the very fact that written texts have become detached from here-and-now situations offers the opportunity for a kind of interaction that is not possible in face-to-face communication. Eagleton describes a text in this way:

> It is a piece of language which has been detached from any specific 'living' relationship and thus subject to the 'reinscriptions' and reinterpretations of many different readers. The work itself cannot 'foresee' its own future history of interpretations, cannot control and delimit these readings as we can do, or try to do, in face-to-face conversation. Its 'anonymity' is part of its very structure, not just an unfortunate accident which befalls it; and in this sense to be an 'author' – the 'origin' of one's own meanings with 'authority' over them – is a myth. (1983: 119)

94

Various readers may and probably will give different interpretations that depend on their social or historical contexts, just as one reader, on various occasions may give different interpretations.[4] A variety of interpretations may be said to be derived from a text but specific interpretations are dependent on specific interpreters, who find meaning according to the interpretive communities to which they belong.

That point having been made, however, it is necessary to look at the other side of the coin, to provide some grounding for such a relativistic approach. Indeed, it would be foolish to claim that texts are not bounded in any way, that any sort of interpretation is possible. To say that interpretation of a text may vary according to social context is not to say that a text may have an infinite variety of meanings. Writers and readers are not (and cannot be) extreme relativists.[5] Not just any interpretation is possible at a given time but a range of interpretations which is shaped by the attendant interpretive communities. Though the meanings attributed to texts do not remain static over time, interpretations at any given time are meaningful within particular frames of reference. Texts have, by the nature of their constructions, a range of possible interpretations and can be said to "orient" readers according to intended effects. Readers come to the situation (created in the text) expecting to have particular questions answered. Some questions might be expectations brought by the reader to the text; others might be developed within the text itself.[6]

Individual writers attempt to communicate with potential readers in ways which are appropriate within their communities. They write particular readers into their texts inevitably leaving room for readers to make their own interpretations.[7] The structure of discourse is understandable within the social context (structure) in which it is constructed and transmitted. The availability of a system of meanings within an interpretive community allows writers to convey messages (or a particular range of messages) and readers to comprehend them (or be satisfied with the assumption that they have). The directions of interpretations might be suggested by the writer, but are not laid down in the text in a way which leaves room for only one right interpretation. The eventual effect of a text need not be synonymous with the assumptions and intentions of actual authors; in fact, some interpretations might be antithetical to his or her intentions. While it is true that a text, once created, exists independently of its writer, there is no inherent meaning in the text itself. Words imply no necessary interpretation. Writing and reading take place within the shared system of meanings of an interpretive community and it is only within the "institutional nesting" (Fish 1980: 308) of such a community that communication is made intelligible.

Paradox in scientific discourse

Discourse analysis has emerged as an important method in the sociology of science only in recent years. Prior to Gusfield's 1976 paper on drinking driver research, the discourse of science was largely ignored as a site for analysis. In fact, the prevailing attitude was that scientific discourse, by its very nature, was not subject to the same sorts of social and cultural influences we recognize in other types of discourse. The term "scientific" has traditionally been taken to imply a high degree of authenticity and objectivity. Scientific discourse was seen as a kind of black box and we have only recently begun to dismantle it through analysis.[8]

The present project is an analysis of scientific discourse which addresses the manner in which paradox is handled in written science texts; specifically, the discourse of justification which surrounds establishing new scientific journals. In first editorials of new journals we find opening statements in which editors introduce the new journal and describe its development, providing a context for inviting others to join a community of like-minded researchers. First editorials are often the sites of explanations about how research areas have developed, how new disciplines have been formed. They address the "whos" and "whys" surrounding such events and very often offer reflections on the larger enterprise of science itself.

Editorials serve a purpose which is quite different from the technical articles or theoretical papers found in the remainder of the journal. They are written with less technical jargon, to meet more sociable or political aims. In this particular type of editorial the journal–reader relationship is addressed, the parameters spelled out, and an invitation offered to prospective participants and community members.

One of the ways this may be done is through the use of ritual. Wuthnow defines ritual as behavior which is "structured to evoke and communicate meanings" (1987: 99) and warns against the popular stereotypes of ritual which relegate it to the realm of supernatural or primitive rites. It is within the "thought collectives" of communities that rituals develop. Our everyday lives are immersed in rituals and they define our daily activities as culturally significant or not. Activities can be seen as representing a continuum with expressive at one end and instrumental at the other. Instrumental activities are aimed simply at achieving some purpose while expressive activities are symbolic acts which communicate some deeper meaning. As an example, in most cases sending someone a birthday card is an expressive act while writing a note about a telephone message is an instrumental act.

Identifying with traditional science

One of the main purposes of first journal editorials can be associated with the expressive end of this continuum. Given the necessity for the journal to stake a legitimate claim on a portion of the scientific readership, it is essential that the endeavor be identified within the parameters of an acceptable scientific tradition. Thus the editorials must make statements which are culturally significant to the scientific community. Statements which refer to science in the traditional "science as objective knowledge" manner are ritualized accounts and are an attempt (though perhaps an implicit one) by the writers to gain legitimacy among prospective community members by reference to a view of science held by the larger community. In a journal's opening editorial statement, there is an implied need to associate the journal with the established enterprise of science. Ritual-talk about science is a way of identifying with the traditional power structure of the larger scientific community.

New journals as a break from the orthodoxy

New journals always, to some extent, represent a break from the status quo. There must be some sort of split, or there would be no justification for establishing a new journal. This may result from a major schism in a scientific field or may be seen as nothing more than the branching of an established research area into a sub-specialty or separate field of study. In either case, it is necessary for constituents to identify themselves as separate from an existing group. The new journal serves as a concrete representation of the shared interests of a community of reseachers in a particular research problem. Their common interest identifies them as similar to each other and different enough from the larger group to warrant a public statement of their status as a separate group.

The resulting paradox

Since most agree that there is already an abundance of scientific journals,[9] there is an inherent need to justify starting another one. The journal must be portrayed as both different enough to warrant a break from the status quo and conventional enough to be considered legitimate by the scientific community. Thus there is a need to emphasize both legitimacy and differentiation in the opening statements of new journals. To the extent that these are contradictory concepts, the problem takes on a paradoxical dimension, a problem which must be addressed in the text. The discourse analysis presented below focuses on this problem, giving examples of the means by which it is addressed, and the ways which journals representing different disciplines are similar to or different from each other in their handling of the paradox.

The discourse of justification in first editorials

In the preceding sections a case has been made (a) that interpretive communities are constitutive of the understanding of communication taking place within them, and (b) that establishing new scientific journals entails appealing to the conflicting needs of the scientific community for both legitimacy and differentiation – with paradoxical implications. This last and longest section offers a textual analysis which focuses on some of the ways in which this paradox is addressed in journals' first editorial statements.

The texts were collected from journals located at several university libraries and the United States Library of Congress. Drawn from fifteen disciplines, including biological, medical, physical, and social sciences, and liberal arts, the sample consists of 140 editorials written between 1887 and 1986.[10]

The type of discourse analysis presented here is similar, methodologically, to recent analyses in the sociology of science literature (Gilbert and Mulkay 1984; Mulkay 1985). These authors identify frequently occurring "interpretative practices and repertoires" (Mulkay, Potter, and Yearly 1983: 199). Thus, a number of well-defined categories is developed through an incremental, inductive process, out of the texts themselves, to be used in further analysis.

For example, in the editorials it was a common strategy to begin with the statement that there are already too many journals in the field. This seems somewhat strange, given the context of the statement – the opening remarks of yet another new journal. But statements to this effect occurred with enough frequency that one could expect, on reading several first editorials, to come across statements similar to these:[11]

> Not Another Journal!
> The appearance of yet another journal is hardly expected to be greeted with universal acclaim. Statements such as "I can't keep up with the existing ones," or "There is too much unnecessary publication now," are predictable . . . (*Transfusion* 1961)

> The appearance of a new journal will raise both hopes and doubts. Some will argue that we need a new journal as much as we need a new APA division, since our bookshelves are already filled with everything from the austere JEP to the zestful Psychology Today . . . (*Professional Psychology* 1969)

In these two examples, we can see aspects of the ritual Wuthnow identifies as necessary for even everyday interaction. The writers are appealing to recognizable themes. Both begin with an acknowledgement of the kind of ambivalence a researcher is likely to feel when presented with "yet another" new journal. The second one then characterizes the variety of journals in the field, taking further the strategy of asking, implicitly, "So why is this journal worthy of your attention?" Gilbert and Mulkay, in their discussion of the experimental papers of biochemists, identify a very similar technique. Opening sentences are written in such a way as to set up a contrast with what follows. "The nature of the opening sentence prepares us to expect and to welcome the constrasting view which the second sentence reveals" (1980: 273).

These practices or devices, once identified, are used to set up a categorical scheme for further analysis of the texts. The set of categories, established in a preliminary analysis of a few texts, should be applicable to other tests belonging to the same corpus, in this case, other first editorials. When dealing with a large number of texts, categorization and coding become a necessity. Calculating frequencies of category usage can then be used to organize large bodies of textual data. A simple calculation of frequencies, however (though sometimes interesting in itself), is not the ultimate aim of the categorization process. A categorization scheme should be designed to tell us something about how particular problems are addressed in the texts. The emphasis is not on quantification of the texts by way of a coding or classification system, but instead on how particular issues are dealt with in each of the texts included in the analysis.

The issues I will attend to here, as outlined in the previous section, are legitimacy and differentiation, the question of how editorials in new journals address the contradictory problem of claiming to be different enough to warrant beginning a new journal yet remaining within the orthodoxy to the extent that the journal can enjoy the sanctions of legitimate status.

Staking a legitimate claim

The most common theme in these editorials is a description of the growth of a particular research area. Writers give historical narratives, invoking familiar themes of growth in science. The use of biological metaphors is common; discipline formation being likened to childbirth and development, growing interest compared to the growth of plants or trees. Scientific disciplines and research interests are often portrayed as branching and developing, inevitably evolving just as nature is constantly changing and developing. Descriptions of growth in these terms are ritualistic appeals to readers' fundamental assumptions about the orderliness of nature. This is an appeal to legitimacy in the highest order. Who could argue with the claim that living things grow, develop, and reproduce? To analogize organizational growth with natural growth is an effective strategy; the widely accepted legitimacy of one is easily transferred to the other. Consider these examples:

> The history of new journals is that new journals are in turn formed. This reality mirrors the history of investigation: new areas are discovered, flourish, and give rise to other new areas yet again. And so the pursuit of knowledge and its

communication like the universe itself, is ever expanding. The appearance of yet another new journal is justified in the proportion to the need it fulfills – its viability is in turn a function of the quality of its contents. The remarkable growth in the scope and volume of significant contributions to the cellular aspects of the immune response has created the need for a separate journal devoted primarily to cellular immunology. (*Cellular Immunology* 1970)

Additional journals, hence, appear to be an inevitable consequence of the expansion and specialization of a field. New scientific knowledge gained from research is sterile without some degree of publication; with limited or restricted publication it fails to achieve its highest objectives. (*Applied Physiology* 1948)

There is an awakening of interest in geography in the schools of America, wide spread and rapidly growing – an interest shared alike by teachers and students from the lowest grades to the university. A healthy growth is in progress . . . (*Journal of Geography* 1902)

A new star is on the horizon of medicine. In this country and abroad, pediatric surgery has reached the place when we must admit that it now deserves to rank with other specialties concerned with the particular problems of treating specific types of patients. The new journal is in strong hands, and the announcement of its founding has been widely approved by all those who have heard of its stated aims. (*Journal of Pediatric Surgery* 1966)

Some editorials, in addition to statements about growth in their research area, more explicitly associate the journal with a natural dialectic or evolutionary synthesis. This is more than expansion and growth. This is a claim that the journal represents the culmination of particular events or elements which move beyond the past and offer new hope for the future. The following example illustrates the point.

The emergence of solid-state physics as a recognized specialty of physics has taken place over a period of many years. A more recent development, stimulated partly by the growth of industrial interest in the field, has been the growing realization of the common interests between physicists and chemists in the problems of solids. It has been felt by many that the coming of age of solid-state science should be recognized by the publication of a journal devoted exclusively to this field. (*Physics and the Chemistry of Solids* 1956)

While the above examples illustrate claims to legitimacy based on references to nature or to science as an enterprise, there are also more local claims, statements addressing intra-discipline concerns. These are more specific statements, attempts to identify the new journal with well-known people or other journals. This kind of name-dropping can also be considered ritualistic. It has been identified as a "ceremonial" use of names; there is little evidence that the name is used to convey specific information, but it is used to associate the status of a respected name with the user (Wells and Picou 1981). Note the following:

> Early in the 19th century the French philosopher Comte described the emergence of a new occupation: the engineer. Today we are watching the emergence of the professional manager, the man who bears the same relation to the technical specialists of today as the engineers of Comte's generation did to the inventors and to the scientists. (*Management International* 1961)

In this example, the name-dropping technique is used in a variety of ways. (a) "Early in the 19th century" implies the legitimacy of history; (b) "French philosopher" carries the double status of the French intellectual, who has traditionally enjoyed a high status among the educated public, and philosophy, generally considered a well-established and highly regarded intellectual (as opposed to applied) discipline; (c) "Comte" is well known as a founding father in social thought; (d) the engineer is probably the most respected practitioner of the applied sciences; and (e) the analogy of the manager as an engineer draws attention to the ways in which the two professions are similar. Overall, this is a quite creative attempt to establish the legitimacy of both the new journal and the science it represents.

The essential difference

Though establishing legitimacy is a very important part of a new journal's opening editorial statement, it is essential to point out why it is necessary to add this particular journal to the existing literature. There is an imperative for the editor to differentiate this endeavor from others, justifying the claim that the new journal indeed addresses some particular need in the research area. When new journals are differentiated from the existing ones the implication is made that it somehow provides an improvement to the status quo. This is not done in the glowing, quasi-religious manner that is used when talking about nature or the development of science (as in the examples above). It is done by referring to the practical needs of researchers in less abstract, more concrete terms. In this sense, differentiation can be seen as an instrumental aim, as opposed to the expressive goals addressed in appeals for legitimacy.

The need most often cited for starting new journals is to provide a focus for the communication about a particular research topic, bringing together results, usually described as widely scattered in a number of other journals, into one central location. Such statements provide descriptions of development, often characterized as haphazard and disorganized, from a variety of origins. The journal is offered as a solution to the problems it describes, as an arena for addressing the common research interests to which it appeals. For example:

Most genetical papers of medical interest – and these are becoming increasingly numerous – are widely scattered throughout an ever-increasing number of specialized medical journals . . . The *Journal of Medical Genetics* is the first to be exclusively medical and to be broadly based. As such, it is a timely venture. (*Journal of Medical Genetics* 1964)

It is the aim of the *Journal of Insect Physiology* to foster the development of that knowledge by attracting to one focus a selection of the most important new contributions from all parts of the world. (*Journal of Insect Physiology* 1957)

Political Theory fills a long existing need for a journal of political philosophy that is broad in scope and international in coverage. The absence of such a journal was especially unfortunate because dialogue is essential for the practice of political philosophy. (*Political Theory* 1973)

Another need alluded to is the widely recognized one of faster publication of research results. In reference to individual scientists' careers, Bourdieu has observed, "A scientist who makes the same discovery a few weeks or a few months later (than a previously announced discovery) has been wasting his time, and his work is reduced to the status of worthless duplication of work already recognized (and this is why some researchers rush into print for fear of being overtaken)" (1975: 26). Having said it first is valued so highly that painstaking and thorough replication is almost unheard-of in science. Beginning with a promise of speedier publication is therefore a means of setting a journal apart from the status quo. It differentiates this one from the others and offers an advantage to those who join the community of researchers the journal represents. Below are some examples from the editorials.

The purpose of the journal is to provide expert reviewing and rapid publication of research articles in the general field of fluid dynamics of planets . . .
(*Dynamics of Atmospheres and Oceans* 1976)

Linguistic Analysis was conceived so as to provide a medium for the rapid dissemination of lively, high quality research articles in formal syntax, semantics, and phonology. (*Linguistic Analysis* 1975)

While it is expected that by publishing submitted papers within a few months only of their acceptance, this journal may set a new and desirable trend in the field of pharmacological publications in general and thereby contribute to the advancement of pharmacology throughout the world. (*European Journal of Pharmacology* 1967)

Perhaps the most obvious attempts to differentiate a new journal from the existing ones come in the form of an address to militant members of the potential readership. Militancy is a touchy subject, however, considering the strong need to establish the legitimacy of the journal. Only a few of the editorials make outright statements of this sort. One example invites the disenchanted to rally round the new journal as a way of restoring "balance." See below.

> In the interest of those many who have lost their intellectual input into social policy this journal is one place among many needed places which invites views that tend to restore the balance. Therefore, ideas are solicited from those many who have some intellectual views of their own which they are willing to set forth expressing what has happened, what is happening, and how it might be otherwise.
>
> (*Quarterly Journal of Ideology* 1976)

Perhaps my own favourite reference to militancy is the following example:

> Controversy, so far as possible, will be excluded.
>
> (*American Journal of Psychology* 1887)

Though this kind of statement is rare, the sentiment is probably widely shared. Journal publications may seem, at times, slightly controversial. But most would agree that most of what becomes published is well within the limits of acceptability within any particular research area.

Attending to the paradox

The aims of claiming legitimacy for a new journal (by identifying with orthodox, already established referents) while differentiating it from established ones (by emphasizing how this journal is really not like any other) can be seen as conflicting objectives. Yet both of these issues were addressed in the editorials (for frequencies, see Figure 5.1). Describing "natural" growth in a research area, referring to some kind of new synthesis in the evolution of a discipline, or referring to well-known or respected members of the research community are ways of establishing legitimacy in terms of the broader scientific community. Offering the practical benefits of providing speedier publication of results, consolidating scattered work into one journal, or appealing to disenchanted members of the scientific community all serve to differentiate the new journal from the existent ones.

Addressing these issues at different levels of abstraction serves to mask the paradoxical problem which they imply. Statements about legitimacy are expressive activities as described above. They invoke the familiar, ritualistic rhetoric of science as the dominant form of knowledge. Justifying the endeavor in this way associates questions about the new journal with questions about the sovereignty of science. Claiming the necessity of the journal as a solution to a practical problem provides further justification but at a lower level of abstraction and serves a more instrumental aim. This

103

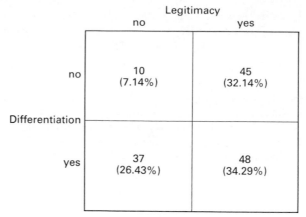

Figure 5.1

appeals to needs which are more immediate if not as weighty. Thus, instead of treating these as conflicting goals, the authors of opening editorials may address them both by treating them as complementary. They need only step up and down rungs of the abstraction ladder, to address expressive and instrumental goals together.

In many cases, that is just what these editorials do. Most addressed one or the other of these issues but a large proportion of them tackled both legitimacy and differentiation within the same editorial.

There are notable differences between disciplines on the use of these rhetorical devices.[12] Geography editorials address issues of legitimacy a great deal more often than they differentiate themselves from others, and sociology editorials follow the same pattern (see Table 5.1). Chemistry editorials tend to follow the opposite pattern; they differentiate the new journal from existing ones more often than they appeal to legitimacy. Across all disciplines, there is a tendency to address one of these concerns more than the other. However in some fields (such as physics, medicine) a majority of new journal editorials address both of these.

Using rhetorical devices which address concerns of both differentiation and legitimacy makes it necessary to pose the problem as a complementary rather than a paradoxical one. The lack of statistically significant differences between disciplines indicates a high degree of similarity on the manner in which new journals are justified.

Conclusion

The examples above provide insight into the justificatory practices which surround the establishment of new scientific journals. The strategy employed in these editorials provides an effective way of addressing the paradox implied by the conflicting goals of seeking both legitimacy and differentiation. By relying on familiar, ritualistic ways of referring to science, writers were able to tap "subtle and implicit messages" (Wuthnow 1987: 99) which are a part of the culture of science. Making statements about the natural growth of a scientific research area associates establishing the new journal with the laws of nature. Dropping the names of well-known members of the research community, organizations, or well respected journals communicates the intention of identifying with the orthodoxy, an acknowledgement of the hierarchy of the scientific community. Appealing to more practical concerns such as the need for speedier publication or the need to focus the field by consolidating the publication of research results under the auspices of one specialized journal is a way of differentiating the journal from the existing literature by offering to meet those needs. By posing these issues at different levels of abstraction, these potentially conflicting aims are recast as complementary ones.

Notes

1. Development of parts of this paper benefited greatly from discussions with both Marsha Witten and Robert Wuthnow. I acknowledge their contributions but take full responsibility for the final form of the argument presented herein.
2. The terms "community" and "interpretive community" are used interchangeably throughout the paper. Unless clearly stated otherwise, they are meant to be synonymous.
3. Fleck's book was written in 1935 but not translated until 1979, and was a precursor to the work of Thomas Kuhn.
4. This is the basis of the claim that it is not possible to formulate an *ultimate* reading of any text. Since the interpretation of a text is an interactive process which may result, at subsequent readings, in different interpretations based on the interpretive community of the reader, an analyst may never be sure that he or she has "gotten it right." This is true both for different readers and for different readings by the same reader. At reading 1 I may not formulate the same interpretation as I might at reading 2. The categories within which I am able to classify and interpret may change in between. This may sound like a wholly relativisitic approach but instead is based on a sort of dialectical determinism which prescribes what I am able to comprehend and is based on the social context of my experience.
5. This perspective is based on "reader-response" criticism and is exemplified in Fish (1980).
6. Woolgar points out some of the ways texts provide for particular readings: preliminary instructions (settings, headings, textual openings); externalizing devices (appeals to nature, the "evidence"); pathing devices (fixing the text in relation to past work); sequencing devices (ordering events in the narrative) (1988: 76–7).
7. This explanation comes from reader-response criticism, or audience-oriented criticism. See, e.g., Susan R. Suleiman and Inge Crosman, *The Reader in the Text* (Princeton: Princeton University Press, 1980).

8. See Bruno Latour, *Science in Action*. Cambridge, Mass.: Harvard University Press, 1987, for a complete discussion of scientific "black boxes," and Woolgar (1988) for a summary of recent developments in the sociology of science.
9. In fact, of the editorials included in the analysis, 13 percent mentioned in the editorial itself that there was already an excess of journals.
10. The proportions were weighted for proportional representativeness, e.g., the number of editorials in the sample were roughly proportionate to the number of journals in existence for a particular discipline.
11. All excerpts from the texts are direct quotes from the editorial, Vol. I, Number 1, of the journals designated.
12. The difference is not large enough, however, to achieve statistical significance (see Table 5.1).

References

Austin, J. L. 1962. *How To Do Things With Words*. London: Oxford University Press.
Berstein, Basil. 1990. *The Structuring of Pedagogic Discourse, Vol. IV: Class, Codes and Control*. London: Routledge.
Bleich, David. 1975. *Readings and Feelings: An Introduction to Subjective Criticism*. Urbana, Ill.: University of Illinois Press.
Bourdieu, Pierre. 1975. The specialty of the scientific field and the social conditions of the progress of reason. *Social Science Information* 14: 19–47.
Cicourel, Aron. 1985. Doctor-Patient Discourse. In *Handbook of Discourse Analysis*, Vol. 4, *Discourse Analysis in Society*. New York: Garland.
Coulthard, Malcolm and Montgomery, Martin (eds). 1981. *Studies in Discourse Analysis*. London: Routledge & Kegan Paul.
Eagleton, Terry. 1983. *Literary Theory: An Introduction*. Minneapolis, Minn.: University of Minnesota Press.
Fabb, Nigel, Attridge, Derek, Durant, Alan, and MacCabe, Colin (eds). 1988. *The Linguistics of Writing*. New York: Methuen.
Fish, Stanley. 1980. *Is There a Text In This Class? The Authority of Interpretive Communities*. Cambridge, Mass.: Harvard University Press.
Fleck, Ludwik. 1979. *Genesis and Development of a Scientific Fact*. Chicago: University of Chicago Press.
Garfinkel, Harold. 1967. *Studies in Ethnomethodology*. Englewood Cliffs, NJ: Prentice-Hall.
Gilbert, Nigel and Mulkay, Michael. 1980. Contexts of Scientific Discourse: Social Accounting in Experimental Papers. In Karin D. Knorr, Roger Krohn, and Roger Whitley (eds) *The Social Process of Scientific Investigation*. Dordrecht: Reidel.
Gilbert, Nigel and Mulkay, Michael. 1984. *Opening Pandora's Box*. Cambridge: Cambridge University Press.
Green, Bryan S. 1983. *Knowing the Poor*. London: Routledge & Kegan Paul.
Gusfield, Joseph. 1976. The literary rhetoric of science: Comedy and pathos in drinking driver research. *American Sociological Review* 41: 16–34.
Halliday, M. A. K. 1978. *Language as Social Semiotic*. London: Edward Arnold.
Heritage, John. 1984. *Garfinkel and Ethnomethodology*. Cambridge: Polity Press.
Hymes, Dell. 1974. *Foundations in Sociolinguistics: An Ethnographic Approach*. Philadelphia, Penn.: University of Pennsylvania Press.
Iser, Wolfgang. 1978. *The Act of Reading*. Baltimore, Md.: Johns Hopkins University Press.
Kuhn, Thomas. 1970. *The Structure of Scientific Revolutions*, 2nd edn. Chicago: University of Chicago Press.

Labov, William. 1972. *Language in the Inner City*. Philadelphia, Penn.: University of Pennsylvania Press.

Leenhardt, Jacques. 1980. Toward a sociology of reading. In Susan R. Suleiman and Inge Crosman (eds) *The Reader in The Text*. Princeton, NJ: Princeton University Press.

Morris, Joan. 1988. Images of community in scientific texts: A grid/group approach to the analysis of journal editorials. *Sociological Inquiry* 58: 240–60.

Mulkay, Michael. 1985. *The Word and The World*. London: George Allen & Unwin.

Mulkay, Michael, Potter, Jonathan, and Yearley, Stephen. 1983. Why an analysis of scientific discourse is needed. In Karin D. Knorr-Cetina and Michael Mulkay (eds) *Science Observed*. London: Sage.

Pratt, Mary L. 1988. Linguistic Utopias. In Nigel Fabb, Derek Attridge, Alan Durant, and Colin MacCabe (eds) *The Linguistics of Writing*. New York: Methuen.

Waddell, Craig. 1988. The fusion of horizons: A dialectical response to the problem of self-exemplifying fallacy in contemporary constructivist arguments. *Philosophy and Rhetoric* 21: 103–15.

Wells, Richard H. and Picou, J. Steven. 1981. *American Sociology: Theoretical and Methodological Structure*. Washington, DC: University Press.

Woolgar, Steve. 1988. *Science: The Very Idea*. Chichester: Ellis Horwood.

White, James Boyd. 1984. *When Words Lose Their Meaning*. Chicago: University of Chicago Press.

Wuthnow, Robert. 1987. *Meaning and the Moral Order: Explorations in Cultural Analysis*. Berkeley, Calif.: University of California Press.

TABLE 5.1

Percentages of journals by discipline referring to "differentiation" and "legitimacy"

Discipline	Differentiation	Legitimacy	Both	Neither
Anthropology	60.0	60.0	20.0	0.0
Biology	66.7	61.9	28.6	0.0
Chemistry	81.8	27.3	18.2	9.1
Economics, Business	33.3	55.6	11.1	22.2
Geography	25.0	100.0	25.0	0.0
Geology	50.0	75.0	25.0	0.0
History	71.4	85.7	57.1	0.0
Linguistics	62.5	62.5	37.5	12.5
Mathematics	40.0	60.0	20.0	20.0
Medicine	60.0	90.0	50.0	0.0
Philosophy	57.1	57.1	28.6	14.3
Physics	66.7	83.3	50.0	0.0
Political science	54.5	63.6	27.3	9.1
Physical science	100.0	62.5	62.5	0.0
Sociology	37.5	75.0	37.5	25.0
For Chi-Square, p. =	0.30	0.17	0.52	0.26

Part II

Vocabularies of Expression: Decoding the Symbolic Structure of Music, Art, and Dance

6

Putting it together: Measuring the syntax of aural and visual symbols

Karen A. Cerulo

"The art of making art," wrote composer Stephen Sondheim, "is *putting it together*" (my emphasis).[1] But Sondheim's contentions need not be restricted to the arts. We derive meaning from any message or symbol – artistic, political, instructive, or personal – by reviewing both the content of the symbol, and the way that content is put together or structured. Indeed, we might expand Sondheim's claim to read, "The art of communicating rests largely on how symbols are put together."

Deriving meaning from content is an easy concept to understand. Capturing meaning from structure is less straightforward. What do variations in symbol structure contribute to the communication process? And can we develop a systematic way to capture and analyze that structure? This chapter attempts to address these questions. I begin by unraveling the ways in which structure conveys meaning. Next, I present a new set of indicators aimed at measuring symbol structure, specifically musical and graphic symbols. To illustrate the construction and utility of these measures, I apply them to national anthems and flags. But readers should note that while national symbols serve as our guide in this journey, the techniques presented here can accurately measure a wide variety of musical and graphic symbols.

Structure as message:
the case of national symbols

National symbols project a message. That message is purposively constructed, with leaders of national governments consciously picking and
choosing the various elements of their message: words, sounds, colors,
images, etc. (See, for example, Deutsch *et al.* 1957: 36; Merritt 1966: chapters
1 and 2; Boli-Bennett 1979: 222–3; Agulhon 1981: 16–22.) Zikmund
emphasized this selectiveness in his study of national anthems, writing "we
must recognize that in virtually all cases, it (constructing the message) was
done consciously and that in the course of concentrating on some themes the
country was generally de-emphasizing others" (1968: 78). Weitman
expressed similar sentiments with regard to flags:

> The national flag is an IMAGE which the nation-state projects of itself, and the
> characteristics of the flag . . . are viewed as specific sign-vehicles through which the
> nation-state communicates more or less specific messages about itself to others.
> (1975: 335)

Conscious decision-making is evident in the construction of other national
symbols as well. Emblems such as the state arms are often altered by national
governments in order to reflect significant changes within the nation. For
example, after the Second World War the Austrian government added a
broken chain to the feet of its traditional Austrian eagle. The broken chain
symbolized the freedom Austria regained in 1945 (Talocci 1977: 43).
Similarly, when the Philippines moved from Spanish to American domina-
tion, they added an eagle (an American symbol) to their state arms (Talocci
1977: 107).

   All national symbols convey a message. We can analyze that message in
two ways. On the one hand, we can examine the content of the symbol: the
colors or emblems used in a flag; the key, tempo, or lyrics of an anthem. In
so doing, we would decipher the meaning of each component of the symbol;
for example, the red stripe of a flag might symbolize bloodshed, the upbeat
tempo of an anthem might stand for triumph over enemies. Such an approach
is a *semantic analysis*: we isolate the symbol's elements and focus on the
meaning of each of those elements. A second alternative would have us study
the design or configuration of a symbol: What colors and emblems occupy
adjacent positions in the flag? How many planes or sections does the flag
contain? What is the contour or shape of an anthem's melody? What is the
relationship between melody notes and the chords that accompany them?
When focusing on elements such as these, we are undertaking a *syntactic
analysis*: we examine the meaning conveyed by a symbol's design or
configuration and the relationship between its parts.

   To date, most of the research on national symbols explores their semantic meaning.[2] This nearly exclusive focus on semantic structure is puzzling. Communication theorists tell us that syntactic structure is as important as semantic structure when it comes to communication effectiveness. (For example, Cassirer 1955: 94, 96; Saussure 1959; Cherry 1961: 66; Barey 1965: 93; Leach 1976: 45–9; Hervey 1982: 219; and Henrotte 1985: 660–1.) This is because syntactic structure orders or organizes a symbol's various elements. So, while the elements – the content – of two symbols may be identical, repeating those elements, emphasizing one element over another, or altering the way in which the elements are combined can change both the meaning and the effectiveness of the symbol's message. Language offers the most accessible example of this idea. Consider the statement: "I love you." As written, it conveys a clear sentiment of affection. However, we can change the syntactic structure of the elements I, love, and you, thus producing an entirely different message. By emphasizing certain elements we can strengthen the message. We might say: "*I* love you" or "I love *you*." In addition to changes in emphasis, we might change the form of the sentence – declarative to interrogative. As a result, a rather incredulous tone would be conveyed: "*I* love *you*?" We might even change the grammatical ordering of the words, thus communicating confusion on the part of the speaker: "*Love* you, . . . *I*?" While the content of these examples is identical, each represents a different syntactic structure. By varying the syntactic structure, we vary the message.

While language affords the clearest example of the importance of syntactic structure, these premises are readily applicable to other forms of communication as well. Two well-known national symbols help to illustrate the point: "God Save the Queen" and "La Marseillaise." Both anthems are written in the same key and use many of the same notes. Their content is similar. It is the juxtapositioning of notes that gives each anthem its character and meaning. In "God Save the Queen," movement from note to note is slow and gradual; the musical distance between each note (that is, their relative position on the musical scale) is small; the melody is consonant and contains little or no ornamentation. The opposite is true for "La Marseillaise." As a result of differences in emphasis, form, and order of the notes – differences in syntactic structure – each anthem conveys a different mood and feeling. "God Save the Queen" is a stately hymn of reverence, while "La Marseillaise" is a rousing call to arms.

Flags, too, illustrate the importance of a symbol's syntactic structure. Consider the history of the French flag. When the revolution of 1848 broke out in France, leaders decided that a restructuring of the flag was needed to capture the tenor of the times. The blue-white-red tripartite flag was changed to a blue-red-white flag. By placing the two primary colors adjacent to one another as opposed to separating them with a white bar, the new flag took on higher contrast, thus conveying more activity and movement than its predecessor (Smith 1975: 135–8). All of these examples illustrate a key point.

113

The *combination* of a symbol's elements conveys a meaning that may differ from that of any single element of the symbol. Meaning, then, is largely contingent on the syntactic structure of the symbol . . . the way in which words, sounds, colors, or image are put together. (For additional support of this premise see, for example, Koffka 1935: 184; Cassirer 1955; Barthes 1967, 1977; Meyer 1967: chapter 1; Nettl 1967: 30; Firth 1973: 46; Leach 1976: 58–9; and Eco 1985: 173–4.)

Given the importance of syntactic structure to communication, devising a way to measure this structure becomes a central research task. Before we can fully explore the determinants and influences of variations in the syntax of symbols, we must develop a precise and easily replicated method of capturing that variation. Such measures would render aural and visual symbols an easily accessible source of social science data, amenable to all of the rigorous methods that are central to the social science tradition. What follows then is a complete set of quantitative indicators aimed at the precise measurement of musical and graphic symbols' syntactic structure. The discussion that follows describes these measures and uses anthems and flags to demonstrate their utility. However, readers will immediately see the generalizability of these measures to other musical and graphic symbols.

Measuring syntactic structure

Musical syntax

We can analyze musical syntax as it exists on a continuum of basic to embellished design.[3] In essence, this continuum addresses the complexity of musical syntax. While it by no means encompasses every quality of musical structure, it does provide a starting point from which to study music's "groundwork." The continuum addresses the factors music theorists would consider in their examination of the structure, the concrete design, of any musical score.

Basic musical syntax is characterized as a stable, constant, and fixed musical structure. Its construction is confined to the foundational elements, the building blocks, of music composition. Basic syntax exhibits a limited range of musical motion. In moving from one point to the next, composers choose the most direct route. This creates a sense of stability and constancy in the music. In addition, basic syntax is free of variation or ornamentation of simple musical patterns. In moving from one point to the next, the syntax is fixed in that the number of musical combinations is limited and the range of musical sounds is restricted. Basic syntax offers the most concise, direct method for fulfilling the rules upon which Western tonal music is based. (For more information on these rules, see Westergaard 1975; Dalhaus 1980a, 1980b; and Lindley 1980.)

Embellished musical syntax embodies opposite qualities. It is a decoration or an ornamentation of basic syntax and presents erratic, wandering motion. In this structure, composers broaden the alternatives for movement. Rather than minimizing input, they inject variation into the music; they develop basic syntactic patterns. Hence, embellished syntax is necessarily flexible, using a wider range of musical sounds and combinations. Unlike basic syntax, embellished syntax elaborates, manipulates, and sometimes disrupts the central elements of Western tonal music composition. (For additional support of the basic–embellished contrast in music, see Meyer 1956: chapter 6; 1967: chapter 1; Youngblood 1958; Moles 1966; Guiraud 1975: 31; Eco 1976: 90; Barthes 1977: 152–3; Bergesen 1979: 336–7; Henrotte 1985: 660.)

These basic–embellished aspects of musical syntax can be quantified. Owing to space constraints, this chapter limits its illustrations to melodic codes. However, illustrations and formulae for measurement of other musical elements (such as phrasing, harmony, form, dynamics, rhythm, and instrumentation) can be found in Cerulo 1988; 1989a; 1989b).

Melody is a succession of single musical tones, a series of pitches arranged horizontally on the musical staff. These tones are organized in mathematical relation to one another and, in general, display a logical and discernible sequence of musical sound. This sequence determines the syntactic structure of a melody. To quantify this structure we must attend to the previously stated characteristics of basic and embellished syntax. Specifically, we must examine the frequency of melodic movement, the magnitude or range of that movement, the method of constructing melodic movement (that is, conjunctness versus disjunctness), and finally the ornamentation or decoration of central melody notes. (For a more detailed explanation of these melodic properties, see Siegmeister 1965; Westergaard 1975; or Ringer 1980.)

Pitch–time plots provide a method for examining frequency, magnitude, method of motion, and ornamentation. Such plots specify two dimensions of the melody: the point in musical time at which the pitch is sounded (measured in single beats) and the location of the pitch, that is, its numerical rank on the musical scale (measured in half steps). Figure 6.1 shows a pitch–time plot of two familiar melodies: Great Britain's national anthem "God Save the Queen," and the French national anthem "La Marseillaise." In these plots, the X axis represents musical time and the Y axis represents the pitch.

Both anthems are written in the key of G. Therefore, each pitch of the melodies is ranked according to the following values:

$$G = 0 \; G\# = 1 \; A = 2 \; A\# = 3 \; B = 4 \; C = 5 \; C\# = 6$$
$$D = 7 \; D\# = 8 \; E = 9 \; F = 10 \; F\# = 11 \; G = 12$$

Given this information, we can match the pitch of each note with the appropriate beat of the anthem at which it appears. Plotting these data gives a visual image of the melodies. More important, the plots illustrate the melodic lines as a function of pitch with respect to time. Therefore, we can

115

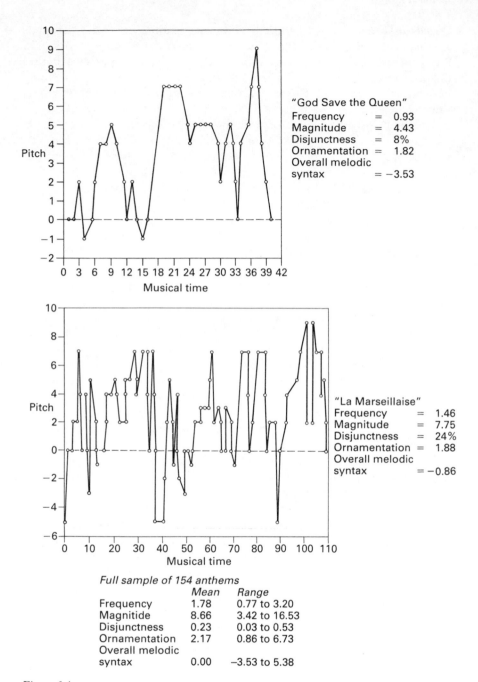

"God Save the Queen"
Frequency   =   0.93
Magnitude   =   4.43
Disjunctness   =   8%
Ornamentation =   1.82
Overall melodic
syntax   = −3.53

"La Marseillaise"
Frequency   =   1.46
Magnitude   =   7.75
Disjunctness   =   24%
Ornamentation =   1.88
Overall melodic
syntax   = −0.86

Full sample of 154 anthems

	Mean	Range
Frequency	1.78	0.77 to 3.20
Magnitide	8.66	3.42 to 16.53
Disjunctness	0.23	0.03 to 0.53
Ornamentation	2.17	0.86 to 6.73
Overall melodic syntax	0.00	−3.53 to 5.38

Figure 6.1

116

analytically determine the aforementioned characteristics of a melody's syntax by calculating certain properties of the line segments connecting each two consecutive points of the line. I have devised a number of formulae for this purpose.

To calculate the frequency of melodic motion I use the formula

$$\text{FREQ} = \frac{1}{m}(p + t)$$

p = the total number of peaks in the melody,
t = the total number of troughs in the melody,
m = the total number of measures in the melody.

The frequency score indicates the number of directional changes in a melody; it tells us how dynamic a melody is. The higher the frequency statistic, the greater the amount of movement in the melody. Dividing the total number of peaks and troughs by the total number of measures in the melody standardizes this score. (Measures are groups of beats marked off from one another by bar lines.) The frequency value for "God Save the Queen" is 0.93; this melody changes direction slightly less than one time per measure. In comparison, "La Marseillaise" has a frequency score of 1.46; its melody changes direction approximately three times every two measures.

The formula for the magnitude of melodic motion is

$$\text{MAG} = \frac{1}{m}\sum_{i=1}^{n} H_i$$

H = the height of the ith peak or the depth of the ith trough,
n = the total number of peaks and troughs in the melody,
m = the total number of measures in the melody.

This formula calculates the average magnitude of melodic motion per measure. By calculating the size of each directional change in the melody, we can determine how drastic the movement in the melody line is. The statistic sums the absolute values of the height of each peak and the depth of each trough in the line. Dividing that value by the number of measures in the melody yields a mean score that tells us the average "musical area" covered in each melody. The higher the magnitude statistic, the more extreme the movement in the melody. The magnitude statistic for "God Save the Queen" is 4.43. The average range of melodic motion in the piece is approximately four half steps. In comparison, the magnitude statistic for "La Marseillaise" is 7.75. The average range of movement in its melody is nearly twice that of "God Save the Queen."

We can examine two different methods of constructing melodic motion: conjunct motion and disjunct motion. Conjunct motion is smooth movement in which notes proceed in successive or nearly successive degrees up and down the musical scale. Conversely, disjunct motion refers to jagged, leapy

117

motion in which notes of a melody are separated by large intervals. To determine conjunct or disjunct method of motion, we use the formula:

$$\text{If } |\triangle P_n| < Q, \text{ melodic line movement is conjunct}$$
$$\text{If } |\triangle P_n| > Q, \text{ melodic line movement is disjunct}$$

$Q = 4.0$ if movement between $\triangle P_n$ is in the same direction as $\triangle P_{n-1}$,
$Q = 3.0$ if movement between $\triangle P_n$ is in the same direction as $\triangle P_{n-1}$,
$\triangle P_n$ is defined as $(P_n - P_{n-1})$,
$P_n =$ the pitch of the nth note.

We can classify each interval in a melody as conjunct or disjunct by comparing $|\triangle P_n|$ to the value of Q. (The values I selected for Q are based on music theory regarding conjunct and disjunct intervals.)[4] Then we can calculate the total number of intervals falling into each category. According to this formula, 92 percent of the consecutive melodic intervals in the British national anthem are conjunct, whereas 8 percent are disjunct. Therefore, "God Save the Queen" is predominantly conjunct. In comparison, only 76 percent of the consecutive melodic intervals in "La Marseillaise' are conjunct; 24 percent are disjunct: three times the amount found in "God Save the Queen." Humming the first line of each anthem illustrates the relative jaggedness and leapiness of "La Marseillaise" as compared to "God Save the Queen."

Finally, the formula for ornamentation is

$$\text{ORN} = \frac{N \sqrt{r}}{v}$$

$N =$ the total number of notes in a melody,
$r =$ the total instances of ornamentation in a melody,
$v =$ the total number of verbal syllables in a melody.

This formula captures the degree of decoration to central melody notes. It measures two aspects of ornamentation. (Each time a single syllable is represented by multiple notes of different pitch, we have an instance of ornamentation.) First, it captures the presence of ornamentation; the formula gives the ratio of notes to verbal syllables in a melody. (Recall, we are dealing with vocal music in this study – national anthems; slight amendments to the formula are necessary for non-vocal music.) Second, the formula captures the frequency with which the technique of ornamentation occurs; it allows us to give extra emphasis to melodies with many instances of ornamentation as against melodies with few, or just a single instance. We provide this emphasis by weighting the formula with the square root of the total instances of ornamentation in the melody. Both presence and frequency are integral to a proper analysis of ornamentation. A melody that is ornamented in only one location will be perceived as more basic than one displaying several distinct instances of ornamentation. This formula ensures that the latter cases receive a higher score. If Ornamentation = 1, the number of notes and syllables are equal, meaning there is no ornamentation. If Ornamentation > 1, the anthem is ornamented.[5] Ornamentation is 1.82 in "God Save the Queen"; "La Marseillaise" has a slightly higher ornamentation score at 1.88.

Each of these measures – frequency, magnitude, method of motion, and ornamentation – addresses a different element of melodic syntax. What is the relationship between the four measures? I explored this question using a sample of national anthems. The sample consists of 154 anthems, representing 150 nations. Cartledge, Reed, Shaw, and Coleman (1978) provided the primary source for compiling this data set. This volume is the most exhaustive collection of national anthems in print. To be included in the sample, an anthem must follow a Western tonal music tradition, that is, be built using the diatonic scales. Anthems based on other musical scales would destroy the stylistic uniformity of the sample, making comparative analysis unreliable.

Earlier, I defined basic syntax as stable, constant, and fixed. In analyzing basic melodic syntax, these qualities should translate to low frequencies of directional change, low magnitudes of change, conjunct methods of melodic motion, and low rates of ornamentation. Embellished melodic syntax should exhibit opposite qualities along these dimensions. The correlation co-efficients for these measures support this conceptualization.[6] All of the coefficients are positive (they range from 0.17 to 0.73) and statistically significant. This indicates a direct relationship between all of the measures. When dealing with national anthems, then, melodic frequency, magnitude, method of motion, and ornamentation are directly correlated with one another: they move in unison. (The behavior of these measures with reference to other musical genres, such as symphonies, songs, operas, is, at this point, an empirical question for future research.) Given this information, it is possible to analyze melodic syntax by using a single summary measure reflecting the basic-embellished continuum.

While the four individual melody measures are correlated, some of the correlations are only moderate. This indicates that there is some independence to these measures, making a simple additive method of combining them inappropriate. However, using factor analysis, we can construct a weight for each of the individual melody indicators; we can use these weights in forming a single summary measure of melodic syntax. To construct such a measure, I standardized the four individual melodic indicators and factor analyzed them. Taking into account the loading for the first factor (which accounted for 58 percent of the total variance), I assigned a weight to each of the individual melody measures and added them. This formed a summary measure of overall melodic syntax:

$$\textit{Overall melodic syntax} = 0.89\ \text{Frequency} + 0.93\ \text{Magnitude} + 0.31\ \text{Disjunctness} + 0.31\ \text{Ornamentation}$$

The factors, of course, may vary somewhat if a different sample of music is used; that remains an empirical question. Yet, when comparing the overall melodic syntax of "God Save the Queen" and "La Marseillaise," we find that the former is comparatively more basic in design (−3.53) than the latter (−0.86).[7] Indeed, were we to hum the melodies to these anthems and review the examples offered in the body of this article, we could hear this difference.

This measure taps many important elements to which musicologists attend when analyzing a melody. The scale systematically classifies a melody's syntactic structure as ranging from basic to embellished in design. Low values are indicative of basic syntax, whereas high values suggest embellished syntax.

Graphic syntax

Like music, the structure of graphic symbols can be analyzed using the basic–embellished continuum. The continuum addresses the complexity of a symbol's graphic syntax. As in our study of music, the continuum does not emcompass every aspect of graphic syntactic structure. However, it provides a starting point from which to study the foundational elements of graphic syntax, addressing those factors that, according to cognitive and color theorists, capture the audience's primary attention when they are processing graphic symbols.

Like music syntax, basic graphic syntax is constant, stable, and fixed. Its construction consists of minimal input, that is, limited points of focus. Basic symbols exhibit few color distinctions or fields (that is, sections). They favor primary colors (blue, red, or yellow) or white over secondary colors. This is because secondary colors are derived from mixing two or more colors, thus representing greater information density. These factors create a sense of constancy in the symbol. Basic symbols also display a limited amount of stark color contrast, making them stable in design. Color theorists tell us that stark contrast is jarring to the eye and thus more difficult to process. (See, for example, Munsell 1946: 37–40; Stockton 1983: 6–8.) Therefore the coloring of a basic symbol is restricted to one part of the spectrum. (A hue indicates the position on the color wheel and is a general name such as "blue," "red," "purple.") The stability of basic syntax is also reflected in the geometric consistency of its design, in other words, if the format of the symbol consists of horizontal or vertical fields, fields of opposing shapes will not be injected or overlaid on the symbol. Finally, basic graphic syntax contains limited ornamentation, that is, few superimposed emblems, signs, or decorations on the field of graphic symbols. In so doing, graphic syntax is fixed, in that information is limited and restricted. In essence, basic syntax represents the building blocks, or the foundational elements, of any graphic symbol; it offers the most concise method of conveying a graphic message.

As with musical syntax, embellished graphic syntax displays opposite qualities along these dimensions. It is a decoration, distortion or, in some cases, a manipulation of basic graphic patterns. (For additional support of the basic–embellished continuum for graphic symbols, or for more information on the characteristics of color composition upon which this continuum is based, see Levi-Strauss 1969: 20; Guiraud 1975: 31; Leach 1976: 58; Marcus and Zajonc 1985: 137–230; Munsell 1946: 13–16, 42–7; Stockton 1983: 4–8; Bergesen 1984: 191–5.

The basic–embellished aspects of graphic syntax can be quantified. To understand fully the development of these measures, readers may find it helpful to picture two national flags: Libya's (a plain, green flag) and the United States flag. Visualizing these flags throughout the following discussion will help to crystallize the concepts captured by the measures of graphic syntax.

I have developed three measures addressing the relative constancy of graphic syntax. First, we count the total number of colors in the flag. This value is represented by test statistic N. Note that in counting these hues, I distinguish and classify them according to the 10 color divisions developed by Munsell (1946): red, yellow-red, yellow, green-yellow, green, blue-green, blue, purple-blue, purple, red-purple. (For the purposes of this study, white and black are also classified as separate hues.[8]) The Munsell system enjoys worldwide acceptance and is used more frequently than any other color classification system. Next, we calculate the flag's number of fields by counting the various sections in the flag. This value is represented by test statistic F. Finally, we calculate the rate of secondary color use in the flag. The percentage of secondary colors is represented by test statistic S and is determined by the formula $S = s/N$, where s equals the number of secondary colors in the flag and N equals the total number of colors in the flag. Libya's flag contains only one color: green. It has one field, composed of a secondary color. Therefore, for the Libyan flag, $N = 1$, $F = 1$, and $S = 1$. Conversely, the US flag contains three colours: red, white, and purple-blue. It has 14 fields: 7 red stripes, six white stripes, and a blue ornamented field. One of its three colors is secondary. Therefore, for the US flag, $N = 3$, $F = 14$, and $S = 0.33$. These figures show, independently of seeing the flags, that the Libyan flag is more constant than the US flag, making it more basic.

To determine the relative stability of a symbol's graphic syntax, we must attend to several components of color contrast and geometric formatting. First, we calculate the degree of contrast by counting the total number of points at which color contrast occurs, that is, points in the symbol where colors meet. This value is represented by test statistic C. Libya's flag contains no color contrast, therefore $C = 0$. In the US flag, red and white meet 12 times, red and blue meet 4 times, and white and blue meet 54 times, therefore $C = 70$. Next, we calculate the nature of the color contrasts used in the symbol: simple versus complex. Simple contrasts are defined as contrasts

121

occurring between colors of the same hue. According to color theorists, these will be most easily processed by viewers. Complex contrasts occur between colors of completely different hues, requiring more effort from viewers when processing the symbol. (See, for example, Munsell 1946: 37–40; Stockton 1983: 6–8). We can calculate X – the degree of complex color contrasts in a symbol – by using the formula $X = x/C$ where x equals the number of complex contrasts in a symbol and C equals the total number of color contrast points. Libya's flag displays no contrast, so $X = 0$. All contrast points in the US flag are complex, therefore $X = 1.00$. On this dimension, the Libyan flag is more basic than the US flag.

In addition to the degree of contrast and the general nature of those contrasts, color theorists tell us that a graphic symbol's stability rests on the intensity of the contrasting colors. Contrast intensity is determined by three aspects of the colors involved in the contrast: hue, value, and chroma. As previously mentioned, the hue tells us a color's position on the color wheel. Value refers to a color's lightness–darkness. Chroma refers to a color's brightness–dullness. These aspects – hue, value, and chroma – have been quantified by color theorists. In Munsell's (1946) quantification system every color is specified by three symbols. The green of Libya's flag, for example, would be specified as G5/8. The G in the notation tells us the hue of the color. In Munsell's system, G stands for green. The 5 refers to the color's value. In Munsell's system, value is represented by a ten point scale, where 1 = dark and 10 = light. Therefore, 5 denotes a color of moderate lightness. The 8 refers to the color's chroma. In Munsell's system, chroma is also represented by a ten point scale, where 1 = dull and 10 = bright. Therefore, 8 denotes a color of relative brightness. We can use Munsell's numerical scores to calculate three dimensions of contrast intensity: hue contrast intensity, value contrast intensity, and chroma contrast intensity.

Hue contrast intensity refers to the magnitude of difference in the hues captured at each point of color contrast. To calculate these differences, we assign numbers to the ten colors on a standard color wheel. Number assignments begin with one and values ascend by units of one as we move clockwise around the color wheel. Such a process yields the following ranks: red = 1; yellow-red = 2; white and yellow = 3, green-yellow = 4; green = 5; blue-green = 6; blue = 7; purple-blue and black = 8; purple = 9; red-purple = 10. Given this information, we can calculate hue contrast intensity using the formula

$$\frac{\sum_{i=1}^{n} |H_n - H_{n-1}| \sqrt{C}}{C}$$

The formula calculates the difference in hue scores found at every point of color contrast, and sums those differences. Next, we multiply that value by the square root of the symbol's degree of contrast, giving added weight to those symbols displaying high incidence of differentiation. Finally, we standardize that figure by dividing the numerator by the total number of contrast points in the symbol. In essence, this yields a mean score that tells us the average intensity of the hue contrasts found in each symbol. Hue contrast intensity for Libya's flag is 0. The same statistic for the US flag is 38.49. These figures in themselves show that minimal use of color makes the Libyan flag more basic than the US flag.

Value contrast intensity refers to the magnitude of lightness or shade differences found at each point of color contrast. To calculate it, we use the formula

$$\frac{\sum_{i=1}^{n} |V_n - V_{n-1}| \sqrt{C}}{C}$$

The formula addresses each point of color contrast and computes the differences in value scores found there. We then sum the value differences and multiply that sum by the square root of the symbol's degree of contrast. This gives added weight to those symbols displaying high incidence of contrast. Finally, we standardize that figure by dividing the numerator by the total number of contrast points in the symbol. In essence, this yields a mean score that tells us the average intensity of shade differentiation found in each symbol. Value contrast intensity for Libya's flag is 0 and for the US flag is 31.55. On this dimension as well, the Libyan flag is more basic than the US flag.

The final component of color contrast – chroma contrast intensity – addresses the relative brightness of adjacent colors. To calculate it, we use the formula

$$\frac{\sum_{i=1}^{n} |R_n - R_{n-1}| \sqrt{C}}{C}$$

Like the formulae for hue contrast and value contrast, the formula provides us with the average magnitude of chroma contrast in a symbol. The formula computes the differences in chroma scores found at every point of color contrast, and sums those differences. Again, we multiply that value by the square root of the total number of points at which color contrast occurs, and we standardize that figure by dividing the numerator by the total number of contrast points in the symbol. Chroma contrast intensity for Libya's flag is 0; for the US flag it is 31.55. Again, the Libyan flag displays a more basic structure than the US flag.

Aspects of color contrast are not the sole determinants of syntax stability. The consistency of geometric patterns plays a role in stability as well. The stable symbol displays uniformity of pattern. For example, in a geometrically consistent flag, we expect to see all of the fields complementing one another by maintaining the same geometric shape, for example, all fields being horizontal, or all being vertical. If a contradictory shape is inserted in the symbol, geometric consistency is jarred. For example, inserting one vertical field over several horizontal fields, or inserting a triangular field over a collection of horizontal fields, disrupts the symbol's dominant geometric pattern. Such disruption makes the symbol unstable, thus requiring more attention from the audience. To capture a graphic symbol's degree of geometric inconsistency, we count the number of contradictory geometric shapes in a symbol. That figure is represented by test statistic G. Neither the Libyan nor the US flag displays geometrically inconsistent shapes; therefore G = 0 in both cases. Both flags are equally basic on this dimension.

Ornamentation is the final dimension of graphic syntax. To calculate the level of ornamentation in a graphic symbol, we count the number of emblems, ornaments, or decorations found on the symbol. The total number of ornaments is represented by test statistic O. Libya's flag contains no ornaments; therefore, O = 0. The US flag contains 50 stars; therefore, O = 50. Again, the Libyan flag is more basic than the US flag.

The ten measures just described address different elements of graphic syntax. As with the music indicators, it is important to explore the relationship between the graphic measures. To do so, I collected a sample of national flags. The sample consists of 164 flags representing as many nations. Smith (1975) and Talocci (1977) provided the primary sources for compiling this data set.

Recall that my definition of basic syntax suggests that basic graphic symbols will display fewer colors and fields than embellished symbols. Basic graphic symbols will display more primary than secondary colors, and exhibit both a low degree and a low intensity of hue, value, and chroma contrast. Basic graphic symbols will be more geometrically consistent than their embellished counterparts. Finally, they will contain less ornamentation than embellished symbols. Correlation coefficients for the graphic syntax indicators support this conceptualization. The coefficients are positive at a statistically significant level. (They range from 0.10 to 0.86.[9]) Thus, when dealing with national flags, there is a direct relationship between all of the measures. On the basis of this information, we can create a summary measure reflecting the basic–embellished continuum, just as we did in the analysis of anthems. Using the method described for the construction of overall melodic syntax, I formed the following summary measure:

Overall graphic syntax =
        0.41 total number colors + 0.52 number fields +
        0.10 percentage secondary colors + 0.91 degree contrast +
        0.22 degree complex contrast + 0.95 hue intensity +
        0.95 value intensity + 0.76 chroma intensity +
        0.05 geometric inconsistency + 0.70 ornamentation

Interested readers should note that this summary measure is based on a factor analysis of the ten individual graphic indicators. I used the loadings from the first factor, which accounted for 51 percent of the variance. As with the music measure, this summary measure draws on important elements to which color and graphic theorists attend when analyzing symbols such as flags. Low values on this scale are indicative of basic syntax, whereas high values suggest embellished syntax. As was true for national anthems, the factors may vary somewhat if these measures are applied to other forms of graphic symbols. This remains an empirical issue. When comparing the overall graphic syntax of the Libyan and US flags, the former is comparatively more basic in design. In fact, using this summary measure, Libya's flag displays the most basic structure in the sample (−6.68), while the American flag is the most embellished (29.16).[10]

Discussion

The measures presented in this chapter provide a reliable method for analyzing the ways in which musical and graphic symbols are "put together." In essence, these measures duplicate qualitative classifications traditionally used by music, color, and cognitive theorists; they capture the same dimensions to which musical or visual specialists would attend in their preliminary analyses of symbols. Yet, by using these measures, musical and graphic symbol structures become accessible to specialists and non-specialists alike. In addition, the measures allow dichotomous categories like basic versus embellished syntax to be analyzed on a continuous scale. Given these points, the indicators presented in this chapter render musical and graphic symbols an extremely accessible source of social science data, amenable to all of the rigorous methods that are central to the social science tradition.

Elsewhere, I have argued that variations in symbol syntax represent different communication strategies, that is, different methods of conveying a message (Cerulo 1988, 1989a). Using the measures presented here, we can explore the factors that influence a communicator's choice of strategy and the precise degree of that influence. For example, I have devoted a good deal of research to variations in the structure of national symbols. What factors are linked to the creation and adoption of basic versus embellished symbols? Thus far, I have discovered several factors. First, my findings are that levels of social disruption influence syntax selection. During periods of high disruption, political leaders create and adopt symbols with basic syntactic structures. During periods of relative stability, they create and adopt symbols with embellished syntax. Second, authoritarian regimes tend to create and adopt symbols more basic in design than those of their democratic counterparts (Cerulo 1989b). Finally, certain socioeconomic and historical factors influence syntax selection. For example, a nation's world position is significantly related to the structure of its symbols. Leaders of core nations tend to adopt symbols with basic syntax, while leaders of semi-peripheral and peripheral nations adopt symbols that are comparatively embellished in design. In the historical realm, my research shows that the nature of a nation's modernization experience is linked to the structure of the symbols it adopts. Leaders of rapidly modernizing nations adopt embellished symbols while those in gradually modernizing nations favor basic symbols (Cerulo 1990). In essence, these findings suggest that different communication strategies are called for by varying sociopolitical conditions, socioeconomic conditions, and periods of historical development. This work on national symbols is only the beginning of a promising line of inquiry. Using the measures presented here, we can examine a wide variety of cultural symbols, precisely determining the nature of society's influence on their production.

Measures such as the ones presented in this article will also allow for the systematic comparison of musical and graphic symbol syntax. We might ask: If syntactic structure represents a communication strategy, does that strategy change from medium to medium? Are musical and graphic structures responsive to different influences? Again, in the realm of national symbols, my work suggests that the relationship between social factors and symbol syntax differs according to medium. For example, comparisons of national anthems and national flags reveal that internal forces such as a nation's form of government, or levels of social disruption, exert the strongest influence on anthem syntax formation. For flags, however, external characteristics like the syntax of the mother country's flag or a nation's geographic region exert the strongest influence on graphic syntax selection. Usage patterns may help to explain some of these differences. However, research regarding the differences involved in the cognitive processing of aural and visual messages is also called for (Cerulo 1990).

Laboratory research could also benefit from the development of measures such as those presented here. Such research could reveal much about the relationship between symbol syntax and strategies of action. For example, do certain structures produce greater physiological arousal? Are certain structures more easily recalled? Are some structures more effective than others at motivating action? Is basic versus embellished syntax differentially interpreted and do they convey different messages or systems of meaning? The answers to these questions hold implications for both scholarly and applied research. With regard to political symbols, for example, we could determine which symbol structures are most stimulating to populations at large or specific blocks of voters. Such knowledge would also be valuable to market research. Advertisers could determine how to structure jingles or graphic displays in order to stimulate the desired results. Finally, classifying symbol structure could offer important information to the therapeutic domain. With the increased use of music and art as treatment for the mentally ill, determining the effects of various musical and graphic structures could prove highly useful in designing treatment programs. In all of these areas, our attention to symbol structures will be greatly enhanced by the availability of tools for their accurate measurement.

These applications suggest only a few of the many benefits and research possibilities afforded by these new measures. Such indicators will provide us with the tools needed to develop and expand the base of cultural studies. Availing ourselves of these tools brings us one step closer to exploring and verifying the links between the social and cultural domains.

Notes

1. Taken from the song "Putting it together." The song is from the Broadway musical *Sunday in the Park with George*.
2. Some examples of this extensive literature include Elting and Folsom 1968; Barraclough 1969; Pedersen 1971; Firth 1973; Smith 1975; Weitmen 1975; Talocci 1977 on flags. For anthems, see e.g. Sousa 1890; Griffith 1952; Nettl 1967; Zikmund 1968; Cartledge, Reed, and Shaw 1978; Lichtenwanger 1979; Mead 1980.
3. Readers will immediately note the similarities between my approach and researchers using the concept of "codes" to analyze symbols. While the characteristics of my continuum differ from these other scholarly attempts, my approach is certainly indebted to works such as Saussure (1959), Douglas (1970), Bernstein (1975), Eco (1976), and Bergesen (1979, 1984). For a good review of this literature, see Corner (1986) or Giles and Wiemann (1987).
4. We know that four musical half steps equals a major third interval. In general, any interval larger than this is considered disjunct. When melodies are moving in a single direction, large interval leaps (intervals larger than major thirds) are required to break a conjunct melody pattern. Therefore, when melodies are moving in a single direction, $G = 4.0$; in essence, $G = $ a major third interval. However, when a melody shifts direction, a smaller interval will be disruptive to listeners. Therefore, I assigned a value of $G = 3.0$ to the opposite direction condition. For more details, see Westergaard (1975).
5. If $r = 0$, r is dropped from the equation. Calculations are then based on n/v.
6. Because of space limitations, the matrix is not presented here, but is available upon request.
7. The most basic melody in the sample is Mali's, at -4.07, and the most embellished is Ecuador's, at 5.38. The range and mean of the summary measure for melody's syntactic code is presented in Figure 6.1. Recall that the indicators forming this summary measure were standardized before they were combined. Thus many of the values are negative.
8. Color theorists usually consider white to be the absence of color and black as the ultimate mixture of colors. However, since accounts of flag construction indicate that white and black are routinely and purposively chosen as integral parts of these symbols, I consider them on a par with the ten color hues. I treat white as a primary color and black as a secondary color.
9. Because of space limitations, the matrix is not presented here, but is available upon request.
10. Note that for this summary measure, $x = 0$; with a standard deviation of 4.17 and a range of -6.68 to 29.16.

References

Agulhon, Maurice. 1981. *Marianne Into Battle*, trans. J. Lloyd. Cambridge: Cambridge University Press.

Barey, G. 1965. *Communication and Language: Networks of Thought and Action*. Garden City, NY: Doubleday.

Barraclough, E. M. C. 1969. *Flags of the World*. London: Warne.

Barthes, R. 1967. *Elements of Semiology*. New York: Hill & Wang.

Barthes, R. 1977. *Image–Music–Text: Essays Selected and Translated by S. Heath*. Glasgow: Fontana.

Bergesen, A. 1979. Spirituals, Jazz, Blues, and Folk Music. In R. Wuthnow (ed.) *The Religious Dimension*. New York: Academic Press.

Bergesen, A. 1984. The semantic equation: A theory of the social origins of art styles. In R. Collins (ed.) *Sociological Theory*. San Francisco: Jossey-Bass.

Bernstein, B. 1975. *Class, Codes, and Control*, 3 vols. London: Routledge & Kegan Paul.

Boli-Bennett, J. 1979. The ideology of expanding state authority in national constitutions. In J. Meyer and M. Hannan (eds) *National Development and the World-System*. Chicago: University of Chicago Press.

Cartledge, T., Reed, W. L., Shaw, M., and Coleman, H. 1978. *National Anthems of the World*. New York: Arco.

Cassirer, E. 1955. *The Philosophy of Symbolic Forms*, trans. R. Manheim. New Haven, Conn.: Yale University Press.

Cerulo, K. A. 1988. Analyzing cultural products: A new method of measurement. *Social Science Research* 17: 317–52.

Cerulo, K. A. 1989a. Variations in musical syntax: Patterns of usage and methods of measurement. *Communication Research* 16, 2: 204–35.

Cerulo, K. A. 1989b. Socio-political control and the structure of national anthems: An empirical analysis of national anthems. *Social Forces* 68, 1: 76–99.

Cerulo, K. A. 1990. Modernization, world-systems, and communication strategies: The case of national symbols. Unpublished manuscript.

Cherry, C. 1961. *On Human Communication*. New York: Science Editions.

Corner, J. 1986. Codes and cultural analysis. In R. Collins *et al.* (eds) *Media, Culture, and Society*. London: Sage.

Cowen, W., Stone, M., and Ware, C. 1987. *Colour Perception*. Toronto: National Research Council of Canada.

Dahlhaus, C. 1980a. Harmony. In S. Sadie (ed.) *The New Grove Dictionary of Music and Musicians*. London: Macmillan.

Dahlhaus, C. 1980b. Tonality. In S. Sadie (ed.) *The New Grove Dictionary of Music and Musicians*. London: Macmillan.

Deutsch, K., Barrell, S., Kann, R., Lee, M., Lichterman, M., Lindgrem, R., Loewenheim, F., and Van Wagenen, R. 1957. *Political Community and the North Atlantic Area*. Princeton: Princeton University Press.

Douglas, M. 1970. *Natural Symbols*. New York: Pantheon Books.

Eco, U. 1976. *A Theory of Semiotics*. Bloomington, Ind.: University of Indiana Press.

Eco, U. 1985. How culture conditions the colors we see. In M. Blonsky (ed.) *On Signs*. Baltimore, Md.: Johns Hopkins Press.

Elting, M. and Folsom, F. 1968. *Flags of All Nations*. New York: Grossett & Dunlap.

Firth, R. 1973. *Symbols: Public and Private*. London: Allen & Unwin.

Giles, H. and Wiemann, J. M. 1987. Language, social comparison, and power. In C. Berger and S. Chaffee (eds) *Handbook of Communication Science*. Newbury Park, Calif.: Sage.

Griffith, B. 1952. *National Anthems and How They Came to be Written*, revised edn. Boston, Mass.: Christopher.

Guiraud, P. 1975. *Semiology*, trans. G. Gross. London: Routledge & Kegan Paul.

Henrotte, G. 1985. Music and linguistics: The semiotic connection. In J. Deely (ed.) *Semiotics*. New York: Lanham.

Hervey, S. 1982. *Semiotic Perspectives*. New York: Academic Press.

Koffka, K. 1935. *Principles of Gestalt Psychology*. New York: Harcourt, Brace, and Co.

Leach, E. 1976. *Culture and Communication*. Cambridge: Cambridge University Press.

Lévi-Strauss, C. 1969. *The Raw and the Cooked*, trans. J. and D. Weightman. New York: Harper & Row.

Lichtenwanger, N. A. 1979. National anthems. In *Colliers Encyclopedia*. New York: Colliers.

Lindley, M. 1980. Composition. In S. Sadie (ed.) *The New Grove Dictionary of Music and Musicians*. London: Macmillan.

Marcus, H. and Zajonc, R. B. 1985. The cognitive perspective in social psychology. In G. Lindzey and E. Aronson (eds) *The Handbook of Social Psychology*, 3rd edn, Vol. 1. New York: Random House.

Mead, R. 1980. The national anthem. In S. Sadie (ed.) *The New Grove Dictionary of Music and Musicians*. London: Macmillan.

Merritt, R. L. 1966. *Symbols of American Community 1735–1775*. New Haven, Conn.: Yale University Press.

Meyer, L. 1956. *Emotion and Meaning in Music*. Chicago: University of Chicago Press.

Meyer, L. 1967. *Music, the Arts, and Ideas*. Chicago: University of Chicago Press.

Moles, A. 1966. *Information Theory and Esthetic Perception*, trans. J. E. Cohen. Urbana, Ill.: University of Illinois Press.

Munsell, A. H. 1946. *A Color Notation*. Baltimore, Md.: Macbeth.

Nettl, P. 1967. *National Anthems*, trans. A. Gode. 2nd edn. New York: Frederick Ungar.

Pedersen, C. 1971. *The International Flag Book in Color*. New York: Morrow.

Ringer, A. 1980. Melody. In S. Sadie (ed.) *The New Grove Dictionary of Music and Musicians*, Vol. 12. London: Macmillan.

de Saussure, F. 1959. *Course in General Linguistics*. New York: Philosophical Library.

Siegmeister, E. 1965. *Harmony and Melody*, 2 vols. Belmont, Calif.: Wadsworth.

Smith, W. 1975. *Flags Through the Ages and Across the World*. New York: McGraw-Hill.

Sousa, J. P. 1890. *National, Patriotic, and Typical Airs of All Lands*. New York: DaCapo Press.

Stockton, J. 1983. *Designer's Guide to Color*. San Francisco: Chronicle Books.

Talocci, M. 1977. *Guide to the Flags of the World*. New York: Quill.

Weitman, S. 1975. National flags. *Semiotica* 8, 4: 328–67.

Westergaard, P. 1975. *An Introduction to Tonal Theory*. New York: Norton.

Youngblood, J. 1958. Style as information. *Journal of Music Theory* 2, 1: 23–35.

Zikmund, J. 1968. National anthems as political symbols. *Journal of Politics and History* 14: 73–80.

7

The musical structure and social context of number one songs, 1955 to 1988: an exploratory analysis

Timothy Jon Dowd

A survey of the sociology of music could very well be entitled "Music As . . .," owing to the fact that music is often treated as an indicator of social conditions or arrangements. Music is used to indicate such things as: subculture (Hebdige 1979), cultural manipulation (Horkheimer and Adorno 1988), organizational output (Hirsch 1972), class structure (Bourdieu 1984; DiMaggio 1982), and quality of life (Blau 1988). The use of music as an indicator is both understandable and appropriate. Yet there is much more to music than merely what it reflects. To reduce it to mere reflection overlooks the fact that music is a relatively autonomous cultural code. In other words, there is an aesthetic agenda in music that is not reducible to class relations, ideology, or organizational arrangements (Barrett 1988; Jensen 1984; Wolff 1983). Hence, a sociology of music should also address how musical structure changes and what social contexts are associated with such changes. Such a focus transforms musical structure from an explanatory variable to a variable which merits explanation.

Albert Bergesen and Karen Cerulo are two sociologists who have made musical structure the focus of study. Bergesen (1979, 1984) suggests that music is a type of language which has its own basic units and syntax.[1] Like spoken language, the structure of these musical units is conditioned by social context. In particular, certain social conditions may be associated with either restricted or elaborated musical codes: restricted codes possess simpler melodic, harmonic, and rhythmic structures while elaborated codes have a more complicated structure. Cerulo (1985, 1988, 1989) builds on the work of Bergesen by crafting a method which quantitatively measures these melodic, harmonic, and rhythmic structures of music. These measures range along a continuum of complexity where lower scores refer to more restricted codes and higher scores to more elaborated codes.

The present study[2] draws on Bergesen's notion of musical code and Cerulo's quantitative measures by examining how changes in the musical structure of songs are associated with changes in the social context in which these songs are created. More specifically, this study explores how the musical codes of number one songs from 1955 to 1988 are affected by four classes of phenomena: (a) the market structure of the recording industry, (b) the organization of the production process, (c) attributes of the musical performers, and (d) instrument technology.

This empirical study can be seen as addressing several issues in the sociology of music and culture. First, claims regarding the relative autonomy (Barrett 1988; Wolff 1983) of musical and cultural codes are supported because variations in musical codes are in part due to characteristics of songs themselves that are independent of institutional or organizational factors. In particular one musical element is found to increase in complexity over time – once again, independent of any institutional or organizational factors. Second, claims that mass media lead to a rigid standardization of cultural products (Hauser 1982; Hennion 1983; Lowenthal 1950; Wilensky 1964) are called into question by this finding of increasing complexity of musical structure across time. Furthermore, claims that mass media lead to a homogenization of diverse cultural forms (Jacobs 1959; Macdonald 1957; van den Haag 1957) are tempered by the findings that (a) the musical codes of black performers are found to differ from those of white performers and (b) the musical codes of American performers are found to differ from those of performers from other countries.[3] Finally, the results do not support the notion that the market structure of the recording industry strongly determines the musical structure of songs it produces (Peterson and Berger 1972, 1975; Rothenbuhler and Dimmick 1982). Specifically, the concentration of the recording industry has no direct relation to the musical structure of songs in this analysis.

Musical structure:
the dependent variables

There are three measures of musical structure used in this study. Melodic ornamentation assesses the relationship between the notes of the melody and the words of the lyrics by measuring the degree to which single verbal syllables are represented by more than one musical note. Melodic form is a summary measure that captures the overall shape of the melody with regards to how the melody changes direction and the size of those changes. Chordal structure is a summary measure that describes the harmonic nature of a song with regards to the particular chords it employs. All three of the musical measures are based on a continuum of complexity where low scores signify low complexity. In the language of Bergesen and Cerulo, basic codes are those with low complexity and stable forms whereas elaborated codes are those with high complexity and expanded forms. A more explicit discussion as to how these measures are constructed is found in Appendix A.

It should be noted that these types of musical measurements are meant to capture formal aspects of the musical structure. They are not to be construed as being indicators of meaning or aesthetics. Intead, this approach is similar to work in the structuralist tradition in that it focuses on the internal organization of a song's musical structure (Alexander 1990; Dahlhaus 1985; Wuthnow 1987).[4] In particular, codes of ornamentation, melodic form, and chordal structure result from the various combinations of underlying musical elements (Bergesen 1984; Cerulo 1988).

Social context:
the independent variables

There are four classes of phenomenon implicated in the sociological literature which are thought to have an effect on musical codes: the market structure of the recording industry, the organization of the production process, performer attributes, and instrument technology. It is conceivable that some of the variation in the melodic form and chordal structure is due to characteristics of the songs themselves (for instance, fast songs may have different melodic forms from slow songs). Therefore, appropriate variables which control for internal song characteristics are also included. The basic question being posed is whether variations in the dimensions of ornamentation, melodic form, and chordal structure from song to song can be explained by associated changes in any of the independent variables.

Market structure of the recording industry

It is asserted that the market structure of the recording industry directly affects the musical structure of songs that it releases (Hirsch 1977, 1978). When the market is stable and concentrated, the musical structure of songs is thought to be homogeneous and restricted (DiMaggio 1977). In the present study we see if market structure does in fact affect the ornamentation, melodic form, and chordal structure of number one songs. In particular we focus on three elements of the market: (a) the annual number of competing firms, (b) the annual level of firm concentration, and (c) the annual turnover of hits.

The annual number of competing firms is the number of firms which have released Top 10 songs in the given year. "Firms" are the major labels that are ultimately responsible for the release of the song, through labels they either own or distribute (Rothenbuhler and Dimmick 1982). Hence, in 1973 a Top 10 song release on the Epic label is attributed to its parent company CBS Records. The annual concentration of these firms is assessed by way of four-firm and eight-firm concentration ratios.[5] Finally, the annual turnover of hits is measured by the number of Top 10 and number one songs in the given year: the more hits there are in a year, the greater the turnover.[6]

Peterson and Berger (1972, 1975) have said that the level of market concentration in the record industry *directly* affects the musical structure of songs released by record labels. They arrive at this conclusion by measuring the degree of industry concentration from 1948 to 1973 by means of four-firm and eight-firm concentration ratios. They then compare each year's level of concentration to the annual level of "musical diversity" by examining the lyrical content of each song and the sheer number of records reaching the Top 10 each year. Peterson and Berger (1975) find that over this 28-year period there are cycles of long periods of high concentration and low musical diversity followed by short, intense periods of market competition (de-concentration) and increased musical diversity. As concentration is re-established, the musical diversity that occurs in times of competition fades. When labels are secure in their dominance and secure in their environment, the musical products that they continue to release will be similar to the ones that brought them success in the past.

This study, like Peterson and Berger (1975) and Rothenbuhler and Dimmick (1982), explores the effect of market concentration on musical structure by way of concentration ratios. The consideration of the annual number of competing firms in relation to musical structure is another similarity between this study and that of Rothenbuhler and Dimmick. But this study differs from both sets of authors in that musical diversity is not being examined here. Instead, varying complexity of ornamentation, melodic form, and chordal structure is the focus.[7] Nevertheless, the argument the authors make strongly implies that musical complexity should also vary from times of concentration to times of competition. Complexity of codes, like diversity, should be more restricted in times of firm concentration. Another difference is that the annual number of hits is used here as an indicator of turnover of hits, not of musical diversity. Still, it is interesting to follow up on the authors' notion that decreasing turnover is associated with more restricted musical codes. A final difference is that the effect of each market variable in the year prior to the release of a given song is examined as well as the effect of the market variables in the same year a song is released (for example, concentration in 1977 may affect the musical structure of songs in 1978 instead of 1977). In light of the work of these authors, we will examine whether (a) a declining number of competing

133

firms, (b) increasing concentration of these firms, and (c) lower turnover of hits are associated with more restricted levels of ornamentation, melodic form, and chordal structure.

Organization of the production process

The market concentration argument assumes that organizational elements at the industry level directly affect the musical structure of the songs record companies release. Yet it could be argued that organization of the process by which songs are actually produced would affect the musical structure much more than concentration does. It is relevant here to focus on the impact of two types of professionals involved in the production process: songwriters and producers. These two intermediaries are often the means by which record companies exercise control over performers' selection of songs as well as the final recorded version of these songs (Wadhams 1990). Granted, there are celebrated occasions when such personnel are seen as liberating the artistic potential of performers (Tobler and Grundy 1982). Still, the reality is that both songwriters and producers are employed by record companies on the basis of their past delivery of success as well as their present ability to deliver success (Peterson and Berger 1971; Shemel and Krasilovsky 1985). Such an emphasis on success leads to a restricted musical code being employed by both types of personnel (Rothenbuhler and Dimmick 1982). The argument is analogous to that made for the major labels in that songwriters and producers are seen as attempting to reproduce the "formula" that has brought them success in the past.

Two variables are constructed to examine whether the organization of production – in reference to songwriters and producers – has an effect on the ornamentation, melodic form, and chord structure of number one songs. Each number one song is coded as to whether the song is written by one or more performer, by one or more outsider, or by both together. "Outsider" refers to an individual who is not part of the performing act. The same coding is used in reference to the producer role.[8]

Barbara Rosenblum finds that the organization of the production process is one source of explanation for variation in artistic codes. Her (1978) study analyzes which social factors lead to differences in "style" between the following categories of photography: news photography, advertising photography, and fine art photography. Her usage of "style" refers to conventions regarding various elements that are fairly stable over time. Rosenblum's premise is that such patterned regularities can be partly accounted for by the organization of photographic production. For example, the similarities that exist between news photographs are due in part to news photographers' lack of control in two areas: typically, they do not select the material which they shoot and they do not have a final say over which of their photographs are selected for use. Rosenblum finds an organized production process which assumes control of decisions in both areas where news photographers lack control. The fine art photographer, on the other hand, faces none of these organizational constraints during the production process. The photographic styles between these two categories of photographers differ partly because photographic codes grow more restricted as the division of labor increases. We follow up on Rosenblum's work by seeing if the inclusion of one or more outsiders in the production process will be associated with a more restricted ornamentation, melodic form, and chordal structure of the number one songs.

Performer attributes

Any attempt to explain variation in the melodic form of number one songs which does not consider the attributes of performers is likely to miss an important source of explanation (Bjorn 1981). For instance, ignoring performers while focusing on market factors as a source of variation in musical structure implies that all performers, regardless of various attributes, will perform roughly the same musical material if the market situation is constant. Several performer attributes mentioned in the literature are seen as associated with changes in the musical structure of songs. Four are examined in this study. The first attribute is the performers' previous level of success. The remaining three attributes are typical demographic variables: the performers' race, gender, and nationality.

As performers earn money for labels, the labels often extend privileges to them which result in greater autonomy in business affairs as well as artistic and technical autonomy in the recording process (Frith 1983; Kealy 1990; Sanjek 1983; Wright 1983). One feasible result is that as a performer becomes more successful, the musical structure of his or her songs will increasingly differ from the songs of the less successful. This is due to the increased autonomy and creative license that will probably accompany success, which allows the performer to pursue his or her musical agenda more readily than artists more constrained by "commercial" concerns. In this study, previous success is measured in three different ways: the number of previous number one singles, the number of previous Top 40 singles, and the number of previous Top 40 albums the given performer has enjoyed.[9]

Ethnographic research has shown that musicians often face conflicting situations (Becker 1963; Bennett 1980; Faulkner 1971). On one hand, they want to express themselves creatively by exploring new musical vocabularies. On the other hand, they realize that they often have to forgo their initial desires in order to make a living. In other words, the musicians studied lacked the resources to follow their own musical agendas. We will see whether the previous success of a performer is associated with greater elaboration in ornamentation, melodic form, and chordal structure.

The preceding discussion of performers' previous success posits that resources lead to musical autonomy. Work on class and stratification (Beeghley 1989; Giddens 1975; Wright 1989) indicates that two demographic attributes in modern capitalism significantly shape acess to resources: race and gender. Both attributes are relevant in recorded music since black and female performers are each concentrated in certain musical styles (Denisoff and Bridges 1982). Thus the musical structure of songs performed by blacks or women could differ from those of whites or men because of the association of the former categories with certain musical formats. Race is also relevant because the history of American mass media includes periods when music by black performers has been borrowed by white performers in a "sanitized" derivative, or has co-existed with music of white performers, or has been largely ignored (Clarke 1983; Denisoff 1989; Frith 1983; Sanjek 1983; Tunstall 1987). [10] The point remains that music by black performers is often seen as being different from music by white performers. This study allows us to see whether the race composition of performing acts (black, white, and mixed) is associated with changes in ornamentation, melodic form, and chordal structure. Bradby (1990) suggests that gender is additionally relevant because songs performed by women differ from those of men in the use of pronouns in lyrics and the rhythmic relation of the lead vocal to the background vocals. This study explores the impact of gender by seeing whether the gender composition of performing acts (female, male, mixed) is associated with changes in ornamentation, melodic form, and chordal structure.

In addition to race and gender, the nationality of performers is another demographic attribute considered. This study focuses on the nationality of the performers to see whether there are associated changes in the ornamentation, melodic form, and chord structure of their respective number one songs. Nationality in this study is defined as the performers' country of origin: the United States, Great Britain, and "Other."[11] This focus is relevant since Cerulo's (1988) study of national anthems shows that musical structures of songs are affected by the nationality of the composer. Note that no direction of effect is specified with these three demographic attributes. Given the context of this study, the literature is ambiguous as to whether these attributes promote restricted or elaborated musical forms. Therefore, the empirical analysis asks if there is indeed an effect, and if so, the direction of that effect.

Instrument technology

The preceding three classes of independent variables are employed with the assumption that musical structure reflects its surrounding organizational arrangements or the people involved in its construction. However, it is unlikely that variation in musical structure is *only* attributable to such factors.

136

In particular, any discussion of changes in musical structure should seriously consider associated changes in instrument technology (Durant 1985; Goodwin 1990). Instrument technology does not refer only to electric or electronic developments. For instance, Weber (1958) has noted that the design of the ancient aulos contributed to the exploration of chromaticism.

Instrument technology, particularly that of an electronic nature, can sometimes lead to mechanization of production and to more restricted musical codes (Clapton and Williams 1983; Rosenblum 1978). For example, record labels that produced disco singles in the 1970s used new instrument technology such as drum machines and synthesizers to "churn out" inexpensive and homogeneous songs (Sanjek 1988). Durant (1985) agrees that technology can constrain musical structure; however, increasing instrument technology means that such constraints occur at a higher level of musical complexity. In other words, if a performer relies solely on drum machines to create the percussion part, the complexity of that part is limited by the technology of the machine. However, as drum machines advance technologically, the musical limitations should correspondingly decrease (Clignet 1979).

Instrument technology is coded in this study by focusing on the four groups of instruments central to the number one songs: keyboards, guitars, basses, and drums (Hamm 1981; Lent 1984; Newquist 1989). Technology is treated as a hierarchy where acoustic forms for each instrument group occupy the lowest level, electrical forms occupy the middle level, and electronic forms occupy the top level.[12] For each instrument group present in a given number one song, the highest hierarchical level is noted. Thus each group is coded as to whether its highest hierarchical level is acoustic, electric, or electronic.[13] This allows us to see if higher levels of instrument technology are associated with more elaboration in the ornamentation, melodic form, and chord structures of number one songs.

Song characteristics

As mentioned earlier, some of the variation in melodic form and chordal structure from song to song may be due simply to the characteristics of the songs themselves. Therefore, certain elements of the songs are controlled for before there is an examination of the variables. The variation in melodic forms could very well be due to the increase in the "repertoire" of possibilities that grows with the passage of time. Time is modeled here as simply the year that the respective song reaches its number one position. Three other song characteristics are controlled for in the analysis of melodic form: (a) whether or not a song is an instrumental, (b) the tempo in beats per minute of each song, and (c) the duration of the song in minutes.

Sample

The purpose of this study is to explore how changes in the musical structure of songs are associated with changes in the social context in which these songs are created. The particular class of songs analyzed in this study are number one songs, those which top the ratings charts of various trade papers associated with the recording industry. This study relies on the charts of *Billboard*, which are generally held to be the most reliable and the most prestigious (Hesbacher 1974; Peterson and Berger 1975; Sanjek 1988). According to a *Billboard* publication there have been 700 number one songs between July 9, 1955 and June 25, 1988 (Bronson 1988). A 15 percent sample (105 songs) of these 700 songs has been generated by means of computer selection. Random sampling is beneficial because it offers a selection criterion that is unbiased with regards to preference and taste (Brooks 1982). The focus is on number one songs because they comprise a coherent group, owing to their chart-topping popularity. There is no assumption that the songs are number one because of similar musical characteristics. Instead, there is a focus on how the structures of these popular songs are similarly affected by social factors. The songs that comprise this sample are listed in Appendix B.

The gathering of the original recordings of each of these 105 number one songs began with the specification of the sample. Next began the process of translating these aural performances to written music so that the methods of musical coding developed by Cerulo (1985, 1988) could be applied to each song. Published sheet music is rarely an appropriate way to make this transference because the emphasis is on marketability, not musical accuracy (Stich 1990). Instead, in this study, most of the songs have been transcribed so as to detail accurately the music contained in the recorded performances.[14]

All the songs in the sample have been scored on an assortment of quantitative measures which describe their respective melodic, rhythmic, tonal, phrase and temporal structures. All in all, over 40 measures of musical structure for each of the 105 songs have been coded. What is presented in this paper is an initial exploration of how changes in ornamentation, melodic form, and chordal structure are associated with changes in the social context of number one songs. Future research will focus on creating a single summary measure of musical structure for each song as well as expanding the sample to include "less popular" songs.

Statistical method

Multiple regression is the tool used to analyze the data. This technique allows for an investigation of the relationship that results when the independent variables systematically vary with the dependent variable. This technique also permits an examination of the scattering of observations not accounted for by this systematic relationship. The proportion of variation that is explained by the set of selected independent variables is indicated by the R^2 statistic. Unfortunately, the R^2 statistic is made larger by the simple inclusion of more independent variables. As a result, the adjusted R^2 is stressed in this analysis (Neter, Wasserman, and Kutner 1983).

The task at hand is to select the set of variables that will explain the greatest amount of variation. This selection is tempered by the limited degrees of freedom in this small sample, the significance of the adjusted R^2, and the significance of each variable estimate. The method used to select the set of dependent variables is the stepwise procedure. This procedure has been augmented by replication with different subsets of independent variables to assure the reliability of the final set of variables selected (Neter, Wasserman and Kutner 1983).[15]

Results

Melodic ornamentation

Each of the number one songs in the sample is coded in reference to its level of ornamentation. The scores range from 1.00 to 5.84, where the mean equals 2.25. The set of variables associated with variations in the level of ornamentation is presented in Table 7.1. Variables that represent internal song characteristics as well as three of the four classes of social phenomenon are found in this model. Together these variables explain 34 percent of the variation in melodic form. Additionally, all the variables are significant at the 0.05 or 0.01 level.

Two types of internal song characteristics are associated with varying levels of ornamentation. First, we see that instrumentals have a more basic ornamentation than non-instrumentals. This is merely a function of definition since instrumentals are coded as having no ornamentation (see note 19). Additionally, we see that as the duration of songs increases, their level of ornamentation becomes more elaborate. One aspect of the production process is found to be significant: songs jointly produced by the performer and an outsider have a more basic ornamentation than songs produced solely by the performer or solely by an outsider. Performer attributes are associated with ornamentation in two ways. First, performers from the USA have a more elaborate ornamentation than performers from Britain or other nations. Furthermore, black performing acts have a more elaborate ornamentation than performing acts which are either white or racially mixed. Note that the effect of being black is separate and independent from the effect of being from the USA. Finally, referring to instrument technology, we see ornamentation is more basic when the lowest level of guitar technology – the acoustic guitar – is present, rather than electric or electronic.

Melodic form

The scores of melodic form range from −1.39 to 3.09 where the mean equals 0. The set of variables associated with variations in the level of melodic form is presented in Table 7.2. Variables that represent internal song characteristics as well as two of the four classes of social phenomenon are found in this model. The set of variables presented here accounts for 37 percent of the variation in overall melodic form. Once again, all the variables are significant at the 0.05 level or better.

Only one internal song characteristic is associated with variation in melodic form. Instrumentals are found to have a more elaborate melodic form than non-instrumentals. This is probably because instruments are typically more agile and far-ranging than the human voice. Two aspects of the organization of the production process show a significant relationship with the overall melodic form. Songs which are produced by both the performer and an outsider have a more restricted melodic form than songs produced solely by the performer or solely by an outsider. Additionally, songs that are written by the performer are found to have a more elaborated melodic form than songs written by both the performer and an outsider or solely by an outsider. Instrumental technology has a significant effect in that number one songs where there is no keyboard technology have a more restricted melodic form than those songs with any type of keyboard technology.

Chordal structure

The chordal structure scores range from −2.56 to 2.64 where the mean equals 0. The set of variables associated with variations in the level of chordal structure is presented in Table 7.3. The chordal structure model includes variables which represent internal song characteristics and market structure. These variables taken together account for 34 percent of the variation in the chordal structure of number one songs. As before, all the variables are significant at the 0.05 or 0.01 level.

Three variables representing internal song characteristics are associated with variation in the chordal structure of songs. We find that with each passing year, the chordal structure of number one songs becomes more elaborated. Number one songs that are instrumentals are also found to have a more elaborated chordal structure than non-instrumentals. Additionally, the longer the duration of number one songs, the more elaborated the chordal structure. Unlike the previous two models, the present model contains two market structure variables. We see that the greater the number of firms with Top 10 songs in the previous year, the more elaborated are the chordal structures of songs in the current year. In addition, an increasing amount of turnover in number one songs is associated with a more restricted chordal structure for each of the number one songs in that same year.

140

Discussion

Song characteristics

This study demonstrates that it is imperative to consider the amount of variation in musical structure which is due to the characteristics of the songs themselves. For instance, we find that instrumentals have a significantly different level of ornamentation, melodic form, and chordal structure from non-instrumentals. Additionally, we see that as songs increase in duration, so does the elaboration of their ornamentation and chordal structure. Cerulo's (1988) work also demonstrates the need for considering song characteristics; she finds that national anthems which employ marches have a more elaborated code than do those which are hymns.

Perhaps the most important finding of this study is that some elements of musical structure may linearly increase in complexity over time while other elements may remain fairly stable. Consider that both the variation in ornamentation and melodic form is explained by factors other than time. Chordal structure, in contrast, displays a trend of increasing embellishment over time. In fact, the passage of time by itself explains 17 percent of the variation in chordal structure. Further analysis shows that number one songs are marked by a decreasing proportion of major chords, I chords, IV chords, and V chords over time. Additionally, these songs contain an increasingly higher proportion of minor chords and "residual chords" (chords that are neither major nor minor). So to understand how musical codes change across time means identifying which internal elements are effected by time and which are not.

Market structure of the recording industry

The notion that the concentration of the record industry brings about a restriction in the musical codes of its songs is an influential one (Frith and Goodwin 1990). Interestingly enough, the concentration ratios used by both Peterson and Berger (1975) and Rothenbuhler and Dimmick (1982) are not associated with variations in the ornamentation, melodic form, or chordal structure of number one songs.[16] The use of both the four- and eight-firm ratios as well as the examination of their effects from the previous year as well as the current year produce no results. There are several reasons why the concentration of the industry may have no effect on these musical structures. Frith (1988) says that the concentration model is no longer appropriate. Major labels do not attempt to put independent labels out of competition. Instead, the majors allow the independents to operate as barometers for what types of music are currently selling. Bradby (1990) suggests that periods which Peterson and Berger assume to offer musical homogeneity actually offer musical innovation. In particular, she sees the "girl-groups" of the 1960s as introducing innovations overlooked by the Peterson and Berger argument. Rosenblum (1978) argues that the concentration model is flawed in that it uses non-musical elements to model musical diversity.

The present models offer a clue as to why the concentration ratios do not offer any significant effects. Peterson and Berger's concentration argument is based on a cyclical pattern over time. As shown above, the variation of ornamentation and melodic form is accounted for by factors other than time. Hence, it is not surprising that concentration has no effect on these musical elements. Chordal structure, however, involves a linear increase in complexity across time. Hence it is not surprising that a cyclical variable is not significantly associated with chordal structure.

Two other indicators of market structure are found to have a significant association with chordal structure. But the resulting associations do not quite match what is portrayed in the concentration model of Peterson and Berger. On one hand, we do find that the annual number of firms with Top 10 songs is associated with an embellishment of the chordal structure of number one songs. But this association is lagged, since the number of firms in the *previous* year is what affects the chordal structure of number one songs in the current year. On the other hand, we see that the greater the turnover of number one songs, the more restricted is the chordal structure of these songs. This finding does not match their notion that a greater number of annual Top 10 songs is equal to greater musical diversity. The findings here support an alternative interpretation: the faster turnover of number one songs in a year is due to a greater supply of potential hits. Perhaps when there is a paucity of songs from which hits are selected, there is a greater likelihood that songs with a more elaborated chordal structure are selected. Hence, a lower density of annual number ones is associated with a more elaborated chordal structure.

The organization of the production process

The notion of the restrictive impact of outsiders in the production process fares only moderately well with regards to ornamentation and melodic form. We do find that the melodic form is more elaborated when the performer writes the song as opposed to either the performer writing with an outsider or an outsider writing the song. However, we find that both ornamentation and melodic form are more restricted when a number one song is produced by the performer and an outsider as opposed to solely the performer or solely the outsider. Furthermore, neither the melodic form nor ornamentation is found to be restricted when an outsider is the producer. This finding may be due to the transformation of the producer role from technician to artist (Culshaw 1976; Denisoff 1986; Frith 1983; Tobler and Grundy 1982). In this context, it is very easy to imagine how a producer can encourage a more elaborated musical structure. Perhaps the restricted codes associated with joint production by performer and outsider are due to an increased number of decision-makers and a diffusion of musical control.

Performer attributes

In terms of demographic attributes, we find that race and nationality offer explanation for a variation in the ornamentation of number one songs. The charge that black performers who find "crossover" success have to lose their musical "blackness" in order to appeal to a wider audience (Perry 1988) is not supported by this finding. However, black performers do not significantly differ from white performers on overall melodic form or chordal structure. Interestingly, gender offers no explanation for variation in any of the three musical elements. Likewise, the previous level of success by an artist does not affect the structure of ornamentation, melodic form, or chordal structure. However, an exploratory analysis of the various melodic elements shows that the more previous Top 40 albums a performer has, the more elaborated is his or her melodic range. Exploratory analysis yields no such findings for gender. The lack of explanation provided by performers' previous success and gender may be due in part to the nature of this sample. It is possible that if this sample were expanded to include songs of lower popularity, the performers' previous success as well as gender might become more important.

Instrument technology

Instrument technology is associated with variations in musical codes. However, these resulting associations offer only limited support to the expectations set forth earlier in the paper. We find that low or no levels of instrument technology are associated with more restricted levels of ornamentation and melodic form than are high levels of technology. But we do not find higher levels of instrument technology to be associated with more elaborated codes than low or no levels of technology. This may be due to the fact that increasing instrument technology is not necessarily applied to increasing musical advances. Technology is often used instead to create the same product with less cost and more efficiency (Goodwin 1990; Sanjek 1988; Tully 1989). Those songs which do maximize the potentials of increasing instrument technology are most likely not heard on Top 40 radio. Hence, a sample that includes songs of varying popularity might capture a greater impact of technology on musical codes.

Conclusions

The goal of this study was to see how changes in the musical structure of songs are associated with changes in social contexts. It has been pursued by focusing on the melodic form, ornamentation, and chordal structure of number one songs over a 33-year time period. In particular, there is a concern with which social contexts are associated with a restriction or elaboration of these musical structures. Four classes of social context were specified: the market structure of the recording industry, the organization of the production process, performer attributes, and instrument technology. The results of this study should not be extrapolated beyond the scope of this sample nor the context of these variables.

We find that several social variables are associated with greater elaboration in each of these musical structures. Performers who are from the United States and performers who are black have more complex levels of ornamentation than other performers. Number one songs which are written by the performer have more elaborated melodic forms than songs whose writers include an outsider. The chordal structures of number one songs are also found to be increasingly elaborated as the number of firms having Top 10 songs in the previous year increases. Put another way, an increasing number of competing firms in the previous year is associated with an increasing chordal complexity for songs in the current year.

We also find that several social variables are associated with more restrictive musical structures. Number one songs that are jointly produced by the performer and an outsider have more restricted melodic ornamentation and overall melodic form than songs produced solely by the performer or solely by an outsider. Number one songs which employ no level of keyboard technology have more restricted melodic forms than songs which use any type of keyboard. Similarly, a more restricted ornamentation is found in songs whose level of guitar technology is no higher than acoustic. Finally, the chordal structure of number one songs becomes more restricted as the annual turnover of number one songs increases.

In addition to explaining variations in musical structure by social context, we find that some variation is due to characteristics of the songs themselves. For instance, number one songs which are instrumentals have more elaborated melodic forms and chordal structures as well as more restricted ornamentation than other songs. An increasing duration of number one songs is associated with an increasing elaboration of melodic form and chordal structure. Finally, we see that the chordal structure of number one songs becomes more elaborated over the years of the period studied.

Appendix A:
Construction of the musical measurements

Melodic structure

It is useful in understanding the following approach to think of melody as the mathematical division of time and pitch. A melody divides time by placing its notes at successive points in its duration (for example, the first note may fall on the third beat of the melody while the second note falls on the fifth beat). A melody divides pitch by placing each successive note at a higher or a lower pitch or the same pitch as its predecessor. If we think of time and pitch together, we see that each note has a unique position in relation to the other notes of the melody.

Cerulo (1985, 1988) states that there are four elements to consider when evaluating how all the notes of a melody are located in pitch and time: (a) the frequency with which the pitch of the melody changes direction, (b) the magnitude of these directional changes, (c) the proportion of intervals between successive notes that are large (disjunct), and (d) the degree to which several musical notes are sung for one corresponding verbal syllable (ornamentation). To these four elements will be added the total number of pitches the melody contains (range).

To make these dimensions more intuitive, they will be discussed in the light of the time–pitch graph for "My Love" presented in Figure 7.1. Note that the horizontal axis represents the division of time in terms of the beat. The vertical axis represents the division of melodic pitch. Pitch is scored by labeling the first note of the scale, the tonic, as "0". The number of half steps

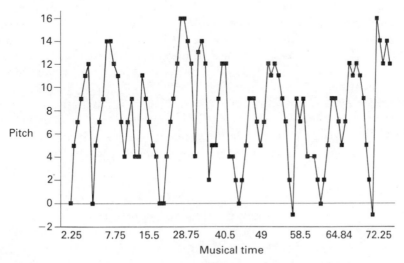

Figure 7.1

that a pitch departs from the tonic yields the score for that note. This means that in the key of C major, we establish a baseline by coding one particular C as "0". As the pitch rises from this baseline we get higher scores. Thus a C sharp is scored as "1", a D is scored as "2" and so on. As the pitch falls from this baseline C, we simply use negative scores.

Frequency of melodic change refers to how many times a melody changes direction. In the graphs, such a change is represented by each of the "sawtooths." The first half of the sawtooth results as the melody changes direction. The second half of the sawtooth signals the occurrence of another directional change. The number of times that the melody changes direction are summed. The measure is then standardized by dividing by the number of measures that the melody entails. Thus the score of 1.83 indicates that the melody changes direction almost two times per measure.

Magnitude of melodic change refers to the size of those changes in direction. For each change the distance from the previous change in direction is counted. All of these distances are then summed. This sum is then standardized by dividing it by the total number of directional changes.[17] So the average size of direction change in pitch for "My Love" is 8 half steps.

Disjunctness is a refinement on the magnitude measure. It refers to how many changes between *individual* notes can be thought of as large or severe. Disjunctness occurs when the interval between notes moving in the same direction exceeds four half steps, or notes moving in a different direction exceeds three half steps. The measure for disjunctness then is the proportion of distances between each of the melodic notes which are disjunct. Nineteen percent of all melodic intervals for the given song are disjunct.

Ornamentation refers to the occurrence of multiple musical notes given to a single verbal syllable. The measure is computed by multiplying the number of musical notes times the square root of the number of incidents of ornamentation and dividing the whole thing by the number of verbal syllables. An ornamentation score of "1" indicates no ornamentation occurs.[18] The further a score departs from one, the more ornamentation is present in a melody. The score of 2.57 shows that there is a fair amount of ornamentation.

Range is the easiest of measures to comprehend. It is simply the number of discrete half steps encompassed by the melody. It is equal to one plus the difference between the score of the highest note in the melody and the lowest note. The range of "My Love" is thus found to contain 18 half steps.

Chordal structure

Chordal structure in this study refers to the proportionate distribution of certain chord types. The chordal structure of each number one song is measured by way of five elements. The first step in doing this is calculating the sheer number of chords employed over the entire length of each song.

The next step consists of calculating the proportion of all chords that are (a) major chords, (b) minor chords, (c) I chords, (d) IV chords, and (e) V chords.[19] This approach differs from Cerulo's (1985, 1988) in three ways. First, all chords are considered as opposed to those that occur only at the dominant beats of each song. Second, there is a distinction made between major and minor chords, as well as a residual category (the proportion that are not major or minor) of diminished, augmented, and suspended chords. Finally, the five elements of chordal structure are continuous measures as opposed to categorical.

Summary measures

An overall summary measure of melodic form is constructed by way of Cerulo's (1988) method. The correlation between each of the five melodic elements is examined. If the correlations are moderate, the elements are standardized and then factor-analyzed. Each element's factor score from the first loading provides a weight which is used in an additive scale. The overall measure for each song is thus made by standardizing each element, multiplying each element by its respective weight and summing these numbers.

The correlation matrix for the elements of melodic form is presented in Table 7.4. The matrix shows that most of the elements are moderately correlated with each other. Ornamentation, however, exhibits a weak relation with all but one of the elements. This does not mean that ornamentation lacks variation or relevance; rather, the variation that occurs in ornamentation does not contribute to an overall measure of melodic form. To deal with this, two measures are employed: one that addresses only melodic ornamentation and one that summarizes overall melodic form. The measure of overall melodic form for each of the songs in the sample is constructed from the following scale:

$$\text{Overall melodic form} = 0.22 \text{ Frequency of directional change} +$$
$$0.78 \text{ Magnitude of directional change} +$$
$$0.66 \text{ Disjunctness} + 0.80 \text{ Melodic range.}$$

The first factor loading from which the weights are derived accounts for 43.3 percent of the variance.

Chordal structure

A summary measure for chordal structure is constructed in the same fashion as for melodic form. The correlation matrix for the chordal structure element is presented in Table 7.5. The matrix indicates that all but one pair of the correlations is strong. Therefore, all the elements are used in the construction of a summary measure for chordal structure. This summary measure is constructed from the following scales:

Overall chordal structure = 0.97 Proportion of major cords −
0.78 Proportion of minor chords +
0.86 Proportion of I chords +
0.64 Proportion of IV chords +
0.53 Proportion of V chords.

The first factor loading from which the weights are derived accounts for 53.4 percent of the variance.

Appendix B:
Random sample of number one songs

Title	Performer	Year
Poor People of Paris	Les Baxter	1956
Heartbreak Hotel	Elvis Presley	1956
I Want You, I Love You, I Need You	Elvis Presley	1956
Love Me Tender	Elvis Presley	1956
Party Doll	Buddy Knox	1957
All Shook Up	Elvis Presley	1957
Witch Doctor	David Seville	1958
Hard Hearted Woman	Elvis Presley	1958
Tom Dooley	The Kingston Trio	1958
To Know Him is to Love Him	The Teddy Bears	1958
Kansas City	Wilbert Harrison	1959
Sleep Walk	Santo and Johnny	1959
Running Bear	Johnny Preston	1960
Alley-Oop	The Hollywood Argyles	1960
I'm Sorry	Brenda Lee	1960
Itsy Bitsy Teenie Weenie Yellow Polka Dot Bikini	Bryan Hyland	1960
It's Now or Never	Elvis Presley	1960
Are You Lonesome Tonight?	Elvis Presley	1960
Will You Love Me Tomorrow?	The Shirelles	1961
Surrender	Elvis Presley	1961
Runaway	Del Shannon	1961
Soldier Boy	The Shirelles	1962
The Loco-Motion	Little Eva	1962
Hey Paula	Paul and Paula	1963
I Will Follow Him	Little Peggy March	1963
Surf City	Jan and Dean	1963
Sugar Shack	Jimmy Gilmer and the Fireballs	1963
Chapel of Love	The Dixie Cups	1964
A Hard Day's Night	The Beatles	1964
Downtown	Petula Clark	1965
You've Lost that Lovin' Feeling	The Righteous Brothers	1965
This Diamond Ring	Gary Lewis and The Playboys	1965
My Girl	The Temptations	1965

Title	Performer	Year
Eight Days a Week	The Beatles	1965
Hang on Sloopy	The McCoys	1965
Turn! Turn! Turn!	The Byrds	1965
These Boots are Made for Walkin'	Nancy Sinatra	1966
The Ballad of the Green Berets	S. Sgt. Barry Sadler	1966
Paperback Writer	The Beatles	1966
Good Vibrations	The Beach Boys	1966
I'm a Believer	The Monkees	1966
Kind of a Drag	The Buckinghams	1967
Somethin' Stupid	Nancy Sinatra and	
	Frank Sinatra	1967
Hello Goodbye	The Beatles	1967
(Sittin' On) Dock of the Bay	Otis Redding	1968
Mrs Robinson	Simon and Garfunkel	1968
Grazing in the Grass	Hugh Masekela	1968
Get Back	The Beatles	1969
The Long and Winding Road	The Beatles	1970
I Think I Love You	The Partridge Family	1970
The Tears of a Clown	Smokey Robinson and	
	The Miracles	1970
You've Got a Friend	James Taylor	1971
Theme from "Shaft"	Isaac Hayes	1971
Brand New Key	Melanie	1971
Song Sung Blue	Neil Diamond	1972
Baby Don't Get Hooked on Me	Mac Davis	1972
Ben	Michael Jackson	1972
I Am Woman	Helen Reddy	1972
Frankenstein	Edgar Winter Group	1973
My Love	Paul McCartney and	
	Wings	1973
Lucy in the Sky with Diamonds	Elton John	1975
(Hey Won't You Play) Another Somebody		
Done Something Wrong Song	B. J. Thomas	1975
Thank God I'm a Country Boy	John Denver	1975
Listen to What the Man Said	Wings	1975
Rhinestone Cowboy	Glen Campbell	1975
Calypso	John Denver	1975
Convoy	C. W. McCall	1976
50 Ways to Leave Your Lover	Paul Simon	1976
Disco Duck (Part 1)	Rick Dees and His	
	Cast of Idiots	1976
You Don't Have to Be a Star (To Be In My	Marilyn McCoo and	
Show)	Billy Davis Jr	1977
Love theme from "A Star is Born"	Barbra Streisand	1977
Got to Give It Up, Part 1	Marvin Gaye	1977
Da Doo Ron Ron	Shawn Cassidy	1977
You're the One that I Want	John Travolta and	
	Olivia Newton-John	1978
Grease	Frankie Valli	1978
Another Brick in the Wall	Pink Floyd	1980
It's Still Rock and Roll to Me	Billy Joel	1980

Title	Performer	Year
Kiss on My List	Daryl Hall and John Oates	1981
Morning Train (Nine to Five)	Sheena Easton	1981
I Can't Go for That (No Can Do)	Daryl Hall and John Oates	1982
Ebony and Ivory	Paul McCartney and Stevie Wonder	1982
Man-eater	Daryl Hall and John Oates	1982
Baby, Come to Me	Patti Austin and James Ingram	1983
Come on Eileen	Dexy's Midnight Runners	1983
Every Breath You Take	The Police	1983
All Night Long (All Night)	Lionel Richie	1983
Owner of a Lonely Heart	Yes	1984
Time after Time	Cyndi Lauper	1984
Wake Me Up Before You Go-Go	Wham!	1984
St. Elmo's Fire (Man in Motion)	John Paar	1985
Money for Nothing	Dire Straits	1985
Miami Vice Theme	Jan Hammer	1985
Say You, Say Me	Lionel Richie	1985
Sara	Starship	1986
Addicted to Love	Robert Palmer	1986
Greatest Love of All	Whitney Houston	1986
On My Own	Patti Labelle and Michael McDonald	1986
Take My Breath Away	Berlin	1986
Stuck with You	Huey Lewis and the News	1986
Lean on Me	Club Nouveau	1987
Nothing's Gonna Stop Us Now	Starship	1987
I Wanna Dance with Somebody (Who Loves Me)	Whitney Houston	1987
Mony Mony	Billy Idol	1987
Father Figure	George Michael	1988
Anything for You	Gloria Estefan and Miami Sound Machine	1988

Notes

1. This is not to imply, however, that the "language" of music is equivalent to a verbal language. Musical elements, unlike spoken and written words, do not portray a specific content, message, or meaning (Attali 1977; Cone 1974; Dahlhaus 1983; Hanslick 1986; Langer 1957).
2. I wish to thank Keith Allum, Tim Clydesdale, Frank Dobbin, Michèle Lamont, Jack Veugelers, Robert Wuthnow, and Yan Yan for all of their comments, suggestions, and support.
3. Blau (1989) and Peterson and DiMaggio (1975) have also found this claim to be unsupported.

4. This approach shares a certain affinity with Weber's (1958) study of Western music. One of his interests was how the mathematical division of the music spectrum into "equal temperaments" emerged in the West.

5. Four-firm and eight-firm concentration ratios refer to the proportion of all Top 10 songs in a given year that are attributable to the four or eight firms with the most Top 10 songs (Peterson and Berger 1975; Rothenbuhler and Dimmick 1982).

6. Sources for the construction of the three market variables are Bronson (1988), Whitburn (1987, 1989), *Billboard's Annual Buyers Directory, Standard and Poor's Industry Survey, Moody's Industrial Manual,* and *Moody's International Manual.* The last three titles are also annual publications.

7. The method in this study ranks songs on a continuum of complexity. Thus "musical complexity" refers to a song's location on that continuum. "Musical diversity" refers to the spread of songs around a reference point such as an average. Such a spread can be concentrated on the low end, middle, or high end of the complexity continuum.

8. The triple-tiered variables for both songwriter and producer are modeled as dummy variables. The source for this coding is Bronson (1988).

9. This information is obtained from Whitburn (1987, 1989).

10. Hamm (1981) notes that while white audiences have responded to musical styles that are distinctly "black," the analogue for black audiences has not emerged.

11. Coding of race, gender and nationality is aided by Bronson (1988), Pareles and Romanowski (1983), and Whitburn (1989). Dummy variables are constructed for all of the categories mentioned.

12. The distinctions between electric and electronic for each instrument group are guided by the discussions in Lent (1984), Darter (1985), Vilardi (1985), and Newquist (1989).

13. Four dummy variables are constructed for each instrument group with the fourth dummy referring to whether or not the group is present in the song.

14. Contrary to Bennett (1980: 107) the pitch and rhythmic aspects of performed music, such as rock, are amenable to transcription in a manner that accurately reflects the performed material. The transcriptions in publications such as *Bass Player, Guitar Player,* and *Keyboard* are excellent examples.

15. The models presented in this study are found to meet the assumptions implicit in the use of multiple regression: VIF scores indicate no problems of multi-collinearity, residual plots indicate no nonconstant error variance, and Durbin-Watson test statistics reject the present of autocorrelation.

16. A preliminary analysis of musical diversity, based on the combined melodic, rhythmic, and harmonic elements of each number one song, finds that the concentration ratios are not significantly related to diversity after considering the effects of time.

17. Note that Cerulo (1988) standardizes by dividing by the number of measures in the melody, whereas here the scores are standardized by the number of directional changes. Both are appropriate in that they produce systematic results.

18. Instrumentals have an ornamentation score of "1" since they have no verbal syllables.

19. For those unfamiliar with chord labels, the I (tonic) chord, the IV (subdominant) chord, and the V (dominant) chord are the first three chords heard in both "Louie, Louie" and "Wild Thing." These three chords are considered the primary chords in contemporary music genres such as rock.

References

Alexander, Jeffery C. 1990. Analytic debates: Understanding the relative autonomy of culture. In Jeffery C. Alexander and Steven Seidman (eds) *Culture and Society: Contemporary Debates*. Cambridge: Cambridge University Press.

Attali, Jacques. 1987. *Noise: The Political Economy of Music*, trans. Brian Massumi. Minneapolis, Minn.: University of Minnesota Press.

Barrett, Michele. 1988. The place of aesthetics in Marxist criticism. In Cary Nelson and Lawrence Grossberg (eds) *Marxism and the Interpretation of Culture*, pp. 697–713. Urbana, Ill.: University of Illinois Press.

Becker, Howard. 1963. *The Outsiders: Studies in the Sociology of Deviance*. New York: Free Press.

Beeghley, Leonard. 1989. *The Structure of Social Stratification in the United States*. Boston, Mass.: Allyn & Bacon.

Bennett, H. Stith. 1980. *On Becoming a Rock Musician*. Amherst, Mass.: University of Massachusetts Press.

Bergesen, Albert. 1979. Spirituals, jazz, blues, and soul music: The role of elaborated and restricted codes. In Robert Wuthnow (ed.) *The Religious Dimension: New Directions in Quantitative Research*, pp. 333–50. New York: Academic Press.

Bergesen, Albert. 1984. The semantic equation: A theory of the social origins of art styles. In Randall Collins (ed.) *Sociological Theory 1984*, pp. 187–221. San Francisco: Jossey-Bass.

Bjorn, Lars. 1981. The mass society and group action theories of cultural production: The case of stylistic innovation in jazz. *Social Forces* 60: 377–94.

Blau, Judith R. 1988. Music as social circumstance. *Social Forces* 66: 883–902.

Blau, Judith R. 1989. High culture as mass culture. In Arnold W. Foster and Judith R. Blau (eds) *Art and Society: Readings in the Sociology of the Arts*, pp. 429–39. Albany, NY: State University of New York Press.

Bourdieu, Pierre. 1984. *Distinction: A Social Critique of the Judgement of Taste*, trans. Richard Nice. Cambridge, Mass.: Harvard University Press.

Bradby, Barbara. 1990. Do-talk and don't-talk: The division of the subject in girl-group music. In Simon Frith and Andrew Goodwin (eds) *On Record: Rock, Pop, and the Written Word*, pp. 341–68. New York: Pantheon.

Bronson, Fred. 1988. *The Billboard Book of Number One Hits*, rev. edn. New York: Billboard Publications.

Brooks, William. 1982. On being tasteless. *Popular Music* 2: 9–18.

Cerulo, Karen. 1988. Analyzing cultural products: A new method of measurement. *Social Science Research* 17: 317–52.

Cerulo, Karen. 1985. Social solidarity and its effect on musical communication: An empirical analysis of national anthems. PhD diss., Princeton University.

Cerulo, Karen. 1989. Sociopolitical control and the structure of national symbols: An empirical analysis of national anthems. *Social Forces* 68: 76–99.

Clapton, Eric and Williams, John. 1983. Playing guitar. In George Martin (ed.) *Making Music: The Guide to Writing, Performing and Recording*, pp. 138–42. New York: Quill.

Clarke, Paul. 1983. "A Magic Science": Rock as a record art. *Popular Music* 3: 195–213.

Clignet, Remi. 1979. The variability of paradigms in the production of culture: A comparison of the arts and sciences. *American Sociological Review* 44: 392–409.

Cone, Edward T. 1974. *The Composer's Voice*. Berkeley, Calif.: University of California Press.

Culshaw, John. 1976. The role of the producer. In John Borwick (ed.) *Sound Recording Practice*, pp. 225–61. London: Oxford University Press.

Dahlhaus, Carl. 1983. *Esthetics of Music*, trans. William Austin. Cambridge: Cambridge University Press.

Dahlhaus, Carl. 1985. *Foundations of Music History*, trans. J. B. Robinson. Cambridge: Cambridge University Press.

Darter, Tom. 1985. *The Whole Synthesizer Catalogue*. Milwaukee, Wis.: Hal Leonard Publishing.

Denisoff, R. Serge. 1986. *Tarnished Gold: The Record Industry Revisited*. New Brunswick, NJ: Transaction Press.

Denisoff, R. Serge. 1989. *Inside MTV*. New Brunswick, NJ: Transaction Press.

Denisoff, R. Serge and Bridges, John. 1982. Popular music: Who are the recording artists? *Journal of Communication* 32, 1: 132–42.

DiMaggio, Paul. 1977. Market structure, the creative process, and popular culture: Toward an organizational reinterpretation of mass culture theory. *Journal of Popular Culture* 11: 436–52.

DiMaggio, Paul. 1982. Cultural entrepreneurship in nineteenth-century Boston: The creation of an organizational base for high culture in America. *Media, Culture and Society* 4: 33–50.

Durant, Alan. 1985. Rock revolution or time-no-changes: Visions of change and continuity in rock music. *Popular Music* 5: 97–121.

Faulkner, Robert P. 1971. *Hollywood Studio Musicians*. Chicago: Aldine Atherton.

Frith, Simon. 1983. Popular music 1950–1980. In George Martin (ed.) *Making Music: The Guide to Writing, Performing and Recording*, pp. 18–49. New York: Quill.

Frith, Simon. 1988. Picking up the pieces. In Simon Frith (ed.) *Facing the Music*, pp. 88–130. New York: Pantheon.

Frith, Simon and Goodwin, Andrew. 1990. The organization of the music business. In Simon Frith and Andrew Goodwin (eds) *On Record: Rock, Pop and the Written Word*, pp. 125–56. New York: Pantheon.

Giddens, Anthony. 1975. *The Class Structure of the Advanced Societies*. New York: Harper & Row.

Goodwin, Andrew. 1990. Sample and hold: Pop music in the digital age of reproduction. In Simon Frith and Andrew Goodwin (eds) *On Record: Rock, Pop and the Written Word*, pp. 258–73. New York: Pantheon.

Hamm, Charles. 1981. The fourth audience. *Popular Music* 1: 123–42.

Hanslick, Eduard. 1986. *On the Musically Beautiful*, trans. and ed. Geoffrey Payzant. Indianapolis, Ind.: Hackett.

Hauser, Arnold. 1982. *The Sociology of Art*, trans. Kenneth J. Northcott. Chicago: University of Chicago Press.

Hebdige, Dick. 1979. *Subculture: The Meaning of Style*. London: Methuen.

Hennion, Antoine. 1983. The production of success: An anti-musicology of the pop song. *Popular Music* 3: 159–93.

Hesbacher, Peter. 1974. Sound exposure in radio: The misleading nature of the playlist. *Popular Music and Society* 3: 189–201.

Hirsch, Paul M. 1972. Processing fads and fashions: An organization-set analysis of the culture industry systems. *American Journal of Sociology* 77: 639–59.

Hirsch, Paul M. 1977. Occupational, organizational, and institutional models in mass media research: Toward an integrated framework. In Paul M. Hirsch, Peter V. Miller, and F. Gerald Kline (eds) *Strategies for Communications Research*, pp. 13–42. Beverly Hills, Calif.: Sage.

Hirsch, Paul M. 1978. Production and distribution roles among cultural organizations: On the division of labor across intellectual disciplines. *Social Research* 45: 315–30.

Horkheimer, Max and Adorno, Theodor W. 1988. *Dialectic of Enlightenment*. Trans. John Cumming. New York: Continuum.

Jacobs, Norman. 1959. *Culture for the Millions?* Boston, Mass.: Beacon.

Jensen, Joli. 1984. An interpretive approach to culture production. In Willard D. Rowland and Bruce Watkins (eds) *Interpreting Television: Current Research Perspectives*, pp. 98–118. Beverly Hills, Calif.: Sage.

Kealy, Edward R. 1990. From craft to art: The case of sound mixers and popular music. In Simon Frith and Andrew Goodwin (eds) *On Record: Rock, Pop and the Written Word*, pp. 207–20. New York: Pantheon.

Langer, Susanne K. 1957. *Philosophy in a New Key*. Cambridge, Mass.: Harvard University Press.

Lent, Chris. 1984. *Rockschool 1: Guitar, Bass and Drums*. New York: Simon & Schuster.

Lowenthal, Leo. 1950. Historical perspectives of popular culture. *American Journal of Sociology* 55: 323–32.

Macdonald, Dwight. 1957. A theory of mass culture. In Bernard Rosenberg and Daving Manning White (eds) *Mass Culture: The Popular Arts in America*, pp. 59–73. Glencoe, Ill.: Free Press.

Neter, John, Wasserman, William, and Kutner, Michael H. 1983. *Applied Linear Regression*. Homewook, Ill.: Richard D. Irwin.

Newquist, H. P. 1989. *Music and Technology*. New York: Billboard Books.

Pareles, Jon and Romanowski, Patricia. 1983. *The Rolling Stone Encyclopedia of Rock and Roll*. New York: Rolling Stone Press.

Perry, Steve. 1988. The politics of crossover. In Simon Frith (ed.) *Facing the Music*, pp. 51–87. New York: Pantheon.

Peterson, Richard A. Three eras in the manufacture of popular music lyrics. In R. Serge Denisoff and Richard A. Peterson (eds) *The Sounds of Social Change*, pp. 282–304. Chicago: Rand McNally.

Peterson, Richard A. 1971. Entrepreneurship in organizations: Evidence from the popular music industry. *Administrative Science Quarterly* 16: 97–107.

Peterson, Richard A. and Berger, David G. 1975. Cycles in symbol production: The case of popular music. *American Sociological Review* 40: 158–73.

Peterson, Richard A. and DiMaggio, Paul. 1975. From region to class, the changing locus of country music: A test of the massification hypothesis. *Social Forces* 53: 497–506.

Rosenblum, Barbara. 1978. Style as social process. *American Sociological Review* 43: 422–38.

Rothenbuhler, Eric and Dimmick, John W. 1982. Popular Music: Concentration and diversity in the industry, 1974–1980. *Journal of Communication* 32, 1: 143–9.

Sanjek, Russell. 1983. *From Print to Plastic: Publishing and Promoting America's Popular Music (1900–1980)*. Institute for Studies in American Music Monographs: Number 20.

Sanjek, Russell. 1988. *American Popular Music and Its Business: The First Four Hundred Years. Volume III: 1900 to 1984*. New York: Oxford University Press.

Shemel, Sidney and Krasilovsky, M. William. 1985. *This Business of Music*, rev. edn. New York: Billboard Publications.

Stich, Mark. 1990. Street smarts: Copying from records. *Keyboard* 16, 8: 102.

Tober, John and Grundy, Stuart. 1982. *The Record Producers*. New York: St Martin's Press.

Tully, Tim. 1989. Good vibrations: The PC joins the band. *PC Computing* 2, 2: 173–81.

Tunstall, Jeremy. 1987. Stars, status, mobility. In Donald Lazere (ed.) *American Media and Mass Culture: Left Perspectives*, pp. 116–23. Berkeley, Calif.: University of California Press.

van den Haag, Ernest. 1957. Of happiness and of despair we have no measure. In Bernard Rosenberg and David Manning White (eds *Mass Culture: The Popular Arts in America*, pp. 504–36. Glencoe, Ill.: Free Press.

Vilardi, Frank. 1985. *Electronic Drums*. New York: Amsco Publications.

Wadhams, Wayne. 1990. *Sound Advice: The Musicians' Guide to the Recording Industry*. New York: Schirmer Books.

Weber, Max. 1958. *The Rational and Social Foundations of Music*, trans. and ed. Don Martindale, Johannes Riedel and Gertrude Neuwrith. Carbondale, Ill.: Southern Illinois University Press.

Whitburn, Joel. 1987. *The Billboard Book of Top 40 Albums*. New York: Billboard Books.

Whitburn, Joel. 1989. *The Billboard Book of Top 40 Hits*, 4th edn. New York: Billboard Publications.

Wilensky, Harold. 1964. Mass society and mass culture: Interdependence or independence. *American Sociological Review* 29: 173–97.

Wolff, Janet. 1983. *Aesthetics and the Sociology of Art*. London: George Allen & Unwin.

Wright, Chris. 1983. The record industry. In George Martin (ed.) *Making Music: The Guide to Writing, Performing and Recording*, pp. 290–7. New York: Quill.

Wright, Erik Olin. 1989. *Classes*. London: Verso.

Wuthnow, Robert. 1987. *Meaning and Moral Order: Exploration in Cultural Analysis*. Berkeley, Calif.: University of California Press.

TABLE 7.1
Regression coefficients for melodic ornamentation

Independent variables	Estimate	SE	Beta
Song characteristics			
Instrumental	−1.12	0.45★	−0.20
Duration in minutes	0.45	0.10★★	0.37
Organization of the production process			
Produced by performer and outsider	−0.82	0.30★★	−0.23
Performer attributes			
US nationality	0.64	0.23★★	0.24
Black	0.59	0.26★	0.19
Instrumental technology			
Acoustic guitar	−1.13	0.27★	−0.33
Adjusted R^2	0.34		
F	10.07★★		
N = 105			

★★ P ⩽ 0.01   ★ P ⩽ 0.05

TABLE 7.2
Regression coefficients for overall melodic form

Independent variables	Estimate	SE	Beta
Song characteristics			
Instrumental	3.52	0.64★★	0.43
Organization of the production process			
Produced by performer and outsider	−1.65	0.43★★	−0.32
Song written by performer	0.95	0.30★★	0.26
Instrumental technology			
No keyboards	−1.44	0.35★★	−0.33
Adjusted R^2	0.37		
F	15.66★★		
N = 105			

★★ $P \leqslant 0.01$ ★ $P \leqslant 0.05$

TABLE 7.3
Regression coefficients for overall chord structure

Independent variables	Estimate	SE	Beta
Song characteristics			
Year	0.15	0.04★★	0.66
Instrumental	2.06	0.86★	0.19
Duration in minutes	0.66	0.28★	0.28
Market structure			
Number of firms in the previous year with Top 10s	0.06	0.02★★	0.35
Turnover of number one songs in the current year	−0.15	0.04★★	−0.43
Adjusted R^2	0.34		
F	11.66★★		
N = 105			

★★ $P \leqslant 0.01$ ★ $P \leqslant 0.05$

TABLE 7.4
Pearson correlation coefficients for the five elements of melodic form

	Magnitude of melodic change	Disjunctness	Ornamentation	Range
Frequency of directional change	−0.18★	0.20★	0.27★★	0.21★
Magnitude of melodic change		0.33★★	−0.04	0.49★★
Disjunctness			−0.08	0.23★★
Ornamentation				0.06
N = 105				

★★ $P \leqslant 0.01$ ★ $P \leqslant 0.05$

TABLE 7.5
Pearson correlation coefficients for the five elements of chordal structure

	Proportion of minor chords	*Proportion of I chords*	*Proportion of IV chords*	*Proportion of V chords*
Proportion of major chords	−0.76★★	0.79★★	0.52★★	0.45★★
Proportion of minor chords		−0.64★★	−0.45★★	−0.36★★
Proportion of I chords			0.39★★	0.39★★
Proportion of IV chords				0.05
N = 105				

★★ $P \leqslant 0.01$ ★ $P \leqslant 0.05$

8

A theory of pictorial discourse

Albert Bergesen

There is no better place to begin an understanding of the general semiotics of art as language than by examining the changing styles and social environment of the New York art world since the Second World War. Here, in the form of an expressive gestural abstract art, was a movement that took the lead in modern painting and established New York as the successor to Paris as a focal point of modernism's continuing experimentation in pictorial discourse. While some still splash and smear oil on huge canvases, styles have moved on through the hard edge and geometric abstraction termed Minimalism and the exploration of philosophical themes in Conceptualism, to the various Neo-Realisms and figurative imagery of the 1980s and 1990s.

Obviously, styles of art produced in and around New York have changed over time. But why? To answer this question the semiotics of painting as sign system and form of coded language or discourse will be explored. Some general theoretical notions linking the social organization of the art world with the production of more abstract or realistic art will be put forth, and some data on the rise and fall of abstraction presented.

Art as pictorial discourse

The painting itself – the object on the wall – represents a statement or communicative act, a piece of discourse that is as much a part of the larger community as it is of its individual author. All artists speak in some form of pictorial language,[1] and while Manet certainly says something different from Monet, Braque from Cézanne, and Pollock from Franz Kline, they all speak in common discursive frames, or styles, that we call Impressionism, Cubism, and Abstract Expressionism. Any particular painting, like any particular individual, is both unique and general at the same time. Because the artist uses the discursive conventions of the time, the artist is therefore a carrier of both individual and collective meaning.

A style of art, then, is a social reality, for it represents what is common across a number of artists, not what is unique to any one. We do, of course, speak of individual style – Pollock's drips seem unique to him. Abstract Expressionism, though, is larger than Pollock, and as a reality only comes into existence when there are a number of artists such that their common conventions can appear. A style does not belong to any particular individual, but only to a group. An individual can reflect a style, or have a style of his or her own (like Frank Stella's geometric bands of color) but Minimalism cannot be understood by knowing the particularities of Stella. Styles, as collective realities, represent codes of expression, that is, languages used by communities of painters.

Diachronics of art history

Explanations of styles of art are most often in terms of their authors, and questions of aesthetics are often confused with a sociology of artistic production. When it comes to style change, most explanations focus upon earlier artists and their innovations which in turn influence later painters. Traditional art history has this linear quality. This form of historical narrative is very similar to the linguistic theory encountered by Saussure (1966). It was what he called diachronic analysis, where explanation of present linguistic forms took place by tracing them back into history. Saussure suggested an alternative form of explanation, what he called synchronic analysis, which is often taken by sociologists to be no more than "across time" analysis. Rather it is the heart of distinctly structural analysis. Saussure noted that changes over time of specific words did not affect the larger structure of the language. His classic analogy for how a language operated was the game of chess. The substantive nature of the chess pieces didn't matter, for they were mere placeholders. You could play with pennies, rocks, or elaborately carved pieces of ivory. What mattered were the rules of the game, for it was the structural location of a piece, not its intrinsic nature, which gave it its situational meaning within the overall rules of the game.

I think it is fair to say that conventional explanations of style are similar to the diachronic analysis Saussure encountered. This is clearly seen in the conventional account of how the breakup of the image in late nineteenth-century Impressionism worked its way through Cubism and on to the gestural abstraction of the 1950s, the Minimalism of the 1960s, and the

Conceptualism of the 1970s. This kind of historicist diachronic account is seen in Alfred H. Barr's classic *Cubism and Abstract Art* (1974). In the diagram reproduced from the jacket of the original edition, there is an outline of the diachronic replacement of one style by another from 1890 through 1935. As an explanation for twentieth-century abstraction the form of logic is clearly diachronic, tracing the historical change in stylistic elements over time. There is no analytical set of relations between either the elements of the art, or more broadly between the structured social relations of the art world and the structured relations of the painterly discourse there on the canvas. His account of twentieth-century abstraction is a narrative of historical evolution going from Neo-Impressionism (1890) to Cubism (1905–10) to Constructivism (1910–15) to Geometrical Abstract art (1935). In another line of diachronic development he traces Synthetism (1890) to Fauvism (1905) to Expressionism (1911) to Non-Geometrical Abstract Art (1935). The logic of explanation here is the style at a previous point in time. This represents nothing but a change in the elements of the language of art, not a change in the structural relations between those elements.

Structural language of art

A structural synchronic analysis is also possible, that is one not based on changes in the elements of the style, but in the larger set of rules in which those elements are placeholders. Saussure's key point was that the historical transformation of elements of a semiotic system has nothing to do with their arrangement or structural relations to each other. In the chess example, the elements may change from pebbles to pennies but the structural relations between the positions, say, of pawn and knight, remain the same. It is a kind of sociology of language elements, where instead of social positions determining individual self identities and not psychological dispositions, there are linguistic rules and positions determining the meaning of signifiers and language elements rather than their intrinsic nature. If pennies or stones could serve as placeholders for the situated meaning of pawn and knight, so could different colors, shapes, forms, and pigments of paint, serve as placeholders for a more general structural theory of style. The language of art is governed by rules, as is the language of the written word, and it can be deconstructed into its basic elements, the materials of art: paint, wood, plaster, bronze, colors, brushes, etc. These constitute the vocabulary of art, and are organized into larger structural complexes by art syntax, such as the techniques and rules of drawing, perspective, color compatibility, and all the things more generally learned in art school. This systematic organization of artistic vobaculary and syntax makes up the language of different styles.

The language of abstraction and realism

Art speaks in at least two basic structural languages: abstraction and realism. These are two basic forms of art language that are defined by general rules, which are independent of the specific elements of color, shape, or type of material. Abstraction, as a linguistic code, is a more reduced mode of expression, involving a narrower pool of painterly vocabulary (colors, forms, shapes, line, tones, etc.) and a less flexible set of syntactical alternatives for combining these elements into a larger artistic whole. One thinks here of the simplified geometrical abstraction of the Minimalists of the 1960s, in both their painting and sculpture. There, a simple shape or two often just placed on the floor of a gallery, constituted a meaningful artistic act. This was clearly a reduced use of syntactical skills of drawing, perspective, color compatibilities, tones, or use of foreground and background. Realism is another language of art, and involves a wider pool of pictorial vocabulary and a more flexible and supple set of syntactical alternatives for constructing a painterly act.

These code distinctions are derived from Basil Bernstein's (1975) notions about the elaborated and restricted linguistic codes that he discovered in patterns of British speech. They are also applicable to styles of art (Bergesen 1984). Abstraction is the more restricted code, realism the more elaborated. These are generalizations, and importantly relative. Abstract art can get more restricted, as for example it did in the movement from the already abstract Abstract Expressionism to the even more abstract Minimalism of the 1960s.

The semiotic crisis of abstraction

Abstraction in general and increasing abstraction in particular, faces a general semiotic problem. Because of the restricted use of vocabulary and syntactical flexibility the meanings contained within the visual structure of the painting become more and more general, giving them less and less specific meaning. An abstract painting can not only have multiple meanings, but its very phenomenological status as art, rather than, say, mistake or child's play, is in question. While modern art has been the butt of much popular humor about modern abstraction, it represents a deep semiotic problem of signifying meaning. In this case it is resolved by adding extra-painterly information (art theory, criticism, artist's commentaries) to fill in the specific signification of these restricted signifiers.

The simplest way to approach the semiotic problem of abstraction is to consider a few splashes or dabs of paint on a white background. What is this? A painting by a serious artist? Drips from a house painter? A child's mess? What? It is literally impossible to tell, if all we are faced with are drips and dabs. Uncertainty here is not a product of lack of education or sophistication, but arises because this painterly act does not contain enough internal vocabularic and syntactical differentiation to signify that it is, in fact, an intentional painting. It is a semantic crisis of the painting, not the viewer. In this situation what is required is additional information, and that comes in the form of everything from the painting's positional location – on a stretched canvas, in a museum, gallery, or hanging on someone's wall, to elaborate theories of art.

These supplemental theories serve to fill in the meanings that the restricted art cannot supply on its own painterly terms. The movement toward more abstraction that characterized much of postwar modern art has led to the mistaken belief in many critical circles that art cannot exist without theory. It is true that severe abstraction cannot exist without theory, though spelled-out realism can. Now, toward the end of the twentieth century, it does not seem that modern art *has* to be abstract and difficult. It was at mid-century, but with the passing of American abstraction in favor of a more pluralistic world of figuration and realism that earlier verdict seems premature. Nonetheless, critics continue to pontificate on the inherent difficulty in comprehending art and the necessity of theory. In reality, theory comes and goes, and to understand why we need a closer look at how abstraction works as semiotic sign.

The restricted signifier

To do this, consider a painting in terms of the basic components of a sign: the signifier and signified. First a mental experiment: if we take a painting to be the signifier and the things to which it refers to be the signified and look at the painting of, say, a barn in a corn field, then that imagery, as signifier, clearly points to, or signifies, a barn out there in a field. This is not to say there are not other meanings, obviously, but this signifier at least signifies a barn. But if that painting were to become more and more abstract then the possibilities of what these painterly signifiers are signifying widen dramatically, making it more and more difficult to pin down the exact meaning the painting is intended to convey. This is the crisis of increasing abstraction. For example, say in a second barn painting, Painting 2, it is a more abstract rendition: just four plain walls. The signifier, the painting, is more restricted, which widens the range of possible significations it can be referring to. Is Painting 2 signifying a box, a house, a building, a barn, a school – what? The technical point here is that simplified, reduced, abstract signifiers lose their ability to signify any particular signification. With increasing abstraction there is an atrophy of the signification process.

Now suppose we have Painting 3, a further abstract rendition of the barn, here just four dots with one in the middle (where the four stand for the barn's walls and the one in the middle for the roof). What do these five dots signify?

The range of significations is really wide open now, and can stand for almost anything: five oceans, lonely individuals, the planets, flowers, faces, anything, including a barn in a field.

But, notice what I have done. In parentheses I provided some extra-painterly information saying, "the four stand for the barn's walls and the one in the middle for the roof." Here I provided some additional meaning that pinned down the abstract painting of the five dots, which in more sophisticated ways is what art theory and critical interpretation do for minimal art. In general then, the more minimal, restricted, or limited the signifier, the wider, broader or larger the range of significations that particular signifier can refer to, resulting in the need for extra signifier meanings which pin down, point to, or identify, an appropriate signification. Most movements of abstract art, then, are accompanied by large bodies of discourse, as in Dadaism, Surrealism, Constructivism, Futurism, etc. This fact has clear implications for the theory of the semiotic process. The language or sign system of painting includes more than just the art-work proper when that visual statement is in the form of a restricted painterly signifier.

The semiotic process therefore is not limited to the signs themselves but is distinctly social. To carry out their meanings restricted styles have to rely upon the wider discursive culture to fill in the meaning that restricted signifiers are incapable of identifying on their own. This is a dynamic process, such that the more abstract the painting the more often it will be accompanied by supplemental theory. Case in point: the emergence of Abstract Expressionism also saw the emergence of very prominent art critics who offered theories that explained the meaning or purpose of the more limited and minimal splashes and dabs of the emerging gestural expressionism. Clement Greenburg (1961) and Harold Rosenberg (1972) advanced theories about American abstraction that provided an interpretive frame within which one could explain or interpret the new abstraction.

The progression of New York art from the 1950s into the 1960s saw the already abstract art get even more abstract or minimal. If Abstraction Expressionism was possibly a blueprint of something that could in principle be spelled out in more detail, then 1960s Minimalism was a blueprint of a blueprint. Following the principle of the shrinking signifier, the amount of theory accompanying this art should increase, and it did. Minimalist painters and sculptors seemed to write more often about their art, explaining what it meant or what the issues were.

Sociologically, from the point of view of the art world as a whole, the role of artist and theorist was beginning to merge. There were still artists who only painted and critics who only wrote, but the artist seemed to be taking on more and more of the burden of the shrinking signifier to provide additional meaning through commentary that increasingly accompanied the works themselves. In catalogs for exhibitions, on typed sheets accompanying gallery and museum shows, and in art magazines, it seemed that the artist was taking more and more time to explain exactly what he or she was doing. This trend reached its final point in the Conceptualism of the 1970s where the signifier so shrank that there was art-free art, so to speak, and all that was left was the supplemental theoretical discourse. Supplemental theory had by now become the primary language of art, while the actual art-work was reduced to the accompanying role of "documentation." The role of artist and theorist was completely fused, and theory predominated. The artist-half only provided secondary "documentation" for the larger theories of Conceptualism.

Diachronic versus synchronic art analysis

The social nature of art styles means that the relevant structural relations for a synchronic non-historical analysis include the discursive environment of the larger art world along with the syntactical and vocabularic elements of the art object proper. When the elements of the language of art (vocabulary and syntax) turn toward a more abstract mode, then to communicate meaningfully art relies on the extra-painterly elements of art theory and criticism. Therefore the structural elements in the language of artistic expression include both the solidarity, "in-groupness," or network density of the larger groupings in which the artists participate (commonly called the "art world") and the structure of the style they produce. Actually, these are not two separate entities, for the style is by definition a collective reality and at the same level of analysis as the solidarity networks of the art community. The sociological independent variable, in-group solidarity, is at the same level as the dependent variability, shared artistic conventions, or style.

To illustrate the difference between synchronic analysis and the more traditional art historical diachronic analysis, we can consider the case of Conceptual art. A diachronic analysis would trace the evolution of the elements of New York abstraction since the Abstract Expressionism of the 1950s. Tom Wolfe (1975) conducted a popular and satirical version of just this, and he captured the gradual change in elements of abstraction from thick oils to thinner acrylics; from fixed picture frame to shaped frame and then no frame; from a larger variety of colors to fewer colors in Minimalism, and so forth. In a more serious tone this is the diachronic narrative that passes as an account of what has happened to modern art. Some, taking an even longer view, could trace abstraction back through Dadaism, to Cubism, and Neo-Impressionism at the end of the nineteenth century: the now canonic Museum of Modern Art narrative of the rise of abstraction in the twentieth century.

But, in a more structural synchronic analysis, explanation lies at the level of relations among the elements, not their historical change. The general structural relation here is that the denser the network ties within the art world and the higher the degree of in-group solidarity, the more minimal the structure of the style. This is a general theoretical proposition, not affected by time or space, that is, not affected by historical changes in the specific vocabularic elements of painting.

For instance, if one were to examine the world of Dada artists one would find a close-knit in-group of high solidarity, producing a restricted code of more abstract and Surreal images and the extra-painterly theory in the form of various Dadaist manifestos. So, given the "in-groupness" of the New York art world, with its closely knit group of artists there is once again restricted pictorial discourse. It is changes in the structure of the group – increasing and decreasing solidarity – that is associated with changes in the structure of the language: to more or less abstraction and realism. Here all one has to know is the condition of the relevant social universe and one can predict the structure of the style of art: more or less abstract, more or less realistic. No historical narrative is needed. There is no need to know the history of changing artist elements. All that is needed is to know the structure of the community of artists.

With abstract art representing a more restricted code of expression and realism a more elaborated code, when the network ties amongst members of the New York art world grew more and more dense their language became more and more abstract. The world of the Abstract Expressionists was, by all accounts, a close-knit in-group of relative geographical proximity and close social relations (see Shapiro and Shapiro 1990). These shared identifications and geographical proximity are very similar to the "in-groupness" noted by Basil Bernstein in his British working-class neighborhoods, where he identified the more restricted mode of expression. In New York it was among artists and the language was painting, not speech, but the result was the same: a restricted style. New York as the center of modern art heightened the sense of "in-groupness." Collective identity was accelerated by the increase in writing about the new art, by an increase in galleries and collectors. Structural relations changed; the language became more abstract. Minimalism succeeded Abstract Expressionism, and then Conceptualism followed Minimalism.

Why art turned to realism in the late 1970s

So far the transformation of the New York School was following a linear path, becoming ever more minimal or abstract, or in linguistic terms more restricted. But the next movement in style was the emergence of realism, dubbed Neo-Realism, Super-Realism, or Hyper-Realism. Art was now quite literal, spelled out, explicit, and figurative. The role of theory also declined, with artists engaging in less speculation about the deep meaning of their work.

One way to see this move away from abstraction is to examine the shifting emphasis in a major art magazine, such as *Art News*. To show the rise and fall of abstraction, feature articles which had pictures from 1945 to 1983 were coded as to whether the art was abstract or not. Abstraction was defined as art containing no recognizable representations from the outside world. As Figure 8.1 shows, abstract art rose in the 1950s, reaching a peak in the 1960s and then declining.

Why, though, had art moved in a singular direction for decades, only to reverse itself in the late 1970s? The answer lies in the fact that since a style represents common artistic conventions shared by a group of artists it is changes at the group level that are reflected in changes in styles. What were those 1970s changes?

There are at least two possible scenarios for why the great American experiment with abstraction turned in the later 1970s to various kinds of realism. One has more to do with the inner dynamics of the art world itself. By now it was so arcane and so much an in-group that it was little understood by the larger world; this resulted in something of a crisis. Conceptual art became such a restricted code that it virtually disappeared, leaving only the theoretical justification for abstraction, which when the abstraction abstracted itself out of existence, was all that was left.

The art world became too inner directed, with artists talking only to themselves, and focusing upon ever more exclusive means of expression, leaving everyone else out. Conceptual art is hard to sell, or hang on the wall, and that may very well have forced art outward again, to more elaborated, realistic formats, that is, to the Neo-Realisms of the late 1970s and 1980s (Bergesen 1988).

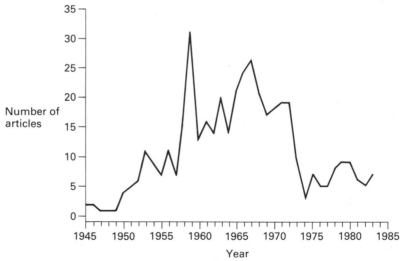

Figure 8.1

A second possible explanation is tied to changes in New York's position in the larger world. At a larger global level there was the "American malaise," in President Carter's words – a loss of confidence, the post-Vietnam syndrome. There was also the growing sense that America faced a challenge from Japan economically, and that the USA was no longer number one. The connecting logic is as follows. New York as the leading American city would feel these reverberations, shattering its sense of global centrality that the country, and with it New York, enjoyed (Bergesen 1987, forthcoming). With that might come a looking outward, and something of a failure of artistic nerve. It is not accidental that this is also the period of a growing interest in European artists and a move away from distinctly American-generated styles.

Second, there is the shift in the predominance of New York within the United States. The "sun belt" phenomenon is growing, as power and population seem to be migrating from the older north-east, of which, again, New York is the capital. This can be seen in the attention given to more regional art (see Figure 8.2) in a prominent art magazine such as *Art News*.

New York as center of American cultural life seemed challenged in the mid-1970s. The decline may be relative, but it was there. With that change in position *vis-à-vis* other American cities has come a loss in confidence. The imperial sense of centrality, of America in the world and New York in America, allowed the growth of a very ingrown community of artists, a self-reflective pictorial discourse. Basil Bernstein observed the linguistic consequences of a closely knit community of close geographical proximity. People's speech became more cryptic and exclusive. They spoke mostly to each other and it showed. It turns out this is not limited to working-class neighborhoods, but applies to any close community, and it is also not

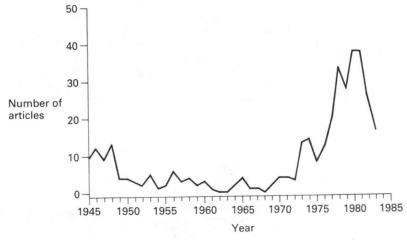

Figure 8.2

limited to speech. Other forms of discourse, like painting and sculpture, are susceptible to the same socio-linguistic processes. The New York art world eventually produced its own version of Bernstein's restricted codes.

That state of affairs, though, did not last. Whether the art changed for its own reasons or because the larger social environment of New York and the United States was changing will be argued. But it is not an accident that the American rise to predominance in world art came at the time of the American rise to predominance in the world economy and world politics. It is also probably not an accident that with American economic decline has come a movement away from American-instigated abstraction as a universal currency of modern painterly discourse in art. The centrality and importance of New York was associated with a confident inward-looking mode of expression, an abstraction that ran its course with the course of American political and economic leadership. As that economic and political leadership showed signs of lagging in the late 1970s it is also the case that American leadership in pictorial expression began to lag. Modern art increasingly had the motifs and feelings of multiple national cultures, rather than the one-world universalism that was the language of abstraction.

Note

1. For a similar analysis of the linguistic elements of music see Bergesen (1979) and for dance see Bergesen and Jones in this volume.

References

Becker, Howard S. 1982. *Art Worlds*. Berkeley, Calif.: University of California Press.
Bergesen, Albert. 1979. Spirituals, jazz, blues, and soul music: The role of elaborated and restricted codes in the maintenance of social solidarity. In R. Wuthnow (ed.) *New Directions in The Empirical Study of Religion*. New York: Academic Press.
Bergesen, Albert. 1984. The semantic equation: A theory of the social origins of art styles. In R. Collins (ed.) *Sociological Theory 1984*. San Francisco: Jossey-Bass.
Bergesen, Albert. 1987. The decline of American art. In T. Boswell and A. Bergesen (eds) *America's Changing Role in the World-System*. New York: Praeger Publications.
Bergesen, Albert. 1988. A tale of two values: Sense and cents. In I. H. Shafer (ed.) *The Incarnate Imagination: Essays in Theology, the Arts, and Social Sciences in Honor of Andrew M. Greeley*. Bowling Green, Ohio: Popular Press.
Bergesen, Albert. 1991. Semiotics of New York's artistic hegemony. In Resat Kasaba (ed.) *Cities in the World-System*. New York: Greenwood Press.
Bernstein, Basil. 1975. *Class, Codes, and Control*. New York: Schocken Books.
Greenberg, Clement. 1961. *Art and Culture: Critical Essays*. Boston, Mass.: Beacon Press.
Rosenberg, Harold. 1972. *The De-Definition of Art*. New York: Horizon.
Saussure, Ferdinand de. 1966. *Course in General Linguistics*. New York: McGraw-Hill.
Shapiro, David and Shapiro, Cecile (eds). 1990. *Abstract Expressionism: A Critical Record*. Cambridge: Cambridge University Press.
Wolfe, Tom. 1975. *The Painted Word*. New York: Bantam.

9

Decoding the syntax of modern dance

Albert Bergesen and Allison Jones

The expressive arts obviously constitute a means of communication, and as such are clearly susceptible to linguistic analysis. Art is a language: "That painting speaks to me," we have heard, or said ourselves. Similarly music is called a "universal language." Modern dance is described in terms of its movement vocabulary and there are syntactical rules for combining these body gestures into a larger structure.[1] Choreography is dance syntax for bodily vocabulary. That the arts are composed of more elemental units, a vocabulary, that is combined through rules or principles, a syntax, into larger structured wholes, seems readily apparent. There is a further step in the linguistic analogy, though. When dance is viewed as a language, then its choreographic structure – as a kind of linguistic structure – is susceptible to the same sociological principles that govern structures of speech. For example, we know that conditions of close geographical proximity and dense network ties among members of a social community are associated with the appearance of certain forms, or codes, of speech. The analogue with dance is that similar conditions in the sociology of the dance-world should also be associated with changes in the code of choreography.

Basil Bernstein's codes

We can begin with the studies of the socio-linguist Basil Bernstein (1975), who upon studying patterns of speech of closely knit British working-class neighborhoods concluded that they had given rise to a different code from that of the middle class. It was short, cryptic, slang-ridden speech. He called this code "restricted" and said it was defined by a narrow pool of vocabularic elements and a rigid or formal set of syntactical alternatives from which the speaker constructed a speech act. This was in contrast to what he called the "elaborated" code of the middle class, where the pool of available vocabulary was wider and the range of syntax both larger and more flexible. He thought the restricted codes of the working class hindered their performance on standardized tests and hence impeded their mobility through the British class system. For claiming limitations on working-class speech he was widely criticized.

But Bernstein had stumbled upon a condition more general than class, for while economic dynamics might be at the heart of why people were clustered in working-class neighborhoods, it was the clustering, the social and moral density of those communities, that was the key to their form of speech. In effect, any dense community, regardless of class, will produce its own slang-like, restricted language. For example, consider other closely knit communities: a laboratory of nuclear scientists, the military, social fraternities, inner city youth gangs, or married couples of long duration. All of these, widely divergent in terms of class, race, gender, and education, tend to produce a coded, exclusive language, whether of nuclear physics or street talk. What they hold in common is degree of "in-groupness," common sentiments, shared values, and solidarity. If group solidarity declines they cannot assume others share common sentiments so they will have to spell out their intentions in full detail. The code becomes more elaborated. As the solidity of a group or community varies, the type of code produced also varies, or the type of choreography varies. The logic is straightforward sociology: variation in group context produces variation in structure of the language. But now the language is modern dance.

Meaningful communication is a balance between what is spelled out in the linguistic act itself (the dance) and what a community brings to that act in terms of supplemental information (Bergesen 1984). With more elaborated codes their broad vocabulary and supple syntax allow them to craft specific meaning or intention without relying upon additional information. With more minimal, restricted, or simplified codes it is not clear from the code itself exactly what is being said. In semiotic terms, when the signifier becomes more restricted it is possible to have any number of significations, such that extra knowledge is required to interpret or understand the group's code of restricted language.

In modern abstract painting this took the form of various art theories which arose with Abstract Expressionism and reached a peak during the Minimalism and Conceptualism of the 1960s and 1970s, when it seemed that theory was as important, or more so, than the actual painting. With Conceptualism the concrete art-object was only an illustrative device to get across the more important conceptual idea or theory. As dance became more minimal and esoteric in the 1960s and 1970s there arose more and more extra-dance interpretations, essays, theories, manifestos, and other sources of information to fill in or explain just what these minimal bodily gestures really meant.

The language of dance

Before going on to see how the language of modern dance changed during the 1960s and 1970s the more formal elements of dance as language will be outlined. Of all the expressive arts, dance is perhaps the easiest to conceptualize as language. In ballet there is a clear pool of vocabulary, a lexicon of some 200 well defined steps, such as *arabesque, pirouette,* and *saunter* (Foster 1986: 90). Modern dance, while much more loose and improvisational a language than ballet, nonetheless has had something of a traditional vocabulary, which is derived from the works of Isadora Duncan, Martha Graham, Doris Humphrey, and Charles Weidman. While different choreographers perfect different movements that are identified as their own language (like the bodily contraction–release and elaborate emotionalism of Graham), at a more general level one can view the totality of a dance presentation as part of dance's vocabulary. Obviously, the most basic element is the body itself. Turns, twists, walks, runs, falls, and somersaults, along with many other movements, are the specific vocabularic elements which make up the lexicon of dance. While the body is the most basic material of dance, it is situated for performance, making the situating environment a potential element in a choreographer's vocabularic pool.

Moving out from the body proper is clothing – from minimal leotards through elaborate costumes depicting situated identities in a larger narrative or dramatic structure. For any clothing there is variation in how elaborate and colorful it is, such that this too becomes a dimension of dance lexicon. Outward from the dressed dancer come the possibilities of props and their ordering into meaningful structures as sets, depicting everything from abstract forms to identifiable places in the outside world: city streets, or a place in the country. A set is lit with various degrees of lighting complexity, and dance is accompanied with sound, from human voices through commissioned orchestral music. Degrees of lighting and music are part of the vocabulary of dance. In general a more minimal or restricted dance code is one where there is less of this dance vocabulary and less elaborate combinations. Conversely, a more elaborated code has more vocabulary and a more complex set of syntactical rules.

171

Elaborated choreography: Martha Graham

As an example of an elaborated dance choreography consider Martha Graham's *Errand into the Maze*, first performed in 1947. The music was composed by Gian Carlo Menotti specifically for this piece. As an elaborated code the set and costume play an important role. The set is symbolic, the most obvious figures being a "Y" and a white tape extending from the "Y". Traditional male and female roles are distinguished by the woman's black and white dress and the man's primitive male costume.

As the music starts, a woman in a white and black dress appears. Her body moves with the music, contracting, as if in agony. She turns and makes big, sweeping gestures with her legs, as if driven. The strain in her face further expresses the agony she is feeling. At the height of her emotion, a man appears on the stage. A bone lines across his shoulders, acting as a yoke. His almost Egyptian-like movements are very forceful and full of strength, in contrast to the woman's. Her fear due to his presence is made obvious by the change in her movement. She begins to dance with the tape which seems to draw her uncontrollably closer to the "Y". When she dances with the man, it seems as if she is almost fighting him, the movement of their legs being so jerky. When he leaves, she seems to calm down somewhat, but her fear returns as the man returns again. She gets behind the "Y" and wraps the tape around it as if to shield herself from this frightening creature. At the end, the man drops to the floor, and the woman unwraps the tape, suggesting the departure of her fear.

Errand into the Maze is full of emotion and energy. Graham had adapted the theme of Adriadne and Theseus to one in which she could examine the emotional state of fear. In the original story, Adriadne gives Theseus, her love, a golden thread to help him find his way out of the maze after killing the Minotaur. In Graham's adaptation, Adriadne uses the "golden thread" to help conquer her overwhelming fear. Graham is careful to portray this fear as originating solely in the mind of the woman. She does this by giving the man a yoke for his arms, which signifies him as incapable of actually hurting the woman (McDonagh 1976: 63–4).

Restricted choreography: Merce Cunningham

In sharp contrast is Merce Cunningham's 1968 *Rainforest*. Instead of movement existing for the sake of the meanings it portrays, it here exists simply for the sake of movement. The performance does not involve a theatrical production of lights, sets, costumes, dramatic gestures, or a decipherable theme as in *Errand into the Maze*. As such, it has a much more minimalist, or restricted, code of choreography.

"There is no rain to be seen or heard in the piece, and the 'forest' is a cluster of inflated pillow shapes" (McDonagh 1976: 292). The stage is bare except for these 2' × 2' pillows made of some sort of metallic silver material. Some have been filled with helium and float in the air, while others linger closer to the floor. The title suggests that the dance is about a rainforest, and there is the sound of running water along with intermittent sounds of birds and other animals. The performers consist of three men and three women, all dressed in beige unitards that make them look almost naked. There are never more than three performers on stage at a time. Their movements are slow, more like stretching movements than actual choreographed dance steps. As the dance proceeds, the movements become stronger until the energy level reaches its peak. The end is signified when the stage is empty, but the sounds of the rainforest continue.

There is none of the emotional narrative of fear, love, hate, or being attracted and repelled as in Graham, nor a structure of beginning, middle, and end. Just movement. No plot, no climax, just movement. The gender identities are also blurred by the unisex dress, whereas Graham clearly demarcated male from female. The use of music as vocabularic element for accent to the structure of the story is also missing, as there are just some background sounds rather than a specifically composed piece. Therefore from music, to set, to dress and movement, Cunningham's dance is a more restricted code of expression than Graham's.

Restricted choreography: Yvonne Rainer

An example of an even more minimal piece is *Trio A* (1966) by Yvonne Rainer.

> A woman stands with profile to the audience and swings one arm across her stomach and the other simultaneously behind her. Smoothly swirling her arms, she joins hands and frames her head. The flow of movement continues in an unbroken and uninflected stream following the weight of the gesture rather than any emotional determinant. She taps one foot in a smooth arc and then the other, extends out to the side and makes tiny circling motions. Resting the weight on one leg, she lowers herself to the floor and then pushes herself up and kicks to one side; she stands to repeat the swinging motion of the arms that started the dance. She sits and rolls over backward, rises to face away from the audience, wiggles a bit, and, turning in profile, she adjusts a little like an athlete ready to compete. She bends all the way forward, spreads her legs, and then drops into a squat to thrust a leg to the side. A sequence of rolling like a log is started, and she stops to offer a little spasmodic variation followed by bouncy leaps, and with her back to the audience she tilts her head to the left, arcs her body to the right, and concludes on the balls of her feet.
> The piece is resolutely physical without any emotional overtones. No dramatic accents are used and the parts of the dance flow into one another without a break. (McDonagh 1976: 447)

This is a very minimal piece: four and a half minutes of almost everyday movement. The absence of sets, props, elaborate lighting, together with very ordinary movement, represent a very reduced pool of traditional dance moves.

Elaborated code: Twyla Tharp

A more elaborated piece of choreography is seen in Twyla Tharp's *The Catherine Wheel* of 1982. As a full-scale theatrical production on Broadway, this represents quite a contrast to some of her earlier works, such as her 1969 piece, *Medley*. The earlier Tharp was involved with the minimalist dance movement in New York until she was commissioned by the Joffrey Ballet in 1973 to choreograph *Deuce Coup* (Livet 1976). It was a huge success and other ballet companies, most notably the American Ballet Theatre, began to commission her work.

Tharp's biggest undertaking came with *The Catherine Wheel*, taken from the legend of St Catherine, the Christian martyr whose only crime was striving to be the perfect human being. The characters consist of the leader, Sarah, the chorus, the parents, the children, the pet, the poet, and the maid. The characters all wear wild street clothes, as well as red jazz shoes. According to Tharp, this family is presented in a "cartoon style" of wacky dress.

The performance begins at a castle on the ocean. A woman, Sarah, enters and sees the perfection in the computerized image of the body of Catherine. While she is deciding to try to emulate that perfection, the scene changes and the music of David Byrne is heard. On the stage, dark figures, the chorus, dance in a line with one person passing a glowing ball through the line. As it comes back through the line, it is evident that this is a pineapple. Behind the screen, characters don costumes in the shadows. The screen rises to reveal a house with a worn armchair, end table, lamp, and kitchen table. The maid is dusting when the bride and groom enter. Their dance is somewhat slapstick – loose, like rag dolls. They jump from one side to another, in a manner resembling the rock dance of the 1980s. While the two are engaged in a joyous dance, a pineapple drops on the husband's head, and he mistakenly thinks his wife has hit him. The fighting begins and the house becomes a site of tumultuous uproar.

The scene switches back to the one where Sarah is imitating the perfect movements of the computerized Catherine. She dances with all the conviction of someone who is extremely determined. The next scene returns to the house, only this time the pineapple is bigger. The members of the family vie for possession of the growing pineapple, and then the scene flips back to Sarah, now dancing with the chorus. The pineapple continues to grow and Sarah is forced on to the torture wheel, her fear evident in the agonizing contortions of her face. Back at the house, the pineapple has become enormous. The turning point is when the pineapple is torn up. The maid becomes hysterical, her face assuming all sorts of ugly expressions. Suddenly, broken bits and pieces of junk are thrown on to the stage. The chorus and Sarah arrive to clean it up. It is all accumulated in a net, and the wife must climb over the bodies of the chorus to give it all to Sarah. The scene switches back to the ocean, and Sarah remembers everything that has happened in reverse order.

These different dances come from the 1940s, 1960s, and 1980s. *Errand into the Maze* is an example of traditional modern dance. *Rainforest* and *Trio A* are examples of the period of minimalist dance of the 1960s and 1970s. *The Catherine Wheel* is an example of the 1980s–90s use of props, narrative, emotion, and all the vocabularic elements shunned in the 1960s and 1970s. Along with illustrating different choreographic codes, these dances are also examples of how modern dance moved from narrative, elaborated modes of structuring dance to a phase of increasing abstraction and restricted minimalism during the 1960s and 1970s, only to flip back again in the 1980s and 1990s to less minimal dance and a generally wider pool of movement vocabulary. To obtain a fuller sense of these changes a systematic analysis of the shifting range of dance vocabulary can be made.

Coding the language of dance

These general shifts in dance forms can be seen by coding the extensiveness of the dance vocabulary of a number of choreographers. To accomplish this a dance vocabulary scale was created which measured the presence or absence of different elements in a dance performance, such as movement, costume, props, lights, etc. (for the complete coding scheme see the Appendix). The data were obtained by coding thirteen dances previously recorded on video tape. Dances were selected from the 1940s through the early 1980s, and represent many important choreographers: Martha Graham, Merce Cunningham, Yvonne Rainer, Steve Paxton, David Gordon, Twyla Tharp, and Paul Taylor. Sample size was constrained by the availability of video tapes, and is not a representative sample of all choreographers. The total score for each dance is presented in Figure 9.1. This figure shows a clear drop in the range of dance vocabulary in the 1960s and early 1970s, a range to be regained in the later 1970s and early 1980s.

Why minimal dance?

The next question is why? Why did modern dance turn to more minimalist formats, or codes, in the 1960s and 1970s? And just as interesting, why did

175

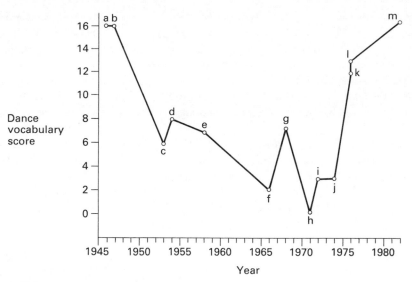

Figure 9.1

dance move back again in the 1980s toward more spelled-out, elaborated, less abstract, modes of choreography? Much of the explanation about change in the world of dance is the largely historical tracing of influences, of who studied with whom, of who left what dance company to start his own. Sometimes dance history is divided into cohorts. McDonagh (1976), for instance, divides his choreographers into categories: "the forerunners" (Isadora Duncan, Loie Fuller, Ruth St Denis, Ted Shawn), who are followed by "the founders" (Martha Graham, Lester Horton, Doris Humphrey, Charles Weidman), and so forth. The notion here is that new cohorts bring new ideas, new blood, and hence change in choreography. The limitation of these arguments is that changes in choreographic direction can only be identified once they have occurred. There is no predictive power with historical accounts.

Another variant of this *post hoc* analysis is the action–reaction explanation. Merce Cunningham rebelled against the emotionalism of Martha Graham, the argument goes. Or as one author put it,

> originally reacting against the expressionism of modern dance . . . the post-modernists[2] propose . . . that the formal qualities of dance might be reason enough for choreography, and that the purpose of making dances might be simply to make a framework within which we look at movement for its own sake. (Banes 1980)

Movement for the sake of movement is in fact what the postmodernists stood for, and that was different from the more narratively theme-oriented classical modern dance. To say they rebelled, or explored new territory, is

176

true, but it is not an explanation of why they did what they did. It is description, not explanation. For explanation we need to move outside the specific rhetorical overlay of the participants' actions and look at the larger objective social situation.

Social determinants of dance form

To do this, following the socio-linguistic principles discussed earlier, we use three propositions at different levels of analysis:

(a)   At the level of relations among choreographers, other things being equal, the closer the network ties among choreographers, the more minimal and restricted their choreography. Conversely, the more isolated the choreographer, the more spelled out and elaborated the choreography.
(b)   At the level of the solidarity of the larger art world in which dancers and choreographers are embedded, other things being equal, the more ingrown and unified the art world, the more minimalist and restricted the choreography. Conversely, the less unified the art world, the more elaborated the choreography.
(c)   At the level of the international system, in which the art world is embedded, when a country exercises hegemony or dominance in the world-system, other things being equal, dance choreography will be more minimal, abstract, and restricted. Conversely, during periods of a more competitive world-system, where no one state dominates, choreography will be more elaborated and spelled out.

These three propositions are at different levels of social organization, ranging from immediate choreographer-to-choreographer relations, to relations of choreographers to the larger art world, and finally to the position of a national society in the world-system as a whole. At the lowest level of interactional relations, the sociological variable takes the form of the closeness or density of choreographer network ties. At the community level it takes the form of the solidarity and "in-group" nature of the urban community, and at the international level it takes the form of the hierarchical position of a country in the world-system.

How does each of these propositions apply to the shift of modern dance choreography to more minimal and restricted codes in the 1960s and 1970s and then back again to more elaborated formats in the 1980s?

Close network ties

The first proposition links restricted codes to density of network ties. Given close interpersonal relations, levels of taken-for-granted assumptions about

177

the intentions and purposes of individuals increase, such that there is less necessity to spell out in precise elaborated detail individual intentions. The more things can be taken for granted, the more minimalist codes become. There is a second aspect to minimal communications. They act as micro-rituals, reaffirming common group sentiments. Minimalist communication forces others to rely upon common understandings of what these shortened cryptic messages mean, which activates these common sentiments, thereby reinforcing them.

In the case of the 1960s minimalist dance choreography, much of it seems to have come from a very close-knit group of dancers who met through a composition workshop taught by John Dunn at Merce Cunningham's studio. Lucinda Childs, David Gordon, Alex Hay, Deborah Hay, Robert Morris, Steve Paxton, Yvonne Rainer, Trisha Brown, and others began performing at the Judson Church in 1962 and they went on to form the heart of the Judson Dance Theater (Banes 1980). Here is the classic Bernstein close-knit group: not British, but New York neighborhoods, and not minimally structured speech, but minimally structured dance. With these choreographers there is an emphasis upon form for form's sake, a position similar to the minimalism in painting and sculpture of the same period. This turn toward form of communication as content of communication, raises questions about the foundations of the dance enterprise, just as Minimalist and Conceptual artists raised questions about the essence of painting and sculpture. In this kind of dance,

> the choreographer becomes a critic, educating spectators in ways to look at dance, challenging the expectations the audience brings to the performance, framing parts of the dance for closer inspection, commenting on the dance as it progresses. (Banes 1980: 16)

The growth of commentary, intellectualizing, and theorizing about the meaning of dance itself, is part of the more general dynamics of the semantic equation (Bergesen 1984). As the vocabulary and syntax of a language shrink, extra-linguistic meaning is required to fill in and explain the precise meaning of the shrunken language. In dance, this took the form of the manifestos and intellectual commentary that regularly accompanied minimalist performances.

Declining importance of New York

> In the '70s, once the issues of technique and expression had been identified, tested, and resolved in a variety of ways, and once dance had been reduced to its essential features, a new expressionism arose in the work of Meredith Monk, Kenneth King, and others. Narrative was reinstalled in dance – a virtuosity of inventiveness, skill, and endurance, as in Douglas Dunn's graceful, symmetrical constructions, Lucinda Childs' obsessively precise dances, and David Gordon's elegantly witty works. (Banes 1980: 18)

178

Banes notes the late 1970s shift back to more elaborated choreography, with increases in dance vocabulary and syntactical complexity. But the reason offered is only the description of what happened: "A new expressionism arose"; the implied explanation is that somehow dance had exhausted the experiments of the 1960s–70s and was now ready to move on. There is another explanation, rooted in the declining centrality of New York, the community of origin for much of minimalist dance.[3]

The key point here is that the movement toward a more abstract and minimal form of artistic expression was not limited to dance during these decades. It dramatically occurred in art and one could even argue that the free form jazz of people such as John Coltrane and Pharaoh Saunders represented a very "in-group," abstract, encoded mode of musical language. Minimalism, then, was a movement across a number of arts and raises questions broader than just network ties within the dance world of choreographers. If the minimalist impulse was seen in painting and sculpture too, the explanation has to be rooted in conditions that affect all these different art worlds. This brings us to the linkage between modes of artistic expression and the sense of importance and self-confidence that comes with being society's central point for cultural events.

This was New York after 1945, but it is also the case that by the mid-1970s, with the rise of the "sun belt" and cities such as Los Angeles, New York was no longer the dominant originating point for creating culture. New York began to slide, and with that the self-confidence of being the center also began to crack. With that the incestuous nature of artistic expression gave way to the more spelled-out languages of Neo-Expressionism and Neo-Realism in painting, and a more narrative and decorative modern dance. The beginning of relative decline of New York City, financially and culturally, was also the point at which the artistic production turned from a very encoded, private, "talking to ourselves," abstract minimalism, to a more broadly intelligible narrative, decorative, realistic form of language across the different arts. If the primacy of New York had continued there would have been a continuation of private, inbred art of the abstract–minimal–conceptual variety. But New York declined and the language of its artistic production also began to change.

American decline in the world-system

The second proposition was tricky, for while New York was certainly culturally dominant in the 1960s, it might have also been so during the early twentieth century. If that is so – Greenwich Village in the early twentieth century as a key center of American art – then another factor besides New York's central position within American society must be required. This brings us to the third proposition.

The issue is still the general movement toward abstraction and minimalism

179

in the 1960s and 1970s, but the causal dynamics are now shifted upward from New York's position within the United States, to America's position within the world. Abstraction, and Minimalism as a derivation of that trend, represent a mode of generalized or universal artistic currency that accompanies American hegemony. This is because abstract forms of artistic expression, from dance to painting, do not signify a particular geographic or historical location the way realism does. When a country is in a position of dominance or hegemony, the appearance in it of a universal artistic mode allows other states to express themselves in what is at once a universal and at the same time distinctly American form of expression. The unity of world order under American hegemony is also symbolized by the universalism of an abstract language of expression. Local national cultures are lost in a generalized mode of artistic discourse across national boundaries.

With the relative American decline in the mid-1970s, from the post-Vietnam malaise to the sense of losing the economic race to Japan, the United States no longer imposes a generalized artistic currency on all nations. By analogy the dollar served as the world's monetary currency until, with the waning of American influence came a move away from the dollar. In the arts, abstraction served as a world currency of expression, and that is now also disappearing. With the national decline there has been a shift to more realistic elaborated expression. The sense of centrality and leadership that comes with hegemony allows for a certain "Roman provincialism," that is, a willingness to talk only to immediate peers in the world's leading city. Everything needed is in that center, and intellectually it feeds upon itself, resulting in very restricted codes of discourse. But when that centrality gives way to a shifting world order of increasing pluralism, then the sense of talking only to peers in the center also is shaken, resulting in more spelled-out, or elaborated, modes of cultural expression.

Appendix

Dance vocabulary coding scheme

A total score is compiled from the following degrees of elaboration.

1. *Movement*: 0 = no prior training or technique necessary: simple walking, running, skipping; 1 = minimal training, but some gymnastic ability required: cartwheels, turns, etc.; 2 = intense training, years of formal ballet or modern technique.
2. *Choreography*: 0 = improvisation; 1 = improvisation, some choreography; 2 = definite choreography.
3. *Music*: 0 = silence; 1 = sounds (radio, voices, etc.); 2 = composed music.

4. *Movement synchronized with music*: 0 = no; 1 = yes.
5. *Facial expression*: 0 = blank, or pasted-on smile; 1 = emotion-filled, expressing anger, agony, sadness, etc.
6. *Costume*: 0 = street clothes; 1 = leotard, tights, nudity; 2 = theatrical costume.
7. *Role of hair*: 0 = down, no importance in dance; 1 = important role in dance.
8. *Lighting*: 0 = none, or plain yellow stage light; 1 = special effects, lights that change, etc.
9. *Set or backdrop*: 0 = no; 1 = yes.
10. *Props*: 0 = no; 1 = yes.
11. *Format or theme*: 0 = none; 1 = mathematical, repeating patterns; 2 = traditional: beginning, middle, end.

Notes

1. A recent example is Susan Leigh Foster's *Reading Dancing: Bodies and Subjects in Contemporary American Dance* (1986).
2. Banes refers to the minimalist dance of the 1960s–70s as "postmodernist," and to the extent this means post-Martha Graham, Humphrey, *et al.*, this is fine. But postmodernist sensibilities are actually quite eclectic and narrative, borrowing from past styles and opposed to any sort of theory (opposed, that is, to the evil of logocentricism and of privileging any theoretical position). Actually, the dance of the 1960s–70s is the height, or end of modernism, not an example of postmodernism, and represents the last spasm of abstraction and non-representational form. Post–1970s dance, on the other hand, is much more open to theatricality, much as postmodern architecture is open to decoration. The minimalist "bare bones" glass and steel box of modernist architecture has an analogue with the minimalist "bare bones" dance of Cunningham and the Judson Dance Theater.
3. For a similar argument about changes in the world of painting and sculpture see the chapter by Bergesen in this book.

References

Banes, Sally. 1980. *Terpisichore in Sneakers: Post-Modern Dance.* Boston, Mass.: Houghton Mifflin.
Bergesen, Albert. 1984. The semantic equation: A theory of the social origins of art styles. In R. Collins (ed.) *Sociological Theory 1984.* San Francisco: Jossey-Bass.
Bernstein, Basil. 1975. *Class, Codes and Control.* New York: Schocken Books.
Foster, Susan Leigh. 1986. *Reading Dancing: Bodies and Subjects in Contemporary American Dance.* Berkeley, Calif.: University of California Press.
Livet, Anne. 1976. Introduction. In Anne Livet (ed.) *Contemporary Dance.* New York: Abberville Press.
McDonagh, Don. 1976. *Rise and Fall and Rise of Modern Dance.* New York: E. P. Dutton.

Part III

Vocabularies of Persuasion:
Rationality, Rhetoric, and Social Reality
in Policy, Legal, and Public Discourse

10

Metaphors of industrial rationality: the social construction of electronics policy in the United States and France

Frank Dobbin

For a generation social scientists have located culture outside the boundaries of rationalized institutions. The national character approach linked national policy preferences to shared character traits, suggesting that a national predisposition to authoritarianism would elicit authoritarian regimes (Almond and Verba 1963; Inkeles and Smith 1974; Bell 1980). In that framework culture was an individual-level variable. Structural functionalism, by contrast, situated culture in institutions but divided cultural institutions (integration and latency functions) from instrumental ones (adaptation and goal attainment). In that framework cultural institutions (education, the arts) were self-consciously and explicitly symbolic and normative.

The recent renaissance of culture in the social sciences has, for the most part, perpetuated this sort of compartmentalization. Culture has come to refer to a set of acknowledged symbolic institutions in modern societies rather than to a pervasive dimension of all modern institutions. Social scientists have been particularly slow to analyze intrumental institutions in cultural terms. When they have done so they have taken the exposé approach of the "organizational culture" school to show that factors such as charisma play a role even in rationalized institutions, rather than treating rationality itself as a social construct.

In the last decade or so a few analysts have situated cultural meaning at the core of rationalized institutions. The Birmingham school has explored science from a constructivist perspective (see also Latour 1987). Neo-institutional students of organizations have charted the social construction of rationalized corporate strategies (Meyer and Rowan 1977; Fligstein 1990). At a more macro-level studies have traced the rise of rationality and the social construction of the modern nation-state (Anderson 1983; Thomas and Meyer 1984). In that vein the present study explores the effects of institutionalized constructions of industrial rationality on the policy-making process in modern nations.

Rationalized meaning systems and public policy

Berger and Luckmann (1965) take a constructivist view of social institutions in all settings, insisting that the social construction of reality operates in rationalized societies just as it does where meaning is organized around mysticism or religion. They reject the notion that rationalized meaning systems symbolize ultimate truths while mystic and religious systems raise false gods, a notion that has made it difficult for modern scholars to treat rationality as a meaning system.

Rationalized meaning systems are organized following the principles of science. Institutions embody laws of cause and effect that are purported to be universal and immutable, laws which are subject to revision when they prove to be wrong (Wuthnow 1987).

Core constructions of rationalized meaning systems are demystified and take the form of commonsense understandings of the world. They share the traits of practical knowledge rather than of religious revelation, representing the nature of the social world not as complex and esoteric but as simple and accessible. Such meaning systems are predicated on the notion that the social world can be understood as a series of mundane cause–effect relationships that can be gleaned directly from experience. As Clifford Geertz argues, "it is an inherent characteristic of common-sense thought . . . to affirm that its tenets are immediate deliverances of experience, not deliberated reflections upon it" (1983: 75). Rationality suggests that the social world is reducible to a series of taken-for-granted relationships and that understanding the world is a process of logic and reason, not of faith. As such, rationalized social systems represent the world as composed of transparent and shallow relationships rather than of underlying, unseen influences such as those of deities and phantoms. But as Geertz insists, such commonsense notions of the universe nonetheless comprise meaning systems:

> If common sense is as much an interpretation of the immediacies of experience, a gloss on them, as are myth, painting, epistemology, or whatever, then it is, like

them, historically constructed and, like them, subjected to historically defined standards of judgment . . . [It] can vary dramatically from one people to the next. It is, in short, a cultural system. (1983: 76)

Rationalized meaning systems, mundane, transparent, and accessible as they are, represent a world based on common sense. But they do vary by locale. They may link any one of a number of plausible causes to a particular effect, but that cause stands on its shallow defensibility. There must be a recognizable logic behind the cause–effect link, and frequently such links are rendered defensible by the use of natural analogy. As Mary Douglas argues,

> the incipient institution needs some stabilizing principle to stop its premature demise. That stabilizing principle is the naturalization of social classifications. There needs to be an analogy by which the formal structure of a crucial set of social relations is found in the physical world . . . When the analogy is applied back and forth from one set [of] social relations to another and from these back to nature, its recurring formal structure becomes easily recognized and endowed with self-validating truth. (1986: 48)

My goal here is to explore the nature of the institutionalized logics of industrial policies in the United States and France. Those logics are historical constructs with roots embedded in social institutions. That is, over the past hundred years or so prevailing institutions in nations that experienced rapid industrial revolutions were constructed as the cause of growth. France and the United States credited existing institutions with their industrial takeoffs. They constructed logics of progress around prevailing institutions, and then deliberately applied those logics to promote the growth of new industries.

By looking at electronics industry policy I hope to show two things. As Mary Douglas suggests, both the United States and France constructed logics of progress based on natural analogies. In the United States the logic was that market selection effects economic rationality and in the aggregate results in growth. The analogy was to natural selection in the animate environment – to the survival of the fittest. The French analogy was to a biological system, with a central entity (the brain) coordinating the activities of all of the parts to achieve survival and growth. So first, in the American scheme the failure of market mechanisms would be seen as responsible for economic irrationalities, whereas in France it would be the failure of central coordination that would have this result. Second, those constructed logics of industrial rationality shape policies governing new industries, such as electronics. The United States and France had very different notions about how to stimulate growth in the sector, and what to guard against.

Constructing high technology growth

Recent policies designed to spur the growth of the high technology sector vary widely by country. In each country high technology policies bear a

187

striking resemblance to the policies used to stimulate growth in an array of other sectors. The United States stimulates market mechanisms while French bureaucrats plan and orchestrate industrial development. I will argue that those strategies are not the result of the persisting administrative capacities of these nation-states (Skocpol and Finegold 1982; Krasner 1984; March and Olsen 1984) because in many cases new administrative structures were adopted to install these policies.

Instead I will argue that existing growth policies constructed fundamentally different notions of economic growth in these two countries. Because policies had designated different causes of growth, these countries installed different policies to effect those causes when they sought to promote the growth of electronics. After a brief sketch of traditional industrial policies in these three countries I review the strategies used to promote electronics between 1960 and 1980.

Space limitations prohibit a full comparison of the relative merits of this constructivist approach and of more traditional interest group approaches (pluralist, rational choice, and neo-Marxist variants), but I want at least to describe the advantages of the constructivist perspective. Broadly speaking, institutional studies that chart consistent national policy styles over long periods of time have undermined the power of interest group approaches by showing that in comparative perspective France, for instance, tends to adopt the same policy strategies again and again. The French (or the British or Brazilians) tend to choose the same solutions no matter who prevails in political battles. What those studies have shown is that national policy styles are quite persistent over time, even across regime changes. They suggest that different countries choose among mutually exclusive sets of alternatives when they attack a new problem. In short, interest group conflicts would appear to decide which of several similar strategies will be pursued within a nation, rather than challenging the broad logic of public policy. And it is true that in the United States, for instance, the left and right debate *how* to fortify market mechanisms, but not *whether* to use market enforcement or state industrial planning. The constructivist perspective offers a way to understand the broad regions of consensus within nations that underlie stable national policy styles.

Traditional industrial strategies

The United States

America's first policies to regulate industry were designed to protect the economic liberties of citizens. The two main prongs of American industrial governance, antitrust legislation and industry regulation, aimed to guard economic freedom (Wilson *et al.* 1980: vii). The logic of antitrust policy, beginning with the Sherman Antitrust Act (1890), was that the state had a duty to shield firms from predatory competitors. The Act to Regulate Interstate Commerce (1887) which established the first of many federal regulatory agencies aimed at preventing discriminatory pricing practices that could destroy small firms. As industrial growth progressed these government interventions, designed to guard economic liberty, were constructed as a cause of America's industrial takeoff and soon became a positive prescription for growth. In the nineteenth century the corruption of federal schemes to aid industry had galvanized Americans against interventionist policies, and market enforcement was soon equated with *laissez-faire*. As Andrew Schonfield argues, a series of changes in the last quarter of the nineteenth century led Americans away from a belief in the capacity of states to promote economic growth directly and toward "the view, shared by both political parties, of the natural predominance of private enterprise in the economic sphere" (1965: 302). In the emergent American construction of progress markets were ultimately rational, and public policies supporting markets represented an effort to preserve natural economic conditions. Natural selection became the underlying rhetoric of this form of industrial rationality. Free markets would select the best firms for survival, in the aggregate producing the highest possible rate of economic growth.

France

The organization of the French state at the time of industrialization was another thing altogether. France had prospered and grown under a strong centralized state that could supply a large standing army to rebuff continental invaders (Anderson 1974). State centralization had been the key to France's military successes under feudalism, for it allowed the monarch to suppress local groups in the national interest. Thus industrialization occurred under the auspices of a strong and interventionist state. Louis XIV's finance minister took measures to centralize control over the economy in order to orchestrate growth, and Colbertism was born. In the nineteenth century the French state designed and built a centralized transportation network of highways, canals, and railways (Adam 1972; Pilkington 1973). As industrialization progressed the French bureaucracy assumed control over an array of key industries, from tobacco to porcelain to shipbuilding, whenever private control threatened to bankrupt them (Zeldin 1977: 104). The state nationalized key firms and industrial sectors to ensure that they would be well run, from the national passenger train system (SNCF) to Renault. Those policies were based on the analogy of biological functionalism, in which the organism could not survive and prosper without a complete set of healthy organs (read industries). By contrast, other countries with economies the size of France's have tended to choose a few industries in which they enjoy competitive advantages to support.

The second part of the biological analogy involves state orchestration of industrial growth. Since the Second World War state planners have pursued a new version of Colbertism by coordinating development under a series of five-year plans. Indicative planning has involved elaborate sectoral growth projections and selective interventions to meet national goals (Cohen 1977). The logic of this system is that the state should "mobiliz[e] private interests in the service of public ambitions" such as growth (Hayward 1986). The emergent French understanding of growth revolves around a central state that coordinates the self-interested actions of private entrepreneurs toward national ends. In this scheme the pursuit of self-interest in free markets threatens, without state oversight, to undermine the collective good. The implicit analogy is to a biological system, with a single brain (the state) orchestrating the different parts to achieve growth.

> The essential French view, which goes back to well before the Revolution of 1789, is that the effective conduct of a nation's economic life must depend on the concentration of power in the hands of a small number of exceptionally able people, exercising foresight and judgement . . . The long view and the wide experience, systematically analyzed by persons of authority, are the intellectual foundations of the system. (Schonfield 1965: 72)

After the Second World War both the United States and France recognized the military and industrial potential of electronic miniaturization, and both governments committed massive resources to research and development. Their strategies were shaped by these national constructions of industrial rationality in palpable ways. The United States consistently tried to stimulate market mechanisms by offering incentives to existing firms and encouraging market entry. French bureaucrats tried to rationalize the industry from above by restructuring firms, concentrating research and production expertise, and discouraging the entry of new firms.

American electronics policies

The United States created several new policy instruments to promote the development of the electronics industry, but adhered to the same principles of market enforcement and stimulation that it had used since the nineteenth century. That is, institutional structures were changed to promote the electronics industry, but in an effort to apply the traditional principles of natural selection by market forces. New policy strategies resembled traditional strategies not because they were pursued through old administrative channels, as institutionalist approaches to public policy suggest, but because they drew upon institutionalized constructions of economic rationality.

190

My argument proceeds from the contention that the received wisdom about American industrial policy (the United States has no industrial policy) is mistaken (Magaziner and Reich 1982; Tyson and Zysman 1983). First, American regimes have consistently called their own strategies *laissez-faire* or non-interventionist, arguing that by enforcing market mechanisms they are merely preserving the natural economic order. Yet economists point out that there is nothing natural about market enforcement, which interrupts a tendency for industries to become concentrated in order to achieve stability, economies of scale, and coordination. Second, American regimes are thought not to practice "industrial policy," which has come to mean strategic interventions in particular sectors to promote growth there (cf. Katzenstein 1985). In fact American governments have practiced "industrial policy" since the years after the revolution in the form of stock subscriptions in firms ranging from banks to breweries (Lipset 1963), in the form of land grants to canals and railroads (Kolko 1965), and in the form of research funding and strategic purchasing policies under the auspices of such agencies as the Defense Department (Hooks forthcoming). More broadly, policies to effect market pricing mechanisms and competition *are* industrial policies; in Aaron Wildavsky's words "there is no such thing as not having an industrial policy" (1984: 28).

Since the 1950s federal agencies have promoted the development of the electronics sector with policies designed to foster market competition, by encouraging market entry and discouraging monopolistic pricing and trade practices. While those policies have been pursued independently by different agencies, they constitute a coherent if not coordinated effort to effect growth by enforcing market mechanisms. They have deliberately located authority over the industry in market mechanisms rather than in the federal bureaucracy by limiting the federal role to that of a consumer, or referee, within a free market. Federal agencies have never aspired to establish a central research laboratory, to dictate to firms, or to nationalize the sector (as in France) despite the fact that the state has been the largest consumer of electronics goods.

The market model for R & D

In the years after the Second World War it was clear to the scientific community that electronic miniaturization was within reach, and would have a wide range of military and industrial uses. Yet the Department of Defense did not consider using the national-laboratory model of research and development successfully used at Los Alamos, New Mexico, on the Manhattan Project. Instead federal agencies contracted with private laboratories to carry out their research projects. In the postwar period the federal government spent more, as a proportion of gross national product, on research and development than any other government in the world (Asher and Strom 1977).

191

The decision to give technology development first priority in the postwar period was motivated in part by the belief that technological superiority was a military necessity. A 1945 report from the United States Office of Scientific Research and Development presaged an expanded public role in techno-logical development: "The Government should accept new responsibilities for promoting the flow of scientific knowledge" (Bush 1945: 3).

But instead of building a national laboratory or allocating a single research grant to one large laboratory in order to concentrate scientific expertise, the armed forces stimulated competition among a number of private laboratories in order to develop the technology. The army, navy, and air force competed to find the best approach by financing research on entirely different miniaturization technologies (Borrus 1988). In the late 1940s the army financed a project to improve conventional technology in electronics, and the navy picked up the project in the early 1950s under the name "Project Tinkertoy" (Golding 1971). In 1953 the air force tried to get Department of Defense support for integrated circuit research, and in 1957 it finally received $2 million to finance a "molecular electronics" research at the Westinghouse laboratories (OECD 1968). Meanwhile the navy was supporting the alternative "thin film" technology in private research laboratories, and in 1961 awarded a large grant to IBM to develop production potential (Kleiman 1966). At the same time (1958–64) the army was financing research on the micro-module approach to miniaturization in the laboratories of RCA. By the late 1950s laboratories across the country were racing to find new ways to miniaturize electronics components (Borrus 1988).

Major breakthroughs came at Texas Instruments, where Jack Kilby produced a working integrated circuit in 1958, and at Fairchild which soon afterwards developed a technique for mass-producing integrated circuits. While both breakthroughs came under private research funding, the armed forces' strategy of stimulating research competition by awarding large grants to competing laboratories was credited with the success. Federal funding had kept both of these laboratories alive, but both had the foresight to finance the patentable stage of research privately (Golding 1971; Asher and Strom 1977).

The Department of Defense had deliberately supported competing lines of research in private laboratories during the 1950s and 1960s. They refused to side with one scientific team or another, instead letting the competitive market sort out which technology would prevail. In those years the French government had chosen to pursue only germanium technology, with the result that they were most advanced in that field but had virtually no experience with competing technologies.

Inventing a market for semiconductors

By 1961 Texas Instruments had completed a working prototype computer that was based on integrated circuits. Integrated circuit technology was still extremely expensive, and the Department of Defense (DoD) now sought to bring the price down so that it could use the technology in a wide range of applications (Golding 1971). DoD and NASA adopted a demand side approach to stimulating the development of production technology and the growth of industrial capacity. In short, federal agencies decided to underwrite the cost of the production learning curve rather than wait for the private market to do so. In 1962 federal purchases accounted for 100 percent of integrated circuit sales, valued at $67 million (McKinsey and Company 1983; Henderson and Scott 1988: 52).

The Department and NASA saw important weight advantages for the use of integrated circuits in their new Minuteman II missile and Apollo programs, and they expected military and aerospace applications to proliferate as integrated circuit technology improved. They pursued two strategies to stimulate growth. First, they ordered the technology for every application they could think of, even when the resulting weight reductions over transistor technology did not justify the extra cost (Tilton 1971). Within a few years the armed forces were demanding the technology in seventeen different defense systems, from radar to guided missiles (Asher and Strom 1977: 74). NASA and DoD put out enormous contracts for integrated circuits with the explicit aim of developing more efficient production techniques. As early as 1962 a trade journal noted that avionics research and procurement proposals now demanded the new technology:

> A small but increasing number of proposal requests for studies, and in certain cases hardware, specify microelectronics – at times when the value of its use is dubious . . . not to have a microelectronics capability about which to boast in equipment proposals, is to risk one's chances of winning contracts. (Miller and Piekarz 1982)

Second, they deliberately spread the contracts among multiple suppliers, in a DoD strategy known as "multiple sourcing," in order to stimulate competition among firms rather than concentrating purchasing power to achieve economies of scale and the concentration of expertise in a single firm. In 1962 the Department awarded Texas Instruments the original Minuteman II development and pre-production contracts, with Westinghouse as a principal subcontractor. In 1963 the Department signed contracts with Texas Instruments and RCA for large quantities of integrated circuits, for which they agreed to pay about $100 apiece or roughly three times the market price (Golding 1971; Asher and Strom 1977: 45). In the same year NASA ordered some 200,000 integrated circuits, most of which were provided by Fairchild.

The Defense Department strategy for stimulating production advances worked. Between 1962 and 1967, when defense procurement accounted for over half of all integrated circuit production, the unit price declined from $50 to $3. The air force attributed the development of integrated circuits and the rapid growth of the industry to this strategy of market stimulation. An air

193

force document of 1965 argued that the expansion of the industry resulted from "a combination of wise policy direction by the Department of Defense; initiative, stimulation, and dynamic management by the Air Force Systems Command [the largest federal consumer]; and spirited response by industry" (quoted in Golding 1971: 45).

These policies also successfully encouraged market entry by new firms. Between 1966 and 1973 alone over 30 new integrated circuit firms entered the market (Borrus 1988: 56).

Enforcing market competition through antitrust

In the early phases of integrated circuit development federal policy was to stimulate competition by offering private firms incentives to invent new hardware and new production techniques. In the years since the late 1960s federal agencies, particularly the Defense Advanced Research Projects Administration and NASA, continued to finance technological development by funding research efforts in competing laboratories, yet antitrust policy gained a higher profile in the electronics sector.

Even in the earliest years of the integrated circuit industry antitrust policy played an important role in industry structure. Why didn't IBM and AT&T compete directly in semiconductor production? The Justice Department had successfully sued IBM for antitrust violations associated with requiring its computer customers to buy computer cards from IBM and not from competing firms in 1932, and in 1949 it had sued AT&T for pooling patents with General Electric, RCA, and Westinghouse to prevent market entry by new firms (Soma 1976). IBM understood that competing with its suppliers in the components industry might lead to further antitrust litigation. AT&T's Western Electric division was prohibited from selling any output (for example, integrated circuits) to commercial customers as a result of the 1949 suit, which effectively kept it from getting into that business (Soma 1976). In short, competition among small firms was fostered during the period by "antitrust constraints on potential entry by electronics giants IBM and AT&T into the open market for semiconductor devices" (Stowsky 1989: 245).

Despite its precautions in integrated circuit development, by the late 1960s IBM had become the focus of computer industry antitrust litigation under the Sherman and Clayton Acts, which prohibit efforts to restrain trade, attempts to monopolize industries, and acquisitions that would produce monopolies (Fligstein 1990). Prohibitions against acquisitions that would produce monopolies were, by most accounts, prophylactic in that they prevented industry giants from considering mergers. Restrictions against the restraint of trade were the focus of litigation.

In 1969 the Justice Department filed suit against IBM for restraining the trade of its competitors, principally by bundling software, hardware, and support services and requiring its clients to purchase all three (Soma 1976: 35). After thirteen years of litigation the Justice Department dropped the suit, having effectively put an end to the practices it objected to (McClellan 1984: 61). The longstanding IBM suit stood as a warning to other manufacturers that the Department would not tolerate practices that amounted to the restraint of trade.

IBM has suffered a number of private suits as well. In 1969 Control Data Corporation (CDC) sued IBM for deliberately trying to undermine CDC's business. On the eve of the introduction of a new high-end CDC machine IBM had announced a competing machine which was not yet on the drawing board, causing CDC to drop its price dramatically and to lose a number of orders. In January 1973 the suit was settled out of court for over $100 million worth of subsidies and guarantees (Soma 1976: 37; McClellan 1984: 59–61). At about the same time a number of firms brought suit against IBM for restraining trade by not making system specifications available to competing producers of peripherals and components. Advanced Memory Systems, Telex, and Memorex, as well as a number of smaller firms, won such suits. The Justice Department had opened the way for such suits with its early litigation against IBM and AT&T. The logic of their electronics industry litigation was that large firms in this growing industry must not inhibit market entry or successful competition from their smaller rivals.

The outcome of this set of policies has been easy entry into the semiconductor field and substantial competition among small entrepreneurial firms. This was evident from early on in the semiconductor industry:

> Unlike integrated circuit production in Europe and Japan, which was dominated by large, vertically integrated electronics systems manufacturers, IC production in the United States came to be dominated by a set of independent "merchant" firms whose primary business was the manufacture and open market sale of semiconductor devices. (Stowsky 1989: 245)

In short, at each stage of development American policy toward the electronics industry has been to encourage competition among firms and facilitate market entry. The idea of direct public involvement in production, even in a sector so dominated by public procurement, was anathema. As Andrew Schonfield argues, "Among the Americans there is a general commitment to the view, shared by both political parties, of the natural predominance of private enterprise in the economic sphere" (1965: 302). The logic of American policies was that natural market selection mechanisms serve as a rationalizing force that transforms individual initiative into macroeconomic growth.

Mimicking Japan

While in the 1960s and 1970s these policies were validated by America's dominance of international markets, by the early 1980s it became clear that Japan was overtaking the United States in certain key areas, particularly semiconductor production. The Japanese had gained the lion's share of the market with an industrial strategy based on government sponsorship and industry collaboration on research and development. These experiences tended to disprove American notions of market rationality, at least for the semiconductor sector, and Americans tried to effect the Japanese prescription in several settings. US Memories, a California-based memory chip cooperative involving seven major computer manufacturers, was to expand US production capacities to ensure a steady supply of chips but the venture fell apart in early 1990 over disagreements among the firms. The Austin-based Sematech is a joint venture of 16 high-technology firms; it was established in 1988 to develop and diffuse new semiconductor production techniques that would keep the United States at the cutting edge of the industry. The group has received $100 million annually in federal funding for 1989 and 1990, which amounts to about 40 percent of its budget. The venture has attracted several hundred scientists, yet industry analysts maintain that it is grossly underfunded as compared to the research efforts mounted by Japan's MITI (Vaughan and Pollard 1986; Stowsky 1989). These collaborative efforts represent a response to the apparent failure of "natural selection" in the semiconductor industry. The Americans' capacity to use the decline of the semiconductor industry to disprove that "natural selection" would work suggests that rationalized meaning systems indeed consist of sets of means-ends designations; it suggests also that these are highly susceptible to revision when the means they designate appear to fail (Wuthnow 1987).

French electronics policies

If American electronics policy was motivated by a belief in the efficacy of market processes, French policy was motivated by the belief that economic rationality would result from state orchestration of the efforts of private actors. As Richard Nelson puts it, "The tradition of a strong civil service actively engaged in encouraging, protecting, and subsidizing particular industries goes back to the Bourbons. It was not unnatural, therefore, for the French to assume that the government should play a major role in guiding industrial development" (1984: 33). French policy could hardly have been more different from American policy. Where the Americans outlawed mergers the French brokered them. Where the Americans refused to favor particular firms in their procurement procedures, the French designated "national champions." Where the Americans sought to stimulate competition and market entry the French sought to eliminate both. Where the Americans made agreements to make product competition illegal, the French encouraged it.

French research and procurement policies did not aim to multiply efforts to reach a particular goal, but to concentrate them under a rational central plan. When it came to research and development, this meant that policies supported research into one promising technology rather than competing technologies. When it came to production and marketing it meant that policy was aimed at concentrating the electronics sectors rather than encouraging competition. The "national champion" strategy pursued by the French has involved inducements for competing firms to combine, through horizontal mergers and restructuring; this has created large firms specializing in different high technology products that face no competition within France. Part of the logic was that France should develop every pertinent sector of the computer industry rather than specialize in a particular product.

France has seen three principal national electronics plans since the 1960s: the Plan Calcul (1966), Giscard d'Estaing's internationalization strategy (1977), and La Filière Electronique (1982). Each was designed to restructure the industry, in order to concentrate electronics capacities in parallel "national champions" that would specialize in mainframe machines, office computers, telecommunications equipment, and semiconductors. The first plan was to develop national self-sufficiency, the second to expand international collaborations to take advantage of technology transfers, and the third was to nationalize key firms to bring them under greater state control. The common logic of these three plans was that (a) state orchestration could rationalize the efforts of individual firms whereas free markets would produce industrial chaos (the brain analogy) and (b) the vitality of the entire industry was dependent on the vitality of every subsector (read organ) and thus state policy involved a plan for each subsector (the biological functionalism analogy). The latter was achieved largely through sectoral consolidation (merging establishments with similar products) and market apportionment (allocating markets for particular products to particular firms).

The single-strategy approach to research

Before the 1960s the French electronics industry enjoyed substantial success. In 1960 Machines Bull still rivalled IBM in the international market for computers, having exported machines to the United States since 1950 under a licensing agreement with Remington Rand (Mazataud 1978: 17). French success had come with their advances in germanium technology, which had been promoted by a government research and procurement strategy that concentrated efforts on that one technology. By demanding germanium technology in weapons in the 1950s, and funding research only on that technology, the French state had made France the world leader in germanium technology.

197

The French strategy of permitting civil servants to choose a single technology to invest in would have proven successful in the long run if integrated circuit break-throughs had not eclipsed germanium technology. Instead, the events at Texas Instruments meant that government policy would have to change course.

What pushed the French government to develop a more ambitious and interventionist policy for the electronics sector was an American embargo on the export of mainframe machines to France – machines which the French government had wanted to use in its nuclear research program. That action catalyzed existing French sentiments in favor of developing every vital industrial sector rather than specializing in certain goods and technologies – what I have been calling the functionalist analogy. The French government now felt that dramatic action was needed to bring its computer industry up to speed, so that it could supply the military and industries that depended on computers. The concurrent acquisition of France's computer industry leader by the American firm General Electric reinforced those sentiments.

To ensure the vitality of the French computer industry the state introduced the "Plan Calcul" in 1966. Under the plan the state established a national laboratory in Le Chesnay, outside of Paris, dubbed the Institut Nationale de Recherche en Informatique et Automatisme (INRIA). INRIA was placed under the direct control of the planning authority and by 1968 was receiving half of France's 9 million franc research and development fund for semi-conductors as well as the bulk of the nation's computer research funding (Mazataud 1978: 29–30).

Private research and development contracting differed in several ways from that in the United States. First, the state's Délégation Générale à la Recherche Scientifique et Technique concentrated financing in four large laboratories by contracting directly for research, rather than encouraging competition for research contracts by putting out requests for proposals as the armed forces did in the United States (Tilton 1971: 128–31). Second, the four principal laboratories, INRIA and three private laboratories, pursued research on different products rather than competing to find the best technology for a particular product. The SESCOSEM laboratory, for instance, specialized in components research while INRIA specialized in mainframes. Research programs were coordinated to the end of developing all of the technologies necessary to build computers. In each sub-field planners and scientists chose a single technological strategy to pursue.

Production: the "national champion" approach

The centerpiece of the Plan Calcul of 1966 was an effort to restructure the computer industry to produce sectoral "national champion" firms. Planners coordinated agreements among the major all-French manufacturers, excluding Machines Bull because of its American ties, and restructured firms to consolidate the industry. In December, under the auspices of the plan, an accord was signed between the state and the three largest French-held computer companies: Schneider, the Compagnie de Télégraphie Sans Fil (CTSF), and the Compagnie Général d'Électricité (CGE), establishing the Compagnie Internationale pour l'Informatique (CII). Under the plan the state promised 420 million francs for research and loan guarantees, totaling 500 million francs, in return for a promise that by 1972 CII would produce four mainframe computers (Mazataud 1978: 30). Over the next few years state planners brokered further mergers, to increase the concentration of the mainframe industry. In 1968 the independent Thomson acquired CSF and their 77 percent share of CII, and in 1970 CII absorbed Sperac. By the early 1970s Thomson-CTSF controlled the lion's share of the industry, including majority interest in CII.

State planners did not stop at designating a national champion in the field of large computers but went on to dictate what that firm would produce. As John Zysman (1977) points out, planners prevented CII from exploring market niches by decreeing that it would produce medium-size mainframe computers for industrial and military purposes that would compete directly with IBM's product line.

The Délégation replicated the Plan Calcul strategy to effect horizontal mergers in the peripherals and components (Plan des Composants) sectors in 1966 and 1967 respectively, in both cases by detaching subsidiaries from their parent companies and combining them with competitors in the same product line, so creating the new SPERAC which would produce peripherals, and SESCOSEM which would produce components. As with CII, state planners decided what these groups would manufacture. The Délégation had decided that CII would build machines based on Texas Instruments' semiconductor components, and as part of the overall plan decided that SESCOSEM should duplicate the TI line of components with the aim of supplying CII with French-made semiconductors. SESCOSEM had no particular strengths in producing semiconductors and was unable to achieve TI's economies of scale, thus the firm continued to require substantial state subsidization (Zysman 1977: 149).

The planners' strategy of dividing up product lines to eliminate competition among French manufacturers received another boost in 1969 when Thomson-CSF and CGE (a CII participant) signed a treaty of "non-belligerence"; in it they agreed to divide up the electronics market so that they would not be in direct competition in any major product line. CGE was to focus on telecommunications and energy devices and Thomson on information technology and business and industrial use electronics equipment (Mazataud 1978: 39).

The Délégation's initial marketing strategy was simple. They decreed that government agencies and corporations would purchase CII products rather than shop for computers on the open market. That strategy was predicated on the market power of the French state, where the railways, air lines, utilities (including nuclear power plants), and telecommunications industries are nationalized (Nelson 1984: 34). French firms were thus guaranteed a 40 percent share of the domestic market for computers and related equipment.

French planners had four principal tools that helped them to gain the compliance of firms in these plans. First, they promised to subsidize firms that followed their wishes, or to make up operating deficits if those firms did not turn a profit. Second, they guaranteed a market to those firms by providing public agencies and other "national champion" firms with incentives to buy exclusively from them. Third, they controlled access to credit. Fourth, they controlled trade barriers to protect particular domestic industries. The ability of the French state to control so much of the environment made it easy for state planners to induce firms to participate in their grand schemes.

The internationalization strategy

By the mid-1970s it was clear that the Plan Calcul's efforts to build internationally competitive firms in each high technology sector had not been successful. The French could build their own computers and components, but not at competitive prices. Giscard d'Estaing's administration blamed the effect on the Plan Calcul's protectionist policy on technology transfers. Now the Government sought to develop joint ventures in each technical area to bring technological advances to France. The Government forged an alliance between CII and the American–French venture Honeywell Bull (the latest incarnation of the General Electric–Machines Bull marriage) with a 53 percent French stake, and brokered joint ventures in components development between Thomson and Motorola; between Matra, Harris, and Intel; and between St Gobain and National Semiconductor (Rushing and Brown 1986: 74). Those components industry collaborations introduced a degree of competition in response to the perceived success of competition in the American semiconductor industry. But the policy of designating three French components firms stopped far short of encouraging market entry; it was to be short-lived, and it did not extend to other sectors, where the national–champion approach still prevailed (Brickman 1989).

La Filière Electronique

The Socialists reorganized the electronics sector once again in 1982 under a five-year plan called la Filière Electronique, which nationalized important firms as it restructured the industry. Mitterand nationalized CGE, St Robain, Rhône-Poulenc, and Thomson, and acquired a majority interest in Matra and a 75 percent interest in CII-Honeywell Bull. Restructuring again involved concentrating expertise in every electronics sector to create a complete set of healthy interdependent firms. Here again the biological analogy fits; "filière" refers to the entire range of activities associated with a particular technology and the plan coordinated every sector, from components to aerospace electronics to software. State planners again redrew boundaries among electronics firms to create a national champion in each sector, in an agreement dubbed the "Yalta of Electronics." It called, for instance, for CGE to trade its consumer and components division for Thomson's telecommunications division in order to concentrate expertise on those technologies (Langlois *et al.* 1988). Thomson was to specialize in components (for example, semi-conductors) and professional electronics, CGE in telecommunications equipment, Bull in computers and office equipment, and so on (Brickman 1989).

The nationalizations of the early 1980s were part of the Socialists' overarching plan to socialize the French economy, yet they had surprisingly little effect on how managerial decisions were made because the state had already played a central role in industry decision-making. Nationalization was just another approach to applying the logic of biological-functionalism to the economy. State planners (in the role of the brain) made key decisions governing technology and industry structure with an eye to maintaining a self-sufficient set of healthy interdependent monopolistic firms (in the roles of vital organs). In the eyes of the French, state orchestration remained the solution to the problem of rationalizing and giving direction to the inchoate actions of self-interested entrepreneurs.

As the economic integration of Europe in 1992 looms large on the horizon French policy has taken a more international flavor. European governments have established a number of joint ventures among competing establishments in an effort to achieve the economies of scale that American firms enjoy, and the benefits of collaborative research and development efforts characteristic of Japanese industry. France has taken a leading role in establishing joint ventures in an array of high technology sectors, in what appears to be an extension of its past biological functionalism strategy to Europe as a whole. In 1989 the European Economic Community announced a $5 billion Joint European Submicron Silicon program, known as Jessi, which brings together European talents with the aim of developing a 64 megabyte chip (currently the largest chips are four megabytes). The principal firms involved are France's Thomson, Philips of the Netherlands, and Germany's Siemens, and the French state has committed more than its share of funding. Other international ventures include Race ($1.5 billion for telecommunications), Esprit (a 14-nation collaboration in integrated circuit design), and Eureka-A (a 19-nation collaboration on 297 high technology research projects).

In short, the French strategy for promoting the growth of electronics was, like the American, stimulated by perceived military needs. But that is where the similarity ends. Since the 1960s the French state has played a strong role in the development of the industry, not only by providing substantial research and development funding, but by repeatedly restructuring firms and telling them what to make and whom to sell it to. If the logic of American policy was that market selection would rationalize the self-interested behavior of individual firms, the logic of French policy has been that only central state coordination of industry could rationalize individual action and guide markets in directions beneficial to the nation as a whole. Moreover, the French have repeatedly pursued the policy of creating national champions and undermining markets. This has happened despite the widespread belief that European electronics firms have lagged behind the United States and Japan precisely because countries such as France have not "nurtured small, innovative companies like those that abound in Silicon Valley. Instead, Europe has relied for its advances on big, slow-moving national champions that grew lazy in protected domestic markets" (Greenhouse 1989). Even the most recent international collaborations have replicated that strategy.

Conclusion

In modern nation-states the means–ends designations that are institutional-ized in public policies vary widely. Under the banner of progress govern-ments try all sorts of policy instruments, from breaking up AT&T to nationalizing Renault to privatizing the post office. I have been arguing that the broad logics undergirding such moves can be best understood as part of institutionalized constructions of economic rationality. Different nations pursue broadly different policy strategies because they hold different understandings of the logic of industrial growth, of how the economy works. Those understandings are roughly isomorphic with existing policy strategies as long as those strategies appear to be effective. When countries seek to promote the development of new industries they think in terms of the logic of existing policies. Unless those policies are in the process of conspicuously failing, as during recessions, nations tend to replicate their logics in new policies. In short, as modern social institutions organize growth in one way or another, via what Chalmers Johnson calls "market-rational" or "plan-rational" strategies for instance, they symbolize particular causes of growth. When they attack new problems they try to simulate those causes.

In the cases of American and French policy the underlying logics of industrial rationality draw on natural analogies, as Mary Douglas suggests. In the United States natural selection has become the prevailing metaphor for industrial rationality, and growth strategies have sought to create competitive situations and to stimulate market entry. In sharp contrast French policy activates a biological functionalism analogy in which the national economy can prosper only under the direction of central expert planners who can coordinate the inchoate actions of individual firms and intervene where market processes lead to outcomes that are irrational in the long run. A core element of that strategy is the notion that an economy must contain all of the parts necessary to self-sufficiency. That stimulated the French to initiate the Plan Calcul, to ensure the nation's capacity to produce computers. It also motivated repeated efforts to create a national champion in each sub-sector of the industry, rather than, following the lead of Korea or Japan, to develop particular market niches where the nation had a competitive advantage.

In both cases it is clear that constructions of industrial rationality are not static but are responsive to feedback, as Robert Wuthnow (1987) suggests they should be as part of rationalized meaning systems. The United States has begun to experiment with novel collaborative policies in response to the American decline in the field of semiconductors and the apparent success of Japan's collaborative strategies. It remains to be seen whether collaborative ventures will survive, but they certainly signify the constructed nature of notions of economic rationality. French policy has changed direction several times, from insularity to internationalism to nationalization and again to internationalism. New policies were installed when it became clear that existing policies were not having the desired effect, that is, when events disproved the logic of policies already in effect. Yet in the French case it was not the core logic of *planification* that was altered with each new scheme, it was the relationship to the wider international market.

The electronics industry has provided one example of how institutionalized social constructions of rationality may shape future policy choices. History influenced American and French policy, but not by leaving these countries with peculiar configurations of interest groups or different state organizational apparatuses. Instead history offered different social constructions of industrial rationality, in the form of substantially different sets of public policies that accompanied industrial prosperity. Future studies of the symbolic content of modern rationalized institutions promise to address two problems in the social sciences. First, the images of industrial rationality discussed here offer a way to understand persistent national policy styles that other paradigms of public policy have not been able to explain. Second, the study of symbolism in rationalized institutions promises to redress the current tendency to treat only "symbolic" (read non-instrumental) institutions as cultural, which has had the unfortunate consequence of preventing students of modern culture from analyzing the construction of rationality itself, which lies at the core of modern meaning systems.[1]

Note

I would like to thank Robert Wuthnow for comments on an earlier version of this paper.

References

Adam, Jean-Paul. 1972. *Instauration de la Politique des Chemins de Fer en France*. Paris: Presses Universitaires de France.

Almond, Gabriel and Verba, Sidney. 1963. *The Civic Culture: Political Attitudes and Democracy in Five Nations*. Princeton, NJ: Princeton University Press.

Anderson, Benedict. 1983. *Imagined Communities*. New York: Cambridge University Press.

Anderson, Perry. 1974. *Lineages of the Absolutist State*. London: New Left Books.

Asher, Norman J. and Strom, Leland D. 1977. *The Role of the Department of Defense in the Development of Integrated Circuits*. Washington, DC: Institute for Defense Analysis.

Bell, Daniel. 1980. *The Winding Passage*. Cambridge, Mass.: ABT Books.

Berger, Peter and Luckmann, Thomas. 1965. *The Social Construction of Reality: A Treatise on the Sociology of Knowledge*. Garden City, NY: Doubleday.

Borrus, Michael G. 1988. *Competing for Control: America's Stake in Microelectronics*. Cambridge, Mass.: Ballinger.

Brickman, Ronald. 1989. France. In Francis W. Rushing and Carole Ganz Brown (eds) *National Policies for Developing High Technology Industries*, pp. 71–88. Boulder, Colo.: Westview.

Bush, Vannevar. 1945. *Science – The Endless Frontier*. Washington: US Office of Scientific Research and Development.

Cohen, Stephen S. 1977. *Modern Capitalist Planning: The French Model*, 2nd edn. Berkeley, Calif.: Campus.

Douglas, Mary. 1986. *How Institutions Think*. Syracuse, NY: Syracuse University Press.

Fligstein, Neil. 1990. *The Transformation of Corporate Control*. Cambridge, Mass.: Harvard University Press.

Geertz, Clifford. 1983. *Local Knowledge: Further Essays in Interpretive Anthropology*. New York: Basic Books.

Golding, A. M. 1971. The semiconductor industry in Britain and the United States: A case study in innovation, growth and the diffusion of technology. PhD thesis, University of Sussex.

Greenhouse, Steven. 1989. Europeans unite to compete with Japan and US. *New York Times*, August 21.

Hayward, Jack. 1986. *The State and the Market Economy*. New York: New York University Press.

Henderson, Jeffrey and Scott, A. J. 1988. The growth and internationalisation of the American semiconductor industry: Labour processes and the changing spatial organisation of production. In Michael J. Breheny and Ronald W. McQuaid (eds) *The Development of High Technology Industries: An International Survey*, pp. 37–79. London: Routledge.

Hooks, Gregory. forthcoming. The rise of the Pentagon and US state building: The defense program as an industrial policy. *American Journal of Sociology*.

Inkeles, Alex and Smith, David. 1974. *Becoming Modern*. Cambridge, Mass.: Harvard University Press.

Katzenstein, Peter. 1985. *Small States in World Markets: Industrial Policy in Europe*. Ithaca, NY: Cornell University Press.

Kleiman, Herbert S. 1966. The integrated circuit: A case study of product innovation in the electronics industry. PhD thesis, George Washington University.

Kolko, Gabriel. 1965. *Railroads and Regulation 1877–1916*. Princeton, NJ: Princeton University Press.

Krasner, Stephen D. 1984. Approaches to the state: Alternative conceptions and historical dynamics. *Comparative Politics* 17: 223–46.

Langlois, Richard N., Pugel, Thomas A., Haklisch, Carmela S., Nelson, Richard R., and Egelhoff, William G. 1988. *Microelectronics: An Industry in Transition*. Boston, Mass.: Unwin Hyman.

Latour, Bruno. 1987. *Science in Action*. Cambridge, Mass.: Harvard University Press.

Lipset, Seymour Martin. 1963. *The First New Nation: The United States in Historical and Comparative Perspective*. New York: Norton.

Magaziner, Ira C. and Reich, Robert B. 1982. *Minding America's Business: The Decline and Rise of the American Economy*. New York: Harcourt Brace Jovanovich.

March, James G. and Olsen, Johan P. 1984. The new institutionalism: Organizational factors in political life. *American Political Science Review* 78: 734–49.

Mazataud, Pierre. 1978. *Les Constructeurs de Matériel Informatique en France*. Paris: Bibliothèque Nationale.

McClellan, Stephen T. 1984. *The Coming Computer Industry Shakeout*. New York: Wiley.

McKinsey and Company. 1983. *A Call to Action: the European Information Technology Industry*. Brussels: Commission of the European Community.

Meyer, John W. and Rowan, Brian. 1977. Institutionalized organizations: Formal structure as myth and ceremony. *American Journal of Sociology* 83: 340–63.

Miller, Hugh H. and Piekarz, Rolf R. (eds). 1982. *Technology, International Economics, and Public Policy*. Boulder, Colo.: Westview.

Nelson, Richard R. 1984. *High-Technology Policies: A Five Nation Comparison*. Washington, DC: American Enterprise Institute.

Organization for Economic Cooperation and Development (OECD). 1968. *Gaps in Technology: Electronic Components*. Paris: OECD.

Pilkington, Roger. 1973. Pierre-Paul Riquet and the Canal du Midi. *History Today* 23: 170–6.

Rushing, Francis W. and Brown, Carole Ganz. 1986. *National Policies for Developing High Technology Industries: International Comparisons*. Boulder, Colo.: Westview.

Schonfield, Alfred. 1965. *Modern Capitalism*. London: Oxford University Press.

Skocpol, Theda and Finegold, Kenneth. 1982. State capacity and economic intervention in the early New Deal. *Political Science Quarterly* 97: 255–78.

Soma, John T. 1976. *The Computer Industry: An Economic-Legal Analysis of its Technology and Growth*. Lexington, Mass.: Lexington Books.

Stowsky, Jay. 1989. Weak links, strong bonds: US–Japanese competition in semiconductor production equipment. In Chalmers Johnson, Laura D'Andrea Tyson, and John Zysman (eds) *Politics and Productivity: The Real Story of Why Japan Works*, pp. 241–74. Boston, Mass.: Ballinger.

Thomas, George M. and Meyer, John W. 1984. The expansion of the state. *Annual Review of Sociology* 10: 461–82.

Tilton, John. 1971. *International Diffusion of Technology: The Case of Semiconductors*. Washington, DC: Brookings.

Tyson, Laura and Zysman, John. 1983. American industry in international competition. In Laura Tyson and John Zysman (eds) *American Industry in International Competition*, pp. 15–59. Ithaca, NY: Cornell University Press.

Vaughan, Roger and Pollard, Robert. 1986. State and federal policies for high-technology development. In John Rees (ed.) *Technology, Regions, and Policy*, pp. 268–81. Totowa, NJ: Rowman & Littlefield.

Wildavsky, Aaron. 1984. Squaring the political circle: Industrial policies and the American dream. In Chalmers Johnson (ed.) *The Industrial Policy Debate*, pp. 27–44. San Francisco: Institute for Contemporary Studies Press.

Wilson, Robert W., Ashton, Peter K., and Egan, Thomas P. 1980. *Innovation, Competition, and Government Policy in the Semiconductor Industry*. Lexington, Mass.: Lexington Books.

Wuthnow, Robert. 1987. *Meaning and Moral Order: Explorations in Cultural Analysis*. Berkeley, Calif.: University of California Press.

Zeldin, Theodore. 1977. *France, 1848–1945: Intellect, Taste and Anxiety*, Vol. 2. Oxford: Clarendon Press.

Zysman, John. 1977. *Political Strategies for Industrial Order: State, Market, and Industry in France*. Berkeley, Calif.: University of California Press.

11

The parameters of possible constitutional interpretation

Benjamin Gregg

The American constitutional document is one of the West's most important repositories of political symbols and ideals, and its interpretation exerts a powerful political, social, and economic influence on American society. Yet some of the document's most politically vital referents such as "equal protection of the laws" or "due process of law" are vague in at least one of several senses. In some cases only limited or otherwise problematic evidence exists as to how the framers intended a referent to apply; in other cases a referent is inherently open-ended in its range of possible meanings. In still other cases the appropriate interpretation has been thought to depend on the pervasive norms of society at the time of interpretation (and therefore to shift as norms change). Within the document the relationship between the text and its meaning, and also between legal rules and the norms they embody, establishes the document's actual authority at any given time. In other words the same legal text may through time, with shifts in textual interpretation, come to found a norm different from the one it originally founded. The norm, then, is not always the same thing as the rule specified in the text. This always complex and often perplexing relationship urges an externalist approach to constitutional interpretation (although, as we shall see, not exclusively so). First, in and of themselves the constitutional document's vague or open-ended referents have no single, conclusive, identifiable meaning. When the document's meaning is unproblematic, interpreters feel constrained to regard its language as authoritative without further inquiry.

But when its meaning is problematic interpreters are inevitably forced outside the text in search of some authority to guide textual interpretation. Second, because a purely formal invocation of rules and the deduction of conclusions from them cannot be sufficient for every authoritative legal choice, jurisprudence must be supplemented by norms or other contents external to itself. Equality, for example, makes non-circular commands and imposes non-empty constraints only in the presence of substantive ideals (Tribe 1978: 991). Positing such ideals is a value choice, not an explication of meaning.[1] Hence at some level constitutional interpretation must reject the notion of narrow fidelity to the written text.[2]

An externalist approach thematizes the problematic relationship between constitutional language and its application, and examines historical changes in that application. Externalism is not universally recognized, most notably by the dominant contemporary jurisprudential approach, legal positivism. From this perspective law consists of data – primarily rules – which can be recognized as such by relatively simple tests or "rules of recognition" (Hart 1961). One such test is that the rules have passed through certain formal stages of a legislative process. Another such test is that they can be derived from the *ratio decidendi* – the essential grounds of decision – of a case decided by a court with the jurisdiction and authority to lay down new rules in such a case. Positivism assumes that these rules of law constitute the law, and in this sense that law is a "given," part of the data of experience. Positivism rejects the more obscure idea that legislation can be the product of an implicit general will or that the truth of a legal proposition might reside in some morality implicit in the common consciousness of everyone.[3] Indeed, jurisprudential scholars in general do not acknowledge an externalist strategy. Theirs is usually the internal point of view of those who make legal claims, those who do not want predictions of the legal claims they will make but arguments about which of these claims is sound and why (Dworkin 1986). It is developed chiefly through rationalization of and speculation on the rules taken to be explicitly or implicitly present in legal doctrine.

Many social scientists, on the other hand, believe that an understanding of law requires not only systematic empirical analysis of legal doctrine and institutions but also of the social environment in which legal institutions exist (Cotterrell 1984: 3).[4] From this perspective law is analyzed as a species not of social norm, but of social action (Grace and Wilkinson 1978).[5] To the extent that social norms are not empirically observable, they are not considered a possible research object; the study of rule adherence, for example, would consider the rules' substantive content completely irrelevant.

Yet unless the externalist method also focuses on legal language and the norms it may embody, it misses what (in a political order based on a written constitution) must be the ultimate carrier of interpretations, even non-textually-based ones. After all, the most important datum bearing on what was intended by legislators is the constitutional language itself, just as the critical record of what was meant to be proposed and ratified is what was in fact proposed and ratified (Ely 1980: 16–17).

I propose a language-oriented, mainly externalist approach to examining the constitutional document's various, vague implications of legal equality. Part I argues that in crucial areas constitutional language offers no adequate foundation for authoritative interpretation.[6] Part II offers an alternative approach by locating the parameters of possible constitutional interpretation in two basic forms of legality. By "form of legality" I refer to the normative presuppositions underlying a jurisprudential line of reasoning. The choice of one set of presuppositions rather than another is not a rule-governed or analytical one, but rather a value choice. As such the interpreter may declare for one option or the other, but can nowhere find that choice ready-made in the document. And choose he or she must, consciously or unreflectively, if any position at all is to be taken.

I derive these two forms of legality by modifying and extending Max Weber's ideas on legal rationality, to develop the twin concepts of *universalism* and *particularism*. As normative presuppositions concerning equality, the first permits no distinctions whatsoever between individuals or groups before the law, whereas the second allows some distinctions as valid. In legal texts these presuppositions are evident in the arguments by which conclusions are justified. A universalist and a particularist form of legality define the parameters of what I call *bounded normative ambiguity* (which I demonstrate in Part III from an externalist standpoint, in Part IV from an internalist one).

Part III applies these terms to American history by examining the discrepancies between the constitutional language of equality, on the one hand, and judicial interpretation and social practice on the other. I identify a trend over the last 200 years from predominantly particularist forms to predominantly universalist forms of legal equality, and a trend since the Second World War toward a combination of universalist and what I call *neo-particularist* forms (neo-particularism permits distinctions between individuals to the benefit of minority groups). These trends represent not so much changes from one kind of law to another, as shifts in the way one and the same law is interpreted. My main thesis is that universalism and particularism define the parameters on a continuum of the possible constitutional interpretations of equality.

Finally, Part IV applies these terms to the 1978 Supreme Court decision on affirmative action, *Regents of the University of California* v. *Bakke*. At this point I retreat from the externalist approach pursued in the first three sections. Unlike many other social phenomena, legal practice is fundamentally argumentative and cannot be grasped except in reference to the grounding and defense of claims about what law permits or forbids. I turn therefore to the internal character of legal argument, specifically to the formal legal arguments from the judge's perspective. My purpose is not to argue for or against affirmative action, but to show that the actual court decision is in fact cast in competing universalist and (neo-) particularist terms. By showing from an internalist perspective that the question of constitutionally-based legal equality (and legal inequality) is tenably framed in these terms, I propose them as an externalist explanation of the very uneven pattern in the historical development of constitutional aspects of equality.

To recapitulate: Part I concludes that constitutional language offers no adequate foundation for authoritative interpretation. Part II shows that this leads not to normative anarchy but to bounded normative ambiguity, in the form of universalist and particularist parameters of constitutional interpretation. In other words, the constitutional text offers no foundation, and hence no guarantee, for either expanded or reduced degrees of legal equality; the interpreter must decide what he or she believes the constitutional document warrants, and that discretion will be defined by the universalist-particularist parameters. Part III demonstrates this thesis in general terms, in a sketch of the history of legal equality and legal inequality in America, 1789 to the present; Part IV demonstrates it in the detailed terms of a 1978 Supreme Court decision on affirmative action.

I

In ordinary adjudication (hence in the vast majority of constitutional decisions) courts follow the principle of *stare decisis*, which invokes the authority of the document as law by remitting the document to one end of a growing line of precedents. An initial judicial decision interprets the document by concentrating attention on specific words or the supposed intention of the framers; the second decision focuses chiefly on the meaning of the first, the third chiefly on the meaning of the second, and so forth until the constitutional text recedes to become something like a "remote ancestor who came over on the Mayflower" (Brest 1980: 234). This approach offers itself as a public, predictable, impersonal basis for decisions, promising stability and continuity in related decisions over time. Yet in any given case *stare decisis* neither leads to nor requires any particular results. Available to choice are a wide variety of precedents and a still wider variety of past interpretive decisions. That choice may be guided, consciously or not, by factors external to the law, such as social and political judgments about the case's substance, parties, and context (Kairys 1982: 14). And even if *stare decisis* were an ideal basis for decision, it applies only after a precedent ruling; the precedent which establishes a rule is, in a sense, outside that rule. Hence *stare decisis* cannot justify the manner in which it interprets the constitutional document in that all-important first decision.[7] The philosophical problems faced by the first court in interpreting the document are similar to those faced by any current court interpreting the latest decision.

Those problems relate to (a) the nature of language, (b) the notion of original intent, and (c) the idea of an ethos as a normative foundation for constitutional interpretation.

(a) For 2,500 years the Western philosophical tradition has sought ultimate categories of thought. Contemporary epistemology concludes that instead only shifting paradigms, changing questions, and new sets of answers exist, all limited by the scope of the temporarily prevailing disciplines (see Rorty 1979). Perhaps no categorical distinction can be drawn between matters of definition and matters of fact; even allegedly "analytical" truths may simply be those for which no one has yet offered any alternatives that might lead us to question them (see Quine 1990).[8] Consequently we can never stand outside our current structure of thought, nor outside our current language. If linguistic facts have meaning, then the explanation for that meaning is not the capacity of syntax to express it but the ability of a reader to confer it; "facts" and texts are unavailable apart from interpretation. Interpretive strategies are not put into execution after reading; instead, they give texts their shape, making them rather than arising from them. Accordingly there can be no exclusively correct or natural or appropriate way of reading, but only ways of reading (Fish 1980: 16). The sole test for our theories and interpretations cannot be "facts," but at best something like their coherence with the rest of our beliefs (see Feyerabend 1988).[9] The activity of interpretation is then one not of demonstration but of persuasion. This does not deny the possibility of truth; a proposition can be true even if no procedure exists for demonstrating its truth in such a way that any rational person must concede that truth. But it does imply that truth is inter-subjective or perspectival, and that language is inherently indeterminate, a "cloudy medium." This quality renders linguistified law indeterminate with regard to the meaning of its language. In that sense a text never has a single meaning nor even a finite number of coherent or otherwise tenable readings. Inevitably the same text will have different meanings for different readers and various meanings for disparate eras.[10] If interpretation is the art not of construing but of constructing (Fish 1980: 327), it might seem as though there are as many plausible readings of the constitutional document as there are versions of Hamlet (Levinson 1982: 391). Yet in its extremism this unremittingly subjectivist conclusion is mistaken, as I show in Part II.

(b) Not only are the constitutive responses of the reader variable; the intentions of the author may well be unavailable. Even if the framers' intent *were* an appropriate guide to interpreting the document – assuming for example that the past should exercise such authority over the present and future – only those long-dead men can have known exactly what that intent was. First of all, the vocabulary of eighteenth-century political discourse was in a state of flux. Many pivotal words were new and not yet in general usage, and others had yet to be coined. Some words were not understood similarly within the same community, or even, perhaps, among the framers and ratifiers of the constitutional document. For example the words "equal" and "equality" as used in the eighteenth century – including the notion of equality before the law – did not necessarily imply a conflict with the institution of slavery (McDonald 1985: 53–5).[11]

Beyond that, legal interpretation displays certain unique features which make attribution of intention nearly impossible. Unlike other kinds of literature, legal texts – notably the constitutional document and judicial decisions[12] – are negotiated and bargained over, beginning their life fashioned by more than one hand. In the genesis of legal texts one or more of several authors may agree to words not wanted or meant, as a result of some exchange relationship or of delegated writing. The text may also be the outcome of a process of assembly in which several authors have been independently at work. And unlike other kinds of literature, writers of legal texts (other than contracts) do not speak for themselves (and were they to do so, would speak without authority: legal authors properly speak for collective entities like the court or legislature) (Vining 1990).

(c) A popular notion suggests that legitimate constitutional interpretation depends on the pervasive norms of society, on a morality or collective will implicit in something like a common consciousness present in a community or nation. This notion is problematic inasmuch as (i) there may be no such thing as a collective will or interpretive community; (ii) knowing what the ethos is, as well as deciding which ethos governs in the presence of multiple ethoi, presents an intractable problem; (iii) the constitutional document itself, to say nothing of a nation of heterogeneous individuals, does not display the kind of normative consensus implied by the notion of a national ethos or collective will.

(i) Some would argue that morality is widely shared, available to reflection, and capable of being discovered rather than created because it is already implicit in the common consciousness of everyone (Rorty 1982: 157). Such a consciousness would seem to posit a level of experience shared by all. A different approach to a similar conclusion assumes that, if the speakers of a language share a system of rules that each of them has somehow internalized, understanding must be uniform (Fish 1980). For both approaches interpretive strategies proceed not from the individual interpreter but from the interpretive community of which he or she is a member. Accordingly, since the thoughts an individual can think have their source in the interpretive community, the meanings and texts proceed not from an isolated individual but from a public and conventional point of view; members of the same community necessarily agree because they see everything in relation to that community's assumed purpose and goals. Interpretation among different readers would be stable because those readers belong to the same community. But this and related notions of a collective normative consciousness are fatally vitiated first by the unyielding epistemological problem of demonstrating the possible existence and actual presence of some such "general mind"; second

212

by the manifest fact that interpretations within most communities at any given time are unlikely to be either stable or consensual or even mutually coherent; and third by the unlikelihood that absolutely everyone (despite all heterogeneity) would be embraced (or homogenized) in the normative community (which leads to the next problem: who shall count as a member of the community, and by what criteria?).

(ii) As norms extrinsic to the law change, legal conceptions which derive their content from these norms will change as well. Shifting interpretations of the constitutional document, like the shifted interpretation of a precedent, declare earlier norms invalid or confess that earlier interpreters erred in their selection of norms. When the court declares an earlier decision wrong, it declares it to have *always* been wrong. In maintaining that the judges and public of an earlier time failed to see the truth, that perhaps they were held captive by misinformation or cultural conditioning whose roots they could not glimpse, today's court does not concede that it may be similarly "blinded" in ways to be discovered by future judges and other interpreters, but may see its own adjudication to represent a growth in moral consciousness or interpretive acuity. After all, judges do not generally cast their disagreements as differences in theories of interpretation but rather as differences in what the law *is* (Dworkin 1986: 5). But if at any time we cannot know with certainty that we ourselves are not "blinded," then never can we be certain that moral or intellectual growth has occurred. Alternatively we make the insupportable assumption that the drafters and ratifiers and earlier interpreters suffered from moral blindness, yet nevertheless had the moral vision to supply us with a general commitment to the very norms to which they were blind. But how can we rectify our predecessors' misconceptions without abandoning their concepts?[13]

If the court appeals to the constitutional document's authority as ethos by resting an interpretation on an overt avowal of a national ideal, it purports to speak for the fundamental ethos of the contemporary community and in the end justifies itself only by what it takes to be the wisdom of its own insight. It finds the principle stuff of constitutional judgment in what it takes to be society's fundamental values rather than in the document itself (Ely 1980: 88, note). This renders the document's content and spirit as transient and contingent as national self-definition, a notion that would trouble more than a few interpreters and other citizens. In any case, the idea of a common normative consciousness cannot account for how we could ever know such an ethos with any certainty, nor can it account for the fact that at any given time reasonable people may disagree as to what the national ethos is – nor, in the presence of a plurality of ethoi, how we choose which one will govern.[14]

(iii) Consensus is not a potentially measurable attribute of social collectivities; at any time a given collectivity can be made to exhibit radically different degrees of consensus (Gilbert and Mulkay 1984).[15] Yet those who posit an ethos or collective will as the basis of proper constitutional interpretation presuppose the existence of both public values and uniquely valid solutions to the conundrums inevitably engendered by such values. This in turn implies the absence of all genuine conflict among the values held by various individuals, and dissimilar social sectors, at any one time as well as at different periods in our nation's history. But such a consensus is certainly not true of the constitutional document, which is a veritable bundle of various conflicting norms: process norms as well as substantive norms; structural and institutional norms as well as those embodying individual rights; those which protect the individual from the power of the state, and norms which assure the superiority of federal to state law; norms that underlie granting powers to the federal government and still other norms that support limiting those same powers (Bator 1981: 633). Nor is there any semblance of a consensus among theories of constitutional interpretation.[16] And contemporary moral discourse is fragmented and inconsistent (for example, MacIntyre 1984). Indeed, it has been argued that much of existing law is a patchwork quilt of competing, often inconsistent moral principles, political commitments, and conceptual schemes (for example, Altman 1986). How, then, could a consensus ever be true of the many heterogeneous individuals to whom it applies under diverse circumstances and over broad expanses of time? In fact we do not and perhaps cannot agree on the normative rules by which people should be governed; neither does the constitutional document.[17]

Taken by itself, the arguments that constitutional law has no single, clearly identifiable normative foundation, hence that in crucial areas constitutional language offers no adequate foundation for authoritative interpretation, imply normative anarchy or perhaps nihilism. I now turn this "deconstructive" exercise around by developing an alternative explanation of interpretive structure. By identifying the parameters of possible constitutional interpretation (at least with respect to legal equality) I point not to value nihilism but to bounded normative ambiguity. Whereas normative anarchy implies something along the lines of "anything goes," value ambiguity suggests a degree of uncertainty within certain stable and definable limits or boundaries.

II

Max Weber categorizes all forms of creation and the finding of law in terms of four intersections of two pairs of concepts: formal in distinction to substantive, and rational as distinct from irrational (Weber 1978). Rational means jurisprudential guidance by general principles or abstract rules; irrational, the absence of any such rules or principles. Formal pertains to the absence of substantive content, of political, ethical, religious, or other nature; substantive, to the presence of such content. Hence substantively rational law has political or religious or other content, and is guided by some principles or rules.[18] Formally rational law-making and law-finding are based on rules or principles free of ethical or political or other content; they identify the legally relevant facts exclusively through the logical interpretation of meaning of legal concepts. Formally rational law entails a principled separation of legal norms from extra-legal norms.

This level of analysis makes possible a distinction between socially acceptable and socially intolerable forms of discrimination. As the vicissitudes of American legal history show, what is considered acceptable, and what intolerable, are not constant. They certainly are not constant over time, nor is there ever consensus. At any given time I see three possibilities, which may be stated as categories developed from Weber's model:

(a) What Weber calls formally rational law is legitimate in the widest possible terms, that is, potentially valid in any given social, cultural, political, or historical context, and equally valid for all individuals and groups therein. I shall call this *universalist* legality. It implies its own validity in the widest possible terms, implies no specific value other than the requirement or desirability of universal validity, and in this sense is contentless.

(b) What Weber terms substantively rational law always has some definite content, "finds" some content, or considers some content relevant. This I term *particularist* law. It implies that the ethically valid is valid only for some human beings, only in some communities, or only for certain periods of time. Hence different individuals and groups may stand in different relation to the law, and in this sense all individuals and groups affected by the law do not stand as equals before it.

(c) For most of American history particularist law has discriminated to the advantage of the majority. Recent decades have seen the incremental reinterpretation of old laws (and sometimes introduction of new ones) that discriminate to the advantage of one or more minority groups. I will term such law *neo-particularist*.

This (non-Weberian) distinction between two types of particularism allows us on the one hand to acknowledge the fact that any form of particularist legality is discriminatory, yet on the other hand to differentiate between stigmatizing (namely particularist) and non-stigmatizing (neo-particularist) discrimination. In other words legal discrimination may be either adverse or benign. Affirmative action legislation, the focus of Part IV, is a form of neo-particularist legality.

In distinguishing between universalist, particularist, and neo-particularist forms of legality, I have disregarded a central element of the Weberian categories which inspired these distinctions in the first place: the notion of rationality. I turn now to justifying that disregard and thereby further distance myself from Weberian structure.

Rationality forms a key element in Weber's theory of the rise of modern capitalism. Weber maintains that this rise was made possible by two historical innovations: the Protestant ethic of the calling and the modern legal system. Both embody a type of moral consciousness guided by self-reflective principles. The principle nature of this morality, and the fact that these principles can themselves be placed into question, distinguish this type of moral consciousness from traditional morality in which norms are conventions, uncritically passed down from generation to generation. Accordingly the modern legal system demands a purposive-rational type of behavior, yet one anchored in value-rational convictions.[19] Weber subsequently loses this dualistic notion of rationality when he proceeds to analyze modern law solely as a type of purposive rationality, namely as "positivized" law, law that has become independent of value rationality as the technical administration of law has been relieved of problems of justification. The sphere of law, says Weber, establishes what is valid according to the rules of juristic thought, and juristic thought obtains when certain legal rules and methods of interpreting them are recognized as binding. But

> [w]hether there should be law and whether one should establish just these rules – such questions [the sphere of law] does not answer. It can only state: If one wishes this result, according to the norms of our legal thought, this legal rule is the appropriate means of getting it. (Weber 1946: 144–5)

Jürgen Habermas argues that while problems of justification in the law can be displaced over broad expanses of time, they cannot be displaced forever, as Weber seems to believe. For if we assume that legitimacy is a necessary condition for the continued existence of every type of legal authority, how can a legality based on decisionism (devaluing all grounding in principle) be legitimate (Habermas 1984: 265)? Weber answers: through strict adherence to procedures in the administration, application, and legislation of law. But this explanation leaves unclear how the belief in legality can bring about legitimation if legality simply means conformity to an existing legal order, and if this order, as arbitrarily enacted law, is not in turn open to moral justification. Indeed such an answer is based on circular reasoning: the belief in legality can produce legitimacy only if we presuppose the legitimacy of the legal order that lays down what is legal.

Habermas shares Weber's view that modern law has become separated from legality, yet against Weber he insists that the domain of legality as a whole nonetheless requires moral (rather than any other type of normative) justification. I agree with Weber that moral and amoral forms of political legitimacy *can* be embedded in or carried by specific types of rationality, but I disagree with Habermas that they *must* be. Universalist legality might be seen to display formal (or means-ends or purposive) rationality insofar as both are value-neutral and formal, in this sense contentless. Further, universalist legality might be thought to be characterized by purposive rationality because it is decisionist: it conceives of law positivistically, as a series of formal propositions that stand in unambiguous logical relationships to each other and for that reason allow for clear decisions that require no extra-legal norms. Correspondingly, particularist legality might be said to embody value rationality inasmuch as both are value-laden and substantive, that is, characterized by particular, non-universalizable contents. Here legal decisions can be made only if based on values external to the law, values which must be introduced into the law as contents for substantive norms (norms which, without content, would be formal, like those of universalist legality).

But value rationality is not necessarily moral rationality: the values carried by a particularist legality are always normative, but that normativity need not be of a moral nature. After all, there are different kinds of particularism, displayed for example in different kinds of inequality. Both chattel slavery and affirmative action are particularist, yet in profoundly different ways: in America the former discriminated adversely against a minority, stigmatizing it, whereas the latter discriminates benignly against a majority and does not stigmatize it. (For that reason I designated the latter type of legality "neo-particularist" to distinguish it from the former type of particularism.)

Habermas's argument also implies that the continued existence of our political order requires particularist legality. Yet even if this implication were true at least on political grounds, it cannot be true on constitutional ones. Today it may be true that a liberal democracy could not long sustain its legitimacy in the presence of widespread adverse legal discrimination (although it is not clear that this *must* be so). In any case that foundational document of the American political order, the constitutional document, requires neither a benignly nor an adversely discriminatory legality, no more than it necessitates a perfectly non-discriminatory one. In that sense the document implies no specific substantive morality.[20] It *can* be interpreted in a particularist (or neo-particularist) manner, but it doesn't have to be; it may be viably interpreted in universalist fashion. The legal must be normatively justified, but those norms need not be specifically moral ones. The norms of the document are ambiguous, though not entirely. In the following section I demonstrate from an externalist standpoint my notion of bounded normative ambiguity.

III

The constitutional document is written in the language of universalist legality. In 1787 it was ratified in the name of "we, the people." Its Ninth Amendment holds that rights of "the people" exist prior to government and constitutions, which must recognize them. The basic individual rights guaranteed in some of the other amendments are similarly universalist, including in 1791 the freedoms of speech, press, assembly, and religion; the inviolability of person and property; and the right to a speedy and public trial and to trial by impartial jury. In 1865: the right not to be enslaved, and in 1868 the right to due process of law and to equal protection of laws. In 1870: the right to vote regardless of race or color. In 1920: the right to vote regardless of sex.

These rights are universalistic because framed without reference to color, ethnic origin, or other possible distinctions between the mass of individuals to whom they would seem to apply. Yet their collective history does not represent the steady expansion of universalist legality since they have not often functioned universalistically. For the greater part of its history American society was based on structural inequality with little dissent among white men. White women were legally and politically inferior to white men; Indians and free blacks were legally and politically inferior to all whites. American society was based on a hierarchy of statuses rather than a universality of rights. Before the Civil War legal equality was unacceptable as a national goal; thereafter it meant at most nominally fair legislative classification and statutory application (Katz 1988: 751, note; 758). In other words the constitutional document's universalist language was interpreted in predominantly particularist fashion until well into the twentieth century. Not until 1954 was the document explicitly interpreted universalistically, to provide for one sole community of rights holders with universal entitlement to equal treatment in all aspects of life.[21] Although during the next thirty years new categories of people entitled to presumptive equality – aliens, the illegitimate, the aged, women – gained constitutional protection in whole or in part, by the retirement of Chief Justice Burger in 1986 the number of suspect categories had not been expanded to include gender, wealth discrimination, exclusionary zoning, inequality in welfare benefits, municipal services, or school finance, among other categories.

Especially with the advent of affirmative action legislation and policy in the 1960s, the interpretation of the constitutional document's universalist language shifted to a combination of universalist and neo-particularist approaches (whereby the trend toward neo-particularist legality has been much slighter than the more general trend toward universalist legality).

This general movement (or even "development") represents an ineradicable tension between the two extremes on the one continuum of universalism and particularism (with neo-particularism falling somewhere in between). This is not so much a shift from one kind of law to another, as it is a series of periodic shifts in the way one and the same law is interpreted. Particularism and universalism have defined the parameters of possible constitutional interpretation of legal equality and legal discrimination both before and after the ratification of the Fourteenth Amendment (1868), and

218

universalism and neo–particularism have defined those parameters particularly after *Brown* v. *Board of Education* (1954).[22]

IV

In America the debate remains, as always, inconclusively framed in the mutually exclusive terms of universalism and particularism.[23] For this reason alone we may expect the future course of legal equality and legal discrimination to be pulled back and forth between the competing norms of purposive- and value-rationality. This bounded normative ambiguity is easily demonstrated from an internalist perspective on a major affirmative action case. The Medical School of the University of California at Davis established an affirmative action admissions program for minority candidates, reserving for them 16 out of the 100 places in each entering class. The school twice denied admission to a white male applicant, Allan Bakke, even though according to school standards he scored much higher than any of the 16 minority admittees. Bakke filed suit in a state court, which, while conceding the plan's compelling race-specific objectives – improved health-care for minorities, greater racial integration of the medical student body and profession – nonetheless found the plan violative of constitutionally guaranteed equal protection because its means were race-based.[24] Both Bakke and Davis appealed. California's Supreme Court held that the Davis plan violated the Fourteenth Amendment[25] as well as Title VI of the 1964 Civil Rights Act,[26] and ordered Bakke's admission. Davis thereupon obtained certiorari from the US Supreme Court. In the 1978 decision *Regents of the University of California* v. *Bakke* (hereafter cited as "Bakke 1978") four justices found the Davis plan constitutional under Title VI and voted to deny Bakke admission, while four argued the opposite case, and the ninth justice (Powell) cast the decisive vote and wrote the majority opinion. On the one hand the opinion affirmed that portion of the California court's judgment holding Davis's special admissions program unconstitutional (with Justices Burger, Stewart, Rehnquist, and Stevens concurring). Bakke's admission to the medical school was ordered. On the other hand the opinion reversed that portion of the California judgment enjoining Davis from considering race in its admissions program (with Justices Brennan, White, Marshall, Blackmun concurring).

I do not reconstruct the decision but rather examine its competing perspectives. These divide into three universalist, and three neo–particularist, positions on equality and discrimination. I confront each position of each side with a counter-argument that might be made by the other side.

Universalist argument (1): The *Bakke* majority opinion held that the "guarantee of equal protection to all persons" does not permit the "recognition of special wards entitled to a degree of protection greater than that accorded other" (Bakke 1978: 2750–1).[27] The principle is clearly contradicted by state-sanctioned remedial preference for individuals or groups, including those historically victimized by state-sanctioned discrimination. It embodies a decisionistic concept of legitimacy: simple logical analysis indicates whether a particular case violates or sustains the principle. Hence the validity of the principle is independent of socio-historical context, and legitimacy is self-referential: legitimate is that which conforms to a principle that cannot itself be placed into question (the mentality of obeying the law simply because it is law).

Neo-particularist counter-argument (1): Exceptions to strict equal protection are permissible as benign discrimination and are necessary because of the legacy of racism. An appreciation of our culture's deep-rooted racism is necessary for achieving the social ideal of overcoming the historic effects of racism, that is, of equalizing the races socially, or at least of ameliorating the gross discrepancy in social standing (Wasserstrom 1977: 618).[28] This counter-argument is value-rational because based on the extra-constitutional norm of "equalization."

A particularist (and neo-particularist) form of legality challenges the very possibility of a universalist-type race-neutrality: the supposedly race-neutral criteria society might otherwise employ (standardized test scores, for example) may not be unbiased. Prior experience suggests that adverse race-consciousness will exist even in a racially neutral process of decision or selection (Tribe 1978: 1045). Moreover, formal and substantive norms of equality are neither self-evident nor ethically empty: equal treatment can be unjust, and unequal treatment can be just (Greenawalt 1983: 1183).

Universalist legality finds government action justified if such action respects the right of all community members to be treated as equals, but not otherwise (Dworkin 1977: 239). By contrast, a neo-particularist legality can provide value-rational reasons why the expansion of opportunities for minorities and the elimination of a racist status quo through benign discrimination legitimates the resulting harm, even to those members of the majority not personally responsible for the plight of the minority (Tribe 1978: 1048).

From the universalist standpoint, those on whom the burden of affirmative action falls are being subjected to retribution, inasmuch as this group usually corresponds (in terms of sex and race) to the traditionally favored majority, and since the burden brings material harm (for example, loss of some opportunities) to those individuals compelled to bear it. Neo-particularist legality might counter-argue that discrimination against one particular group may well differ from discrimination against another particular group: discrimination by white against white is less invidious (because no stigma is suffered) than discrimination by whites against non-whites (which stigmatizes non-whites). Whereas universalism equates all forms of discrimination, particularism makes distinctions (on the basis of extra-legal values), arguing for example that special solicitude for an historically disadvantaged group does not violate the constitutional right to equal protection of historically advantaged groups.[29]

Universalist argument (2): The *Bakke* majority position sees "no principled basis for deciding which groups would merit 'heightened judicial solicitude' and which would not," and finds the "kind of variable sociological and political analysis necessary to produce such rankings [of groups meriting heightened judicial solicitude] simply does not lie within the judicial competence" (Bakke 1978: 2751–2).[30] Legitimacy for decisionism rests on formal principles such as the rational-basis test used to assess ordinary classifications that are claimed to violate the constitutional document's equal protection clause: a classification must be reasonable, not arbitrary, and must rest upon some ground of difference having a fair and substantial relation to the object of the legislation, so that all persons similarly circumstanced shall be treated alike. In this way decisionism (hence universalism) presumes equality as a matter of principle, and places the burden on the proponent of unequal treatment to explain why such treatment is warranted.

Neo-particularist counter-argument (2): Arguments against this type of universalism might identify moral rather than formal bases for deciding which groups merit exception. One such basis might be the political or ethical commitment of the majority to substantive fairness toward the minority. A majority might propose or accept classifications which disadvantage the majority even though the classifications were clearly designed not to have that effect, but rather to assure fair treatment for, or representation of, the minority. Then there would be no reason to regard the governmental choice with suspicion and to scrutinize strictly the results. Further, neo-particularist legality can identify a corollary to the principle that a "more searching judicial inquiry" is provoked by "prejudice *against* discrete and insular minorities" (*United States* v. *Carolene Products Co.* 1938: 152–3, note 4).[31] Judicial scrutiny may not be provoked by prejudice against such a minority when the latter is benefited, rather than burdened, by government.

Again, a neo-particularist answers the question "Who merits exception?" by distinguishing between adverse and benign discrimination: if race-specific targets need not necessarily dilute the political power of whites or disenfranchise them, they are benign. Discrimination against whites may also be benign if it implies no racial slur or stigma with respect to whites or any other race, and if it intends no racial insult or injury to those whites adversely affected.[32]

Universalist argument (3): Consistency is vital to universalism, for which the most corrosive message of legal history is the message of contingency. This emphasis on consistency typifies the formalism and proceduralism of universalist legality. According to the majority *Bakke* opinion, to consider constitutional principles as mutable according to "shifting political and social judgments" would be to allow that "judicial scrutiny of classification touching on racial and ethnic background may vary with the ebb and flow of political forces" and therefore to "undermine the chances for consistent application of the Constitution" (Bakke 1978: 2752). This assumes that the court's role in interpretation is that of discerning norms with roots throughout the community and continuity over significant periods of time, so as to lift the court above the level of the pragmatic political judgments of a particular time and place (Cox 1976: 114).

Neo-particularist counter-arguments (3): The universalist principle of consistency provides no adequate guide to procedure since it is, after all, empty. Our notions of equality derive from norms that first define what we mean by "consistency," "impartiality," and "non-arbitrariness." Consistency and impartiality have their source in the rules being administered, and simply spell out what the rules themselves mean (Westen 1983: 640–1). Hence consistency alone in no way implies good or legitimate interpretation. Moreover, the notion of absolute consistency in constitutional interpretation is contradicted by the long-established practice of judicial review. This points up the fact that, in practice, broad and enduring consistency is impossible to achieve.[33]

I shift now to the principle arguments of the other side.

Neo-particularist argument (4): The notion of a "compelling government purpose" appeals to values external to the constitutional document, values open to diverse contents that cannot be procedurally or otherwise formally selected. Neo-particularist legality justifies a purpose in moral, not legal terms. The majority *Bakke* opinion finds that the preferential treatment of some individuals "perceived as members of a relatively victimized group at the expense of other innocent individuals is permissible only when there are judicial, legislative, or administrative findings of constitutional or statutory violations" and the "government interest in preferring members of the injured groups at the expense of others is substantial" (Bakke 1978: 2734). When political judgments regarding the necessity for a particular classification "touch upon an individual's race or ethnic background, he is entitled to a judicial determination that the burden he is asked to bear on that basis is precisely tailored to serve a compelling governmental interest" (Bakke 1978: 2753). Although the moral purpose of preferential treatment may be protected by legal procedure, it cannot be reduced to legal purpose.

Universalist counter-argument (4): One state-sanctioned violation cannot justify a subsequent state-sanctioned violation; the latter is simply a form of "reverse-violation."

Neo-particularist argument (5): Socially tolerable inequality (affirmative or benign discrimination) is tolerable precisely as a means necessary to ameliorate the effects of a history of socially intolerable inequality. Universalist and neo-particularist may both agree that the state "has a legitimate and substantial interest in ameliorating, or eliminating where feasible, the disabling effects of identified discrimination" (Bakke 1978: 2757), but only the neo-particularist will argue that "in order to achieve minority participation in previously segregated areas of public life, Congress may require or authorize preferential treatment for those likely disadvantaged by societal racial discrimination" (Bakke 1978: 2786–7).[34]

Universalist counter-arguments (5): Affirmative or benign discrimination cannot really solve the problem it was designed to solve, if for example members of the group ostensibly benefited by a supposedly benign or remedial measure object that the measure does not, from the group's perspective, truly benefit it. Or such discrimination may at times act to stigmatize further a "discrete and insular" minority. Or purportedly-benign discrimination may mask an intentional form of adverse discrimination. And benign discrimination that seeks racial assimilation not only implies that society benefits by the erosion of differences, it also ignores the importance to minorities of their own distinctiveness (Tribe 1978: 1044, note, 1049, 1050).

Neo-particularist argument (6): Law and public policy designed to address adverse discrimination have no alternative but to employ benign discrimination, since the universalism of non-discriminatory law offers no practical solution to the problem. The neo-particularist choice of race-conscious means is derived from values not found within the constitutional document but rather from a normative calculus that views benign discrimination as socially tolerable. If "racially neutral remedies for past discrimination were inadequate where consequences of past discriminatory acts influence or control present decisions" (Bakke 1978: 2785),[35] then solely race-conscious means are available to achieve a goal whose desirability and constitutionality are not in question. Since *Plessy* v. *Ferguson* (1896)[36] we know that mandating color-blindness in government would negate efforts against racism: the persistence of social, cultural, and economic realities ensure that purporting to be color-blind in the individual case is likely to mask treatment that in fact will prove biased against minority individuals (Tribe 1978: 1043, 1048).[37]

Univeralist counter-argument (6): A universalist legality places principle before perceived social need or any other non-principled, contingent factors. Indeed, even if a universalist legality made any practical solution to the problem difficult or impossible, the principle underlying such a legality would be no less legitimate and worthy of obedience.

With this account of *Bakke* in competing universalist as distinct from neo-particularist norms I have attempted to demonstrate the inherently problematic nature of constitutional interpretation. I have indicated several of these facets. For example, no system of law – whether judge-made or legislatively enacted – can be so perfectly drafted as to leave no room for dispute. Further, the American constitutional document in particular contains several provisions whose invitation to look beyond their four corners cannot be construed away.[38] Also, beyond a few natural meanings encoded in most languages (basic color terms, for example), the majority of meanings in languages, and in different varieties of a language, are crystallized in response to the social, economic, technological, and theoretical needs of the cultures concerned. Language-use does not simply reflect a stock of pre-existing ideas independently formed within a culture, but is a factor in the formation and reproduction of ideas (Fowler 1981: 21).[39] These factors, among others, render a positivist approach to legal interpretation untenable. Hence constitutional language by itself offers, in crucial areas, no adequate foundation for authoritative interpretation. But as my account of *Bakke* has also sought to demonstrate, this does not imply that normative anarchy is the sole or necessary alternative.

Yet some scholars who share my view of constitutional language conclude that solely a normatively-neutral approach to interpretation is the way to avoid the equally perilous pitfalls of positivism and anarchy. John Hart Ely (1980: 100–1) for example argues that the constitutional document is not an enduring but an evolving statement of general norms, since the selection and accommodation of substantive norms is left almost entirely to the political process. The document does not ground a set of substantive rights entitled to permanent protection, but proceeds from the assumption that an effective majority will not inordinately threaten its own rights. It seeks to assure that such a majority will not systematically treat others less well than it treats itself, by structuring decision processes at all levels to try to ensure that everyone's interests will be actually or virtually represented at the point of substantive decision. Its concern, says Ely, with ensuring broad participation in the processes and distributions of government is a concern with formal process, not normative substance. He fails to see that even this "process" is not value-neutral since it embraces the substantive values of participation and non-prejudice (compare Brest 1981).

A similarly-motivated approach combines jurisprudence and free-market economic theory (for example, Posner 1977). Proponents of the law and economics movement embrace the realist view that legal language, while purporting to be about pre-existing rights, in fact obscures what courts do. They claim that American judges often arrive at solutions that would be reached through unimpeded market exchange, in other words the most efficient (least costly) solutions. They further claim that efficiency provides a neutral and objective standard for judicial decision-making, unlike norm-laden rights analysis.[40] Yet economic efficiency is itself a norm which, while certainly independent of the norms grounding social and political rights, nonetheless represents a substantive evaluation of how social and political rights should be distributed. And as we saw (in Part III) with regard to the history of the "development" of constitutional aspects of equality, the *distribution* of rights directly affects the *content* of those rights. Hence if in America in 1789 legal equality extended only to white landed males, the content of the right to equality was on the order of eighteenth-century "rights of Englishmen"; if today legal equality extends for example to non-whites and the poor, then the content of the right to equality is qualitatively broader than its colonial predecessor.

These two approaches illustrate the futility of an approach to constitutional interpretation that would disregard the law's normative dimension. By contrast my theory attempts to sail between the Scylla of positivism and the Charybdis of interpretive anarchy and yet still account for the fundamentally normative nature of the constitutional document (and of all constitutional interpretation). It does this by reconciling the internal and external approaches to interpretation: an internalist approach to norms, and an externalist approach capable of taking account of the law's self-description in normative terms without being bound to that description. In other words the universalist as distinct from neo-particularist parameters of possible con-stitutional interpretation are normative characterizations of forms of legality, yet they stand outside the law's own normative characterizations of legality.

Notes

I wish to thank Robert Wuthnow for his critical comments on earlier drafts of this chapter.

1. Even the injunction to "treat like cases alike and different cases differently" is by itself incomplete and, until supplemented, cannot guide conduct. Any form of legality is indeterminant in other ways as well. As command it can never be wholly determined since even the most detailed command must leave to the individual executing it some discretion. And if every law-applying act is only partly determined by law and partly undetermined, then the undetermined part must be open to extra-legal determinations. This fundamental indeterminacy entails the discretionary nature of applying law – and where discretion is present, Cartesian certitude is absent.
2. Even Judge Bork (1971: 9) might seem to do this when he maintains that "when the Constitution has not spoken, the Court will be able to find no scale, other than its own value preferences, upon which to weigh the respective claims to pleasure." Yet he also champions narrow textual fidelity as the exclusive legitimate approach to reading the constitutional document, indeed on the basis of putative "neutral principles" in the document. Yet even assuming the existence of such principles, an insistence on them does not by itself tell us anything useful about their appropriate content or how the court should derive the norms they may embody. If Bork had the courage of his convictions, his would be a jurisprudence of (near) silence.

3. Legal positivism derives from Jeremy Bentham, was developed in the nineteenth century by John Austin, and in H. L. A. Hart (1961) has its most influential contemporary exponent. Today positivism dominates in legal theory and social science alike. Legal data for the positivist jurisprudent are rules; legal data for the positivist social scientist are quantifiable observable behavior.

4. See for example the behavior-pattern positivism in a study of judicial "attitudes" using bloc analysis, cumulative scaling, and small-group analysis to describe and predict what are taken to be "voting patterns" of Supreme Court and other judges, summarized in Goldman and Jahnige (1976).

5. For Black (1972: 1091) law "consists in observable acts, not in rules as the concept of rule or norm as employed in both the literature of jurisprudence and in every-day legal language." Law, defined as governmental social control, "behaves" in various ways, increasing or decreasing in measurable extent. Thus the "quantity" of law varies with the quantity of stratification in a society. This approach allows Black to conclude that lower ranks have quantitatively less law to call upon than do higher ranks.

6. This section shares with the American legal realists the conviction that rules are inherently indeterminate; with critical legal studies the belief that in many important instances adjudication collapses into legislation; and with the law and literature movement the view that textual interpretation cannot be formal or "objective." But in all of the following sections of this essay I temper these movements' strongly subjectivist bias by identifying objective parameters to interpretation that cannot itself be objective. In other words, a purely objectivist or a purely subjectivist approach, like a wholly externalist or a wholly internalist perspective, is one-sided.

7. Moreover, the precedent contained in a judicial opinion is inherently uncertain. To recognize that the reading of a holding not only can be unintended, but indeed can be contrary to the intent of the opinion's author, need not imply that just any reading is possible and legitimate. But it does imply that the meaning of a precedent is simply what the latest court held.

8. For example Quine (1990: 11) argues that "a sentence is analytic if the native speaker learns to assent to it in learning one of its words."

9. According to Feyerabend (1988: 63), "Facts contain ideological components, older views which have vanished from sight or were perhaps never formulated in an explicit manner. Such components are highly suspicious. First, because of their age and obscure origin: we do not know why and how they were introduced; secondly, because their very nature protects them, and always has protected them, from critical examination. In the event of a contradiction between a new and interesting theory and a collection of firmly established facts, the best procedure, therefore, is not to abandon the theory but to use it to discover the hidden principles responsible for the contradiction."

10. This is especially true of individual words: generations of legislators, judges, and citizens did not understand the Declaration of Independence's word "men" or the Ninth Amendment's invocation of "the people" or the Fifth Amendment's reference to "person" to include Indians or blacks or women, children or aliens or the illegitimate. Legal equality could not extend to these and other groups today had not the constitutional document been invested with meanings different from those intended by earlier generations.

Perhaps legal semantics shift over time the way natural scientific semantics may. Kuhn (1970: 128–9) suggests that "neither scientists nor laymen learn to see the world piecemeal or item by item," but rather both "sort out whole areas together from the flux of experience. The Copernicans who denied its traditional title 'planet' to the sun were not only learning what 'planet' meant or what the sun was. Instead, they were changing the meaning of 'planet' so that it could continue to make useful distinctions in a world where all celestial bodies, not just the sun, were seen differently from the way they had been seen before."

11. Slaves were not equal in law to freemen, but neither were women or children. Two centuries ago limiting the rights of citizenship to "freemen" was entirely consistent with republican principles, and was considered indispensable in most versions of republican theory. Of this and the four other general usages of "equal" and "equality" current in American political discourse during the late eighteenth century, only one negated the possibility of slavery as a morally acceptable institution.

12. Lone dissenting opinions, of course, are an exception: they are fashioned by one hand only, and may be free of all compromise.

13. Actually Dworkin (1977: 134–6, 226) argues precisely this by distinguishing between "concept" and "conception." He compares constitutional interpretation to the problem faced by a son whose father instructed him to be fair. According to Dworkin, the father charged the son with the *concept* of fairness, not with the particular *conception* of fairness the father happened to hold at the time he gave the instruction.

14. For example the court's decision in *Brown* v. *Board of Education* (1954) embraced the norm of racial equality which – given the controversy engendered by the decision and the widespread refusal for more than a decade to implement the decision – represented at the time and in subsequent years a misreading of the national ethos. Indeed, the ethos was divided.

15. Gilbert and Mulkay (1984) studied natural scientists and found that the individual scientist tends to present his or her theoretical position as an unmediated expression of the natural world, insofar as that world has "revealed" itself in the findings of controlled experiments. By contrast, the individual scientist to whom the actions or judgments of other scientists are depicted as being or as having been in error, characterizes and explains the latter scientists in strongly contingent terms. Scientific speakers seem peculiarly able to construct accounts in which they appear to have privileged access to the realities of the natural world, each conveying the strong impression that his or her voice and that of the natural world are one and the same. Similarly, many legislators, judges, and the jurisprudents (as well as other interpreters) identify their respective voices with that of the constitutional document. Hence in law, too, the apparent presence or absence of consensus may be simply a matter of perspective.

16. Over two hundred years the constitutional document has given rise to a veritable Talmud of theories of interpretation and application. One effort (Murphy, Fleming and Harris 1986) to categorize some of the more widely used theories gives a sense of the diversity in contemporary interpretive methods. According to this three-tiered model, "approaches to interpretation" refer to the most basic ways an interpreter perceives the document: textualism v. transcendence, a fixed v. changing document, the document as rules v. the document as vision. "Modes of analysis" denote how a person utilizes those approaches in the enterprise of constitutional interpretation: verbal, historical, structural, doctrinal, prudential, purpose. "Analytical techniques" signify specific interpretive tools: literalism, deductive inference, inductive reasoning, intent of the Framers, *stare decisis*, balancing, moral and political philosophy. And this list does not even include (in fact, rejects) several dichotomies widely applied in constitutional commentary: strict v. liberal construction, judicial activism v. self-restraint, substance v. procedure, interpretivism v. non-interpretivism.

17. Might this problem be resolved by an alternative to notions of communal opinion or collective representation, such as Foucault's (1972: 117, 63, 55, 122) concept of anonymous knowledge and discourse with a life of its own? On this view, "a body of anonymous, historical rules" operates "according to a sort of uniform anonymity, on all individuals who undertake to speak in this discursive field." By "discourse" Foucault does not mean "the majestically unfolding manifestation of a thinking, knowing, speaking subject." He means the "totality of things said, the relations, the regularities, and the transformations that may be observed in them." Foucault is concerned not with how subjects might form a constitution determining who or what is sovereign, but with how the subjects themselves are constituted. (Foucault's theory surely rejects the notion that in making a constitution subjects might constitute themselves.) He finds that every way in which the individual can think of him- or herself as a person and agent is in fact something that has been constituted within a web of historical events, hence that discourse is determined not by the conscious wishes of the speakers but by the transient because historical conditions for discourse. The history which bears and determines us consists of relations of power and not relations of meaning.

    While devoid of the problematic notions of collective will, ethos, and normative consensus, this conception provides no basis whatsoever for grounding legitimate constitutional interpretation – but rather makes all such grounding impossible. Because he rejects the possibility of noumenal selves, Foucault concludes that human beings cannot determine themselves individually or collectively. Hence he cannot share the presupposition of this essay that political and social affairs can be consciously and willfully molded and changed on the basis of texts. As such Foucault's theory provides no viable solution to the stated problem.

18. Having content, and being rule-bound, are not synonymous. For example a Delphic oracle may have the content of ancient Greek theology, yet is not guided by any set of rules or principles providing consistency between different oracular pronouncements. In Weberian terms oracular law is substantively irrational.

19. The Protestant ethic of the calling, as well as modern capitalism, will not be further considered since they are not relevant to this essay.

20. In a book entitled *The Morality of Law* (1969: 162, 153) Fuller finds no *substantive* morality in law in general. For him the meaning of a law is its purpose, hence it is that purpose rather than the legal text that primarily defines a law's proper application. Fuller describes "purpose" in formal procedural terms such as making or interpreting law in such a way as always to render it coherent and clear. Legal morality is then "neutral over a wide range of ethical issues" and the "internal morality of law may support . . . a wide variety of substantive aims."

21. I refer to *Brown* v. *Board of Education* (1954), unanimously ordering racial integration of public schools.

22. I thus differ from other dualistic accounts of historical change in legal form, for example as a movement from substantive to formal law (Weber 1978; Teubner 1983); from repressive to autonomous law (Nonet and Selznick 1978); from repressive to restitutive penal law (Durkheim 1964); from law to bureaucratic administration (Kamenka and Tay 1975); as a decline of private law and increasing dominance of public law (Friedman 1972); as a conflation of private and public law (Winkler 1975; Unger 1976); or as a continuous cycle of movement between rule and discretion (Pound 1954), or formalism and informalism (Abel 1979), or rule and policy (Atiyah 1978).

23. Universalist and particularist forms of legality, while mutually exclusive in content, need not be mutually exclusive in function. For example conflicts between universalist claims and particularist applications may be "resolved" (or least defused) by dissociating them from each other and locating them at different levels of generality.

24. The court did not order Bakke's admission, on the grounds that he did not show that he would have been admitted in the absence of the affirmative action plan.

25. Section 1 reads in part: "No State shall make or enforce any law which shall abridge the privileges or immunities of citizens of the United States; nor shall any State deprive any person of life, liberty, or property, without due process of law; nor deny to any person within its jurisdiction the equal protection of the laws."

26. Title VI is an integral part of the far-reaching Civil Rights Act of 1964. At the time the problem confronting Congress was discrimination against black citizens at the hands of recipients of federal monies, discrimination inconsistent with anti-discrimination provisions of the constitutional document. The bill's purpose was to give blacks the same rights and opportunities that white people take for granted. It did not create any new standard of equal treatment beyond that seen by the legislators to be contained in the document. When Title VI legislation was being debated, Congress was not concerned with the legality of "reverse discrimination" or "affirmative action" programs. Although the use of a racial quota or "set-aside" by a recipient of federal funds would constitute a direct violation of Title VI if that statute were read to prohibit race-conscious action, the congressional debate at the time did not consider even the possibility that the quota provisions for minority contractors might in any way conflict with or modify Title VI. The court has also declined to adopt a "color-blind" interpretation of other statutes containing non-discrimination provisions similar to that contained in Title VI (for example: *Albemarle Paper Co.* v. *Moody* (1975); *Franks* v. *Bowman Transportation Co.* (1976); *Teamsters* v. *United States* (1977); *United Jewish Organizations of Williamsburg* v. *Carey* (1977)).

    Section 601 of Title VI provides that "No person in the United States shall, on the ground of race, color, or national origin, be excluded from participation in, be denied the benefits of, or be subjected to discrimination under any program or activity receiving Federal financial assistance." 42 USC paragraph 2000d.

27. Justice Powell for the majority. Again: "Preferring members of any one group for no reason other than race or ethnic origin is discrimination for its own sake," and the "guarantee of equal protection cannot mean one thing when applied to one individual and something else when applied to a person of another color" (Bakke 1978: 2734).

28. The "need for effective social policies promoting racial justice in a society beset by deep-rooted racial inequities" rejects the race-neutrality of universalism as it implies the necessity of race-consciousness for effective social policy, according to Justice Brennan in *United Jewish Organizations of Williamsburgh* v. *Carey* (1977: 1014). The majority opinion argued for the constitutionality of congressionally required benign discrimination with respect to voting.

29. "In the most open of political processes, blacks may nevertheless require special solicitude because their status as a 'discrete and insular' class subject to prejudice leaves them particularly vulnerable to oppression by the dominant majority. Due to their monopoly on the attributes of wealth and power and their dominance at the state and national levels, whites simply do not require extraordinary protection from majoritarian politics at the local level" (*City of Richmond* v. *J. A. Croson Co.* (109 S. Ct. 706 (1989: 724)).

30. In fact the presentation to a court by counsel of statistical or social scientific evidence (rather than or in addition to purely legal arguments) has been widespread and extensive since its explicit recognition by the Supreme Court in 1908 (*Muller* v. *Oregon*, concerning the constitutionality of a statute limiting women's work in certain establishments to a maximum of 10 hours per day). In the Supreme Court during five terms between 1954 and 1974 such evidence was relied upon in about one third of the approximately 1,270 majority, concurring or dissenting opinions delivered in a total of 601 cases (Abraham 1980: 248). Of course such evidence was not always crucial to the decision reached. Racial discrimination, incidentally, was one of the four areas where such evidence was most heavily used.

31. Justice Stone. Emphasis added.

32. "Unlike discrimination against racial minorities, the use of racial preferences for remedial purposes does not inflict a pervasive injury upon individual whites in the sense that wherever they go or whatever they do there is a significant likelihood that they will be treated as second-class citizens because of their color" (Bakke 1978: 2791–2). Justices Brennan, White, Marshall, Blackmun, concurring with the judgment in part and dissenting in part.

33. Justice Powell in the passage cited in *Universalist argument (3)* may mean preserving constitutional application from change for "significant" periods of time. But what constitutes a "significant" length? This vagueness is unavoidable, inasmuch as any strict definition cannot but be arbitrary, but it leaves us without practical guidelines for determining which application of the constitutional document is "consistent." Powell's reference to "consistent application of the Constitution from one generation to the next, a critical feature of its coherent interpretation" (Bakke 1978: 2752–3), is more metaphor than measure: for how many generations must an application be preserved in order to count as "consistent"?

34. Justices Brennan, White, Marshall, Blackmun. Indeed, "Where there is a need to overcome the effects of past racially discriminatory or exclusionary practices engaged in by a federally funded institution, race-conscious action is not only permitted but required to accomplish the remedial objectives of Title VI" (Bakke 1978: 2775). The text of Title VI is quoted in note 26.

35. Justices Brennan, White, Marshall, Blackmun.

36. This landmark decision upheld the state's racial segregation of railroad passengers.

37. Elsewhere the Supreme Court recognized that requiring color-blindness "against the background of segregation, would render illusory the promise of *Brown* [v. *Board of Education* (1954)]" (Justice Burger, *North Carolina* v. *Swann* (1971: 45–6).

    A similar argument is made by Feminist Legal Theory against the constitutional interpretation of sexual equality as complete gender-neutrality. Feminist theory argues that an ideal of gender-neutrality cannot bring about a condition of substantive equality when the allegedly "neutral" state of affairs against which moral and social progress is to be judged itself conceals a bias against women. Feminist theory further argues that gender-neutrality ignores certain differences between men and women – notably the unique needs of women arising out of pregnancy and childbirth – which should be treated as a special condition (for example by employers, by granting non-punitive leave) even though no comparable conditions exist for male employees (and consequently no comparable treatment by the employer). See for example West (1988) and Law (1984).

38. For example Ely (1980: 14, 15, 28, 33) argues that the Fourteenth Amendment contains provisions that can be read responsibly only as broad invitations to

import into interpretation considerations not found in the amendment's language or in the debates that led to it. This is especially true of the Fourteenth Amendment's Due Process Clause, which provides that no state shall "deprive any person of life, liberty, or property, without due process of law." Recorded comment at the time of the amendment's replication is devoid of any reference that might give the provision more than a procedural connotation.

Again, Ely maintains that the most plausible interpretation of the Privileges or Immunities Clause – "No State shall make or enforce any law which shall abridge the privileges or immunities of citizens of the United States" – is that it was a delegation to future constitutional interpreters to protect certain rights the document neither lists (at least not exhaustively) nor even gives directions for finding.

Finally, the Equal Protection Clause does not apply to the federal government. Yet according to Ely a concept of equal protection may be seen to apply to the federal government on the basis of the Ninth Amendment ("The enumeration in the Constitution, of certain rights, shall not be construed to deny or disparage others retained by the people."). What Ely takes to be the concept of representation at the Constitution's core allows such an open-ended provision to include an equal protection component.

39. Indeed, Halliday (1970) goes so far as to maintain that any language's grammatical system is itself closely related to the social and personal needs the language is required to serve.

40. Coase (1960) for example offers a supposedly objective, normatively neutral exchange calculus by which courts would simply assign any "right" in question to the party willing to purchase that right were it assigned to the other party (assuming zero transaction costs). By definition any other result would be inefficient (that is, costly): granting the right to the party for whom it had less value (thereby violating exchange equilibrium), or (in order to achieve equilibrium) adding unnecessary exchange transaction costs. Any resulting unwanted distribution consequences are regarded as a political (that is, normative) issue and hence should be ignored by judges and left to the legislators.

References

Abel, Richard L. 1979. Delegalization: A critical review of its ideology, manifestations, and social consequences. In E. Blankenburg, E. Klausa, and H. Rottleuthner (eds) *Alternative Rechtsformen und Alternativen zum Recht*, pp. 27–47. Opladen, West Germany: Westdeutscher Verlag.

Abraham, Henry J. 1980. *The Judicial Process: An Introductory Analysis of the Courts of the United States, England and France*, 4th edn. New York: Oxford University Press.

Altman, Andrew. 1986. Legal realism, critical legal studies, and Dworkin. *Philosophy and Public Affairs* 15: 205–35.

Atiyah, Patrick S. 1978. *From Principles to Pragmatism*. Oxford: Oxford University Press.

Bakke 1978. *Regents of the University of California* v. *Bakke*. 98 S. Ct. 2733.

Bator, Paul. 1981. The state courts and federal constitutional litigation. *William & Mary Law Review* 22: 605–37.

Black, Donald J. 1972. The boundaries of legal sociology. *Yale Law Journal* 81: 1086–100.

Bork, Robert. 1971. Neutral principles and some first amendment problems. *Indiana Law Journal* 47: 21–31.

Brest, Paul. 1980. The misconceived quest for the original understanding. *Boston University Law Review* 60: 204–38.
Brest, Paul. 1981. The substance of process. *Ohio State Law Journal* 42: 131–42.
Brown v. Board of Education. 1954. 347 U.S. 483.
City of Richmond v. J. A. Croson Co. 1989. 109 S. Ct. 706.
Coase, Ronald. 1960. The problem of social cost. *Journal of Law and Economics* 3: 1–44.
Cotterrell, Roger. 1984. *The Sociology of Law*. London: Butterworth.
Cox, Archibald. 1976. *The Role of the Supreme Court in American Government*. New York: Oxford University Press.
Durkheim, Emil. 1964. *The Division of Labour in Society*. London: Free Press.
Dworkin, Ronald. 1977. *Taking Rights Seriously*. Cambridge, Mass.: Harvard University Press.
Dworkin, Ronald. 1986. *Law's Empire*. Cambridge, Mass.: Harvard University Press.
Ely, John Hart. 1980. *Democracy and Distrust*. Cambridge, Mass.: Harvard University Press.
Feyerabend, Paul K. 1988. *Against Method*, rev. edn. London: Verso.
Fish, Stanley. 1980. *Is There a Text in this Class?* Cambridge, Mass.: Harvard University Press.
Foucault, Michel. 1972. *The Archaeology of Knowledge*. New York: Pantheon Books.
Fowler, Roger. 1981. *Literature as Social Discourse*. London: Batsford Academic and Educational.
Friedman, Wolfgang. 1967. *Law in a Changing Society*, 2nd edn. Harmondsworth: Penguin.
Fuller, Lon. 1969. *The Morality of Law*, rev. edn. New Haven, Conn.: Yale University Press.
Gilbert, G. Nigel and Mulkay, Michael. 1984. *Opening Pandora's Box*. Cambridge: Cambridge University Press.
Goldman, Sheldon and Jahnige, Thomas P. 1976. *The Federal Courts as a Political System*, 2nd edn. New York: Harper & Row.
Grace, Clive and Wilkinson, Philip. 1978. *Sociological Inquiry and Legal Phenomena*. New York: St Martin's Press.
Greenawalt, Kent. 1983. How empty is the idea of equality? *Columbia Law Review* 83: 1167–85.
Habermas, Jürgen. 1984. *The Theory of Communicative Action*, Vol. I. Boston, Mass.: Beacon Press.
Halliday, Michael A. K. 1970. Language structure and language function. In J. Lyons (ed.) *New Horizons in Linguistics*, pp. 140–65. Harmondsworth: Penguin.
Hart, H. L. A. 1961. *The Concept of Law*. Oxford: Clarendon Press.
Katz, Stanley N. 1988. The strange birth and unlikely history of constitutional equality. *Journal of American History* 75: 747–62.
Kairys, David. 1982. Legal reasoning. In David Kairys (ed.) *Politics of Law*, pp. 11–17. New York: Pantheon Books.
Kamenka, Eugene and Tay, Alice Erh-Soon. 1975. Beyond bourgeois individualism: The contemporary crisis in law and legal ideology. In Eugene Kamenka and R. S. Neale (eds) *Feudalism, Capitalism and Beyond*, pp. 127–44. London: Edward Arnold.
Kuhn, Thomas. 1970. *The Structure of Scientific Revolutions*, 2nd edn. Chicago: University of Chicago Press.
Law, Sylvia. 1984. Rethinking sex and the Constitution. *University of Pennsylvania Law Review* 132: 955–1040.
Levinson, Sanford. 1982. Law as literature. *Texas Law Review* 60: 373–403.
MacIntyre, Alasdair. 1984. *After Virtue*. Notre Dame, Ind.: University of Notre Dame Press.

McDonald, Forrest. 1985. *Novus Ordo Seclorum*. Lawrence, Kans.: University Press of Kansas.

Muller v. *Oregon*. 1908. 208 U.S. 412.

Murphy, Walter F., Fleming, James E., and Harris, William F. 1986. *American Constitutional Interpretation*. Mineola, NY: Foundation Press.

Nonet, Philippe and Selznick, Philip. 1978. *Law and Society in Transition*. New York: Harper & Row.

North Carolina v. *Swann*. 1971. 402 U.S. 443.

Posner, Richard. 1977. *Economic Analysis of Law*, 2nd edn. Boston: Little, Brown.

Pound, Roscoe. 1954. *Introduction to the Philosophy of Law*, rev. edn. New Haven, Conn.: Yale University Press.

Plessey v. *Ferguson*. 1896. 163 U.S. 537.

Quine, W. V. O. 1990. *Pursuit of Truth*. Cambridge, Mass.: Harvard University Press.

Rorty, Richard. 1979. *Philosophy and the Mirror of Nature*. Princeton, NJ: Princeton University Press.

Rorty, Richard. 1982. *Consequences of Pragmatism*. Minneapolis, Minn.: University of Minnesota Press.

Teubner, Gunther. 1983. Substantive and reflexive elements in modern law. *Law and Society Review* 17: 239–85.

Tribe, Lawrence H. 1978. *American Constitutional Law*. Mineola, NY: Foundation Press.

Unger, Roberto M. 1976. *Law in Modern Society*. New York: Free Press.

United Jewish Organizations of Williamsburgh v. *Carey*. 1977. 97 S. Ct. 996.

United States v. *Carolene Products Co*. 1938. 304 U.S. 144.

Vining, Joseph. 1990. Generalization in interpretive theory. *Representations* 30: 1–12.

Wasserstrom, Richard A. 1977. Racism, sexism, and preferential treatment: An approach to the topics. *UCLA Law Review* 24: 581–622.

Weber, Max. 1946. *From Max Weber*, edited by H. H. Gerth and E. Wright Mills. New York: Oxford University Press.

Weber, Max. 1978. *Economy and Society*. Berkeley, Calif.: University of California Press.

West, Robin. 1988. Jurisprudence and gender. *University of Chicago Law Review* 55: 1–72.

Westen, Peter. 1983. The meaning of equality in law, science, math, and morals: A reply. *Michigan Law Review* 81: 604–63.

Winkler, J. T. 1975. Law, state and economy: The Industry Act 1975 in context. *British Journal of Law and Society* 2: 103–28.

12

The role of elites in setting agendas for public debate: a historical case

Richard L. Rogers

During the late eighteenth and early nineteenth centuries the United States experienced successive waves of religious enthusiasm, now commonly referred to as the Second Great Awakening. Millenarianism was an important component of the awakening.[1] Evangelicals carefully crafted exegeses of Bible prophecy to estimate the time of the coming of the millennium. Millerite itinerants created a major stir with their announcement that Jesus would return on October 22, 1844. Those wishing to pass the "last days" in the security of a setting isolated from contact with the sinful world could chose from a smorgasbord of communitarian groups.[2]

Why was millennialism so prominent in early republican America? In this essay I argue that it was an idiom that became widely disseminated due to elite Protestants who were able to shape the substance of theological discourse through their control of the religious press prior to the start of the nineteenth century. My aims, however, are not solely historiographical. Explanations of the fervor of the era have drawn heavily upon social scientific interpretations of religious movements, and the interpretation of early republican millennialism here offered provides an opportunity to reassess the validity of these general theories.

Millennialism and the Second Great Awakening

Early republican millennialism took three forms – elite, popular, and radical. Although the adherents of each differed tremendously in terms of their social status and the level of their integration into American society, they nevertheless appropriated the same set of symbols in their discussions of the direction of American history.[3]

Elite millennialism

The elite evangelicalism of the Second Great Awakening consisted of an informal network of Congregationalists, Presbyterians, Reformed Dutch, and Episcopalians. This coalition was committed to the preservation of the Standing Order, and they organized numerous societies to promote the spiritual and moral regeneration of the new nation in the face of what they regarded as the deleterious effects of a host of social changes: democratization, urbanization, immigration, the expansion of the frontier, and the spread of Catholicism, deism, and popular religious groups such as the Methodists and Baptists (Andrew 1976; Griffin 1960).

Their eschatology was anchored in a style of biblical exegesis developed in England and Scotland by the Protestant intellectual elite, a group whose leading eschatologists included some of the best mathematical and scientific minds of their time: John Napier, Sir Isaac Newton, and William Whiston (Davidson 1977; Toon 1972). Its distinctive feature was the chronology. The Bible, it was noted, offers numerous hints about the ordering and timing of events before the coming of the last days. For example, the Book of Revelation mentions circumstances that would accompany the opening of each of seven seals (Rev. 6–8), the sounding of each of seven trumpets (Rev. 8–11), and the pouring out of each of the seven vials of God's wrath (Rev. 16). Three events are said to last 1,260 days each: the trampling of the holy city by the Gentiles (Rev. 11: 2), the prophesying of the two witnesses (Rev. 11: 3), and the refuge of the woman in the wilderness (Rev. 12: 6).[4] The vision of Daniel chapter 8 would take 2,300 days to fulfill (Dan. 8: 14), and in Daniel 12 the time from the abolishment of the daily sacrifice to the setting up of the abomination that causes desolation was said to be 1,290 days, and the end would come after 1,335 days (Dan. 12: 11–13).

The chronologies constructed were attempts to discern the direction of history by identifying which prophetic events had already been fulfilled. For example, Joseph Mede, one of the Puritan intellectuals at Cambridge in the early seventeenth century, regarded the seven seals of the Apocalypse as periods within the Roman Empire. He also asserted that the rise of Islam was foreshadowed: the Saracens were the locusts of the fifth trumpet, and with the sounding of the sixth trumpet after the year 1300 the powerful Turkish armies had been released on the world. The three 1,260-day periods were in reality different descriptions of the same epoch in history – the 1,260-year reign of papal Rome, the Antichrist. The judgment of the Antichrist's kingdom would be dispensed through the pouring out of the seven vials, with the Reformation regarded as the turning of the waters into blood during the third vial.

In American Protestant eschatology was modified by the unique conditions under which New England society was organized (Davidson 1977; McLoughlin 1978: ch. 2; Stout 1986). God, it appeared, had reserved a vast amount of land for the establishment of a religious society free from the corruption associated with regions dominated by Catholicism or the Protestant state churches. If the biblical foundations of New England were not a step toward the New Jerusalem, they were at least prefiguring it. Some even raised the possibility that they had a special relationship with God in light of findings that were believed to show that the Indians were of Hebrew origin and quite possibly descendants of Israel's ten lost tribes. Prominent clergymen such as John Cotton, Increase and Cotton Mather, and Jonathan Edwards were among those speculating on the interpretation of prophecy.

The early republican elite consciously worked within the parameters established by previous generations of Anglo-American eschatologists. For example, Samuel Hopkins, the pre-eminent evangelical theologian of the post-Revolutionary period, began his *Treatise on the Millennium* (1793) by acknowledging the contributions of many of the prominent English and American writers of the previous century. *Observations on the Revelation of Jesus to Saint John* (1791) by Samuel Langdon, a prominent Congregational clergyman, and *The Second Advent* (1815) by Elias Boudinot, the president of the American Bible Society, directly refer to Joseph Mede and Isaac Newton. All three texts cite *Dissertations on the Prophecies* by the Anglican bishop Thomas Newton. First published in 1754, Newton's work went through dozens of editions in England and the United States.

The elite millennialism of the early republican period displayed two characteristics. First, it continued the Protestant preoccupation with chronology (Bloch 1985: 119 ff.; Miller 1976). The American Revolution was seen as the first step in the spread of civil and religious liberty globally. The fall of the Catholic monarchy in France was a sign that the dominion of the Antichrist was waning. The decline of the Ottoman Empire, also associated by some with the Antichrist, demonstrated that the forces of infidelity were in retreat.

Many projected that the beginning of the millennium would finally come around the year 2000 (see Hopkins 1793: 83–98). The pope was believed to have gained political power with the Donation of Pepin in AD 756, so the 1,260 years of the Antichrist's reign probably began around that time. Moreover, the world would have reached the six thousandth year of its existence. According to a widely maintained typological rendering of the creation story, the six days represented the duration of the world – a day in the sight of the Lord being a thousand human years (Ps. 90: 4; 2 Pet. 3: 8) – and the day of sabbath rest stood for the millennium. Many believed Old Testament genealogies dated the beginning of the world around 4000 BC, thus placing the expiration of the six millennial days around the year 2000.

Chronologizing, however, was widely recognized as a speculative activity, and there were many who felt free to establish more proximate dates. For instance, in *The Downfall of Mystical Babylon* (1793), David Austin, pastor of the Presbyterian church in Elizabethtown, New Jersey, claimed that the end of the Antichrist's reign would come by about 1810. This was on the grounds that the 1,260 years had started sometime between 500 and 553 as friction between Byzantium and the West enhanced the pope's political influence in Italy.

Second, elite millennialism was postmillennial in outlook.[5] This was a recognition of the symbolic nature of the images of the Book of Revelation (see Hopkins 1793: 44). Rather than looking for Jesus' second coming, the early republican elite believed that the millennium would come about through the conversion of the entire world to Jesus Christ and that they, in particular, had been assigned by God the task of organizing moral and evangelistic crusades to accomplish this (Banner 1973; Morse, Worcester, and Evarts 1811). Recurring waves of religious revivals were seen as proofs of the effectiveness of these endeavors, and the sweeping of revivals across New York state in the 1820s and 1830s convinced the evangelist Charles Finney that a highly mobilized Christian community could bring about the millennium in as little as three months (Johnson 1978: 3–4).

Popular millennialism

Popular evangelists of the early republican era – Methodists, Baptists, the Christian Connexion, the Campbellites, the Stonites – distinguished themselves from elite denominations with their opposition to the Standing Order, their anticlericalism, their reliance on lay leaders and untrained ministers, and their acceptance of the meaning of the Bible and religious emotions at face value (Hatch 1989). However, they shared with elite millennialism an interest in establishing a chronology. For example, the Methodist Lorenzo Dow associated the image of the dragon in the Book of Revelation with the papacy (Dow 1851). The seven heads of the dragon were identified with seven forms of government that existed in succession in pagan Rome, and the ten horns were ten governments rising after the sacking of Rome in 377. The 1,260 days expired in 1809 when Napoleon declared the French annexation of Italy and thereby ended the pope's civil authority. Moreover, the church, represented by the woman in Revelation 13, had made two flights into the wilderness to escape persecution: the one into northern Europe was due to the iconoclast controversy and the other was with the Puritan migration to the New World.

There were, however, at least two deviations from elite millennialism in popular thought. The first pertained to the identity of the Antichrist. In popular millennialism, the Antichrist was not only the pope or infidels like the Turks. The image of the Antichrist was extended to cover anyone setting up a "system of doctrine" or a "code of laws" over against "private judgment" on religious matters (Smith 1832: 50). Popular millennialism was especially critical of New England Congregationalists, who, it contended, had drifted away from the intentions of the original European settlers by mixing church and state (see Dow 1851: 108).

The second deviation was the emergence of premillennialism. Premillennialism cannot be regarded as solely the property of popular culture, nor were all forms of popular millennialism premillennial. But there was a special affinity between premillennialism and popular religion: the literal interpretation of the Scriptures was widely conceded to yield a premillennial eschatology, and those within the orbit of popular religion were most likely to interpret prophecy in this manner.

Thus it is not surprising that the most prominent manifestation of early republican premillennialism, the Millerite movement of the 1840s, was closely identified with popular culture (see Hatch 1989). The heart of Millerism was William Miller's calculation that Jesus would return by 1843 (Miller 1842). Napoleon's capture of Rome in 1798 marked the end of the prophetic 1,260 years that had started in 538, when earnest Christians allegedly moved to north-west Asia and north-east Europe to escape the influence of the Roman Catholic Church in the wake of a controversy over saints, images, and the church's infallibility. In addition, 1798 was 1,290 years after the abandonment of human sacrifice, when the last of the pagan conquerors of the Roman empire was converted to Christianity in 508, an event Miller identified as the abolition of the daily sacrifice. In addition, there would be 45 years between the fall of Babylon and Jesus' return (see Dan. 12: 11–12): 1798 + 45 = 1843 (Miller 1843). A slight revision he would make later put the "time" somewhere in the one-year period commencing March 21, 1843, and ending March 21, 1844.

After Jesus did not come by March, 1844, Miller's followers accepted Samuel Snow's modifications of the chronology, which calculated the date of Jesus' return for October 22, 1844 (Linden 1978). This day was the tenth day of the seventh month of the Old Testament calendar, the day on which the high priest entered the holy place to atone for the sins of the people (Exod. 30: 10; Lev. 26: 26–32). This ritual act, it was argued, foreshadowed the intercessory ministry of Jesus (Heb. 9).

Radical millennialism

The development of numerous communal groups during the Second Great Awakening also contained a millennial component (Barkun 1986). These groups emerged from within the sphere of popular evangelicals, but they were more radical than most popular groups. They established highly cohesive communities in order to isolate themselves from the world and promote alternative visions of society; these included departures from traditional sexual norms and an emphasis on the sharing of wealth. The millennium, they believed, was coming (or had already come) to those who adopted the alternative life-style.

Despite the severe break with the mainstream of American society, radicalism used many of the concepts developed within the other strands of millennialism. One of these was chronologizing. According to John Humphrey Noyes, founder of the Oneida community, the 1,260-year reign of the Antichrist stretched from the destruction of Jerusalem in AD 70 to the year AD 1330 (Noyes 1847: 329). After this latter date, he contended, the demise of the papacy was evident: Wycliff was born in 1324, and "[i]t is true (whether it has any thing to do with our prophecy or not) that the dispensation of the Reformation properly dates from the period between AD 1330 and 1400." Unlike evangelical writers, however, Noyes insisted that the second coming of Jesus had to be around the year AD 70 since the Bible associated Jesus' return with the destruction of Jerusalem and could not be wrong about such matters. The failure of the Christian church to recognize Christ's return had left it in a deluded state, and Noyes looked forward to a third appearance of Christ in the not-too-far distant future (Barkun 1986: 65–6).

Shakers likewise developed a chronology based on Bible prophecy in order to justify their faith in Ann Lee (*A Summary View* 1848: 203–11). They maintained that there were 1,290 prophetic days between the ascendancy of Pope Leo I in the year 457 and the beginning of Ann Lee's ministry in 1747, and the 2,300 days of Scripture stretched from the time of Daniel's prophecy in 553 BC until 1747.

Not all radical groups, however, chronologized; the end was either too close to bother with such an exercise or was seen as having already arrived. This did not prevent the incorporation of other themes that had been part of Anglo-American millennialism. Mormons, for instance, believed that the Indians were descendants of the Hebrews, and the millennial-day theory is mentioned in Joseph Smith's revelations (Bushman 1984: 133–9).

Interpreting early republican millennialism

Explanations of the emergence of early republican millennialism can be divided into two categories. The point of division is whether or not millennialism is seen as part of the mainstream of American society.

Classically, social scientific analyses of millenarian movements have regarded such groups as marginal members of their society, whose perceptions of powerlessness or poverty lead them to use the promise of a better age to come as a means to compensate for their current destitution (Aberle 1962; Barber 1941; Cohn 1970; Talmon 1962, 1968).

During the first part of the twentieth century, this idea shaped the interpretation of the Second Great Awakening by attributing the awakening to frontier origins (Cleveland 1916; Davenport 1917; Sweet 1952; Tyler 1944). The frontier was described as an isolated, culturally backward region settled by people who were lazy and uncivilized. Revival services and camp meetings provided contexts in which charismatic itinerants were able to generate a type of mass hysteria that took the form of religious enthusiasm.

Others have argued that millenarianism is more accurately associated with tightly knit social groups whose cohesion insulates them from the outside world (Barkun 1974; Douglas 1970, 1982). In his book *Crucible of the Millennium* (1986), Michael Barkun uses the Second Great Awakening in making the most extensive test of this notion. Millerism and communitarian groups, he contends, thrived in a context where depleted soil conditions and economic depression produced closely knit groups of family and friends. Postmillennialist groups, however, are not regarded as truly millennialist: the conviction of many elite evangelicals that the millennium would not come until around the year 2000 robbed them of a sense of imminency, and the belief that the millennium could be achieved through human initiatives such as evangelism and moral reform minimized the extensiveness of the transformation anticipated.

Despite the different explanations of millenarian movements offered by these approaches, they share a common conviction that millennialism must of necessity be relegated to groups that are not well integrated into the society. Such statements, however, are of little utility in the explanation of early republican millennialism for at least two reasons. First, millennialism is seen solely as the product of situationally contingent conditions with no reference to the broader trends in the development of Protestant eschatology. The use of a chronology, for example, was not a Millerite innovation; it had been a feature of Anglo-American millennialism since the sixteenth century. Second, the pervasiveness of millennialism in the mainstream of American culture is not recognized. The Millerites cannot be regarded as either poor or rural; their net worth was above average, and their centers of support were rapidly growing manufacturing towns (Rogers 1986; Rowe 1985: 106). Moreover, the millennial expectancy of postmillennialists should not be dismissed as easily as has been done. It provided the motivation for the establishment of national voluntary societies committed to the transformation of American society, and individuals such as David Austin and Charles Finney shared William Miller's anticipation that the culmination of prophecy was near.

Efforts to overcome these deficiencies have heightened the appeal of a second class of interpretations recognizing the continuities of millennial speculation over time and across strands. One approach regards millennialism as a fundamental part of an American cultural consensus having its roots in Puritanism (McLoughlin 1978). This argument, however, stresses only the forces for uniformity in American culture without coping with its diversity. As a result, the idea of cultural continuities in eschatological thought has been recast, in order to stress the importance of one particular subculture within the society in purveying millennial expectation, namely, the Puritans and their descendants, the New England Yankees (Cross 1950: ch. 1; Hammond 1979). This argument has a greater degree of plausibility: Yankees did have an inordinate amount of influence in early republican society, and the New England elite did not shy away from publicly promoting religious and moral causes that, if successful, would have turned American society into a Yankee paradise (Andrew 1976).

In the development of this argument, little attention has been given to the processes of communication on which the dissemination and preservation of ideas depends; most people have been content to attribute the spread of millennialism to some vaguely defined institutionalization of Puritan culture. The failure to investigate these processes has complicated the study of early republican religion once the polarization of elite and popular cultures is considered.

Specifically, the emergence of popular religious culture in many ways marked a break in the continuity of the Puritan influence in American life. The antagonism toward the elite was expressed in the rejection of salient features of Puritanism and elite religion, such as its Calvinistic view of the social hierarchy, the formality of worship, and its elevation of the clergy.

Millennialism and agenda setting

The unresolved problem, then, of current scholarship on early republican millennialism is the discovery of how similar eschatological concepts could develop in both elite and popular religious cultures. In so doing, I have appropriated the concept of agenda setting.

The term "agenda setting" refers to the ability to shape the topics of public discourse (see Iyengar and Kinder 1987; Shaw and McCombs 1977). Research on media influence in presidential elections has found that the public at large sifts through a large number of possible issues and reaches an agreement on which issues are most important. This is in spite of divergence regarding party preference. This phenomenon has been attributed directly to the influence of the mass media: by highlighting certain issues, the media are able to divert public attention toward some topics and away from others. The media, however, do not determine people's conclusions on these matters; information is derived from other sources, such as personal networks and their life experiences. In short, the media control what topics one thinks about but not how one thinks about them.

241

The ability to set agendas, of course, is not limited simply to the media. Any social institution involved in the dissemination of information – churches, schools, and government agencies – has this capacity. Those who control these information-disseminating institutions can influence what topics are given priority in public discourse.

Until the end of the eighteenth century, the ability to set the agenda for theological debate resided primarily with the clergy of elite denominations. Sunday sermons, Thursday lectures, and occasional preaching all provided opportunities to influence public discourse (Stout 1986), and state sponsorship of these denominations restricted the potential threats to authority raised by popular evangelicalism.

Books were the key medium by which elite eschatology permeated popular religious culture. Prior to 1800 ordinary families had few books in their home (Hall 1983). To meet the desire to learn more about the Bible and build oneself spiritually, many of these books were religious in nature. People entering the ministry in popular denominations, or otherwise desirous of extraordinary religious instruction, made special efforts to buy or borrow books in order to supplement their lack of a formal theological education (Rhys 1983: 237–8; Thrift 1823: 18).

This pattern of self-education inadvertently placed popular religious culture under the influence of elites. Prior to the emergence of the popular press in the nineteenth century, publication costs could be prohibitive and printers often raised subscriptions in advance of production to cover their expenses. These high costs minimized popular involvement in the book industry, and as a result those materials that were published often reflected elite tastes. Consequently, ordinary people who wanted reading materials were often forced to think about those topics appealing to elites.

There is considerable evidence that the reading habits of popular religious leaders were a conduit for exposing them to elite millennialism. For instance, at the start of his book of sermons on Bible prophecy (1808: iii), Elias Smith, founder of the Christian Connexion, presents a reading list including Thomas Newton's *Dissertations on the Prophecies* and Samuel Hopkin's *A Treatise on the Millennium*. Isaac Backus, a Baptist leader in the north-east, had evidently read Samuel Langdon's *Observations on the Revelation of Jesus to St. John*, as suggested by a 1792 entry in his diary (McLoughlin 1979: 1335). Methodism's Francis Asbury was also familiar with elite millennialists: his reading list included Edwards' *Thoughts concerning the Present Revival of Religion in New England*, Thomas Newton's *Dissertations* (read at least three times!), and probably Langdon's *Observations* (Clark 1958, I: 236; Lang 1972).

The development of the popular religious press in the early nineteenth century altered the flow of information by providing popular religious leaders the ability to set their own agendas. It created an arena in which they could conduct debates without going through channels dominated by the elite. For example, communitarian Robert Owen published attacks on the credibility of the Bible in his periodical *New Harmony Gazette* (Humble 1952). Alexander Campbell read Owen's paper and responded through his own *Christian Baptist*. Later the two met face-to-face in a highly celebrated debate in Cincinnati.

However, the connection with elite millennialism had already been established, and with the rise of the popular press, interest in it did not diminish. Noyes (1847) published his responses to an essay on Matthew chapter 24 by the editor of *Bibliotheca Sacra*, Edward Robinson, and a book on the resurrection of the dead by George Bush, professor of Hebrew at New York City University. Millerite papers regularly published debates on the interpretation of Bible prophecy and included reviews of recent books.

Discussion

In this essay I have laid the foundations of a case for viewing the widespread dissemination of millennialism in the early republic as a consequence of the ability of religious elites to shape the agenda of theological discourse. My ultimate aim, however, is to address the broader questions of the relationship of society and ideology in the sociology of religion.

The sociology of religion has been shaped considerably by the assumption that there is a one-to-one correspondence between some aspect of society and its belief: specific types of doctrines are the product of particular kinds of social arrangements or, conversely, particular social arrangements emerge as a result of adherence to specific doctrines. This notion permeates classical approaches to religion such as the church-sect typology, the theory of secularization, and Weber's Protestant ethic thesis. Attempts to move away from the limits of classical sociology such as grid-group analysis (Douglas 1970, 1982) or the "world systems" approach to religious movements (see Wuthnow 1987) have yet to abandon this assumption.

However, it is clear that the spread of a religious belief or movement cannot always be related to a single condition. For example, the conditions accounting for the global spread of Protestantism cannot be described solely in terms of the Reformation, nor can Catholicism's appeal be reduced to a set of propositions rooted in the life-style of medieval Europeans. Even fairly specific movements such as Millerism cannot be reduced to any single setting (Rogers 1986). Looking at the setting of theological agendas provides a framework in which the sociology of religion can be fundamentally reworked without the limits imposed on it by the notion of one-to-one correspondence.

The ramifications of such a reorientation could be especially important in the study of millenarian movements. Within the study of American millennialism, the approach presented in this paper can obviously be extended into other time periods in which millennial themes were part of the mainstream of American culture (see McLoughlin 1978; Moorehead 1978; Weber 1979). More intriguing, however, is the extension of this idea to the study of Third-World millenarianism. Here researchers have frequently noted in passing that these movements have appropriated ideas from Christian missionaries without exploring in any detail the process by which this appropriation occurred. If this dissemination of millenarianism can be tied in some way to agenda setting in the cultural realm, the possibility exists that Christian missions may have had a far greater impact on Third-World cultures than has been presently recognized.

Notes

1. The way in which the terms millenarianism and millennialism are used vary considerably in the literature. In this paper I use the term millenarian to refer to any movement, regardless of its religious tradition, that believes that the end of the world or an uncorrupted epoch in human civilization is imminent (see Barkun 1986: 11–12). Millennialism is the form of millenarianism generic to Christianity. The term millennium literally means a thousand years, and in Christian eschatology it refers to the thousand-year reign of Christ on earth as prophesied in Revelation 20: 1–6. Historians and sociologists generally broaden the term millennial to include groups emphasizing the proximity of any of the principal events associated with the "last days" (the second coming of Jesus, the day of judgment, etc.) even if they do not subscribe specifically to the doctrine of the millennium.
2. Excellent summaries of the events of the Second Great Awakening can be found in Ahlstrom (1972), Cross (1950), Griffin (1960), and Hatch (1989).
3. For a more thorough summary of early republican writings on the millennium than is provided here, see Bloch (1985), Davidson (1977), Froom (1954), and Miller (1976). Several exemplary texts are cited where appropriate.
4. The duration of time during which the Gentiles will trample the holy city is literally 42 months. Using thirty-day months, this period can be shown to be 1,260 days long.
5. Within Christian eschatology a number of opinions have been offered regarding the relationship of Jesus' second coming to the millennium. The two most important to Anglo-American evangelicalism have been premillennialism and postmillennialism. Premillennialism is founded on a literal reading of Scripture: Jesus Christ will corporeally return to earth prior to the establishment of the millennium or the end of the world. Postmillennialism interprets the biblical reference to the millennium figuratively: Christ's thousand-year reign is a spiritual (not literal or physical) kingdom brought about by the conversion of the entire world to Christianity. According to this latter position, Christ's physical return, if it happens at all, will be after the millennial kingdom.

References

Aberle, David F. 1962. A note on relative deprivation theory as applied to millenarian and other cult movements. In Sylvia Thrupp (ed.) *Millennial Dreams in Action: Essays in Comparative Study*, pp. 209–14. The Hague: Mouton.

Ahlstrom, Sidney. 1972. *A Religious History of the American People*. New Haven, Conn.: Yale University Press.

Andrew, John, III. 1976. *Rebuilding the Christian Commonwealth: New England Congregationalists and Foreign Missions, 1800–1830*. Lexington, Ky.: University of Kentucky Press.

Austin, David. 1794. The downfall of mystical Babylon; or, a key to the providence of God, in the political operations of 1793–4. In David Austin (comp.) *The Millennium; or, the Thousand Years of Prosperity*, pp. 325–426. Elizabethtown, NJ: Shepard Kollock.

Banner, Lois. 1973. Religious benevolence as social control: A critique of an interpretation. *Journal of American History* 60: 23–41.

Barber, Bernard. 1941. Acculturation and messianic movements. *American Sociological Review* 6: 663–9.

Barkun, Michael. 1974. *Disaster and the Millennium*. New Haven, Conn.: Yale University Press.

Barkun, Michael. 1986. *Crucible of the Millennium: The Burned-Over District of New York in the 1840s*. Syracuse, NY: Syracuse University Press.

Bloch, Ruth H. 1985. *Visionary Republic: Millennial Themes in American Thought, 1756–1800*. Cambridge: Cambridge University Press.

Boudinot, Elias. 1815. *The Second Advent, or Coming of the Messiah in Glory, shown to be a Scripture Doctrine and Taught by Divine Revelation from the Beginning of the World*. Trenton, NJ: D. Fenton & S. Hutchinson.

Bushman, Richard L. 1984. *Joseph Smith and the Beginnings of Mormonism*. Urbana, Ill.: University of Illinois Press.

Clark, Elmer T. (ed.) 1958. *The Journal and Letters of Francis Asbury*. 3 vols. London: Epworth Press.

Cleveland, Catharine C. 1916. *The Great Revival in the West, 1797–1805*. Chicago: University of Chicago Press.

Cohn, Norman R. C. 1970. *The Pursuit of the Millennium: Revolutionary Millenarians and Mystical Anarchists of the Middle Ages*, rev. edn. New York: Oxford University Press.

Cross, Whitney R. 1950. *The Burned-Over District: The Social and Intellectual History of Enthusiastic Religion in Western New York, 1800–1850*. Ithaca, NY: Cornell University Press.

Davidson, James W. 1977. *The Logic of Millennial Thought: Eighteenth-Century New England*. New Haven, Conn.: Yale University Press.

Davenport, Frederick M. 1917. *Primitive Traits in Religious Revivals: A Study in Mental and Social Evolution*. New York: Macmillan.

Douglas, Mary T. 1970. *Natural Symbols: Explorations in Cosmology*. New York: Pantheon Books.

Douglas, Mary (ed.) 1982. *Essays in the Sociology of Perception*. London: Routledge & Kegan Paul.

Dow, Lorenzo. 1851. *The Dealings of God, Man, and the Devil; as exemplified in the Life, Experience, and Travels of Lorenzo Dow*. New York: Cornish, Lamport.

Froom, LeRoy Edwin. 1954. *The Prophetic Faith of our Fathers: The Historical Development of Prophetic Interpretation*. Washington, DC: Review and Herald Publishing Association.

Griffin, Clifford S. 1960. *Their Brothers' Keepers: Moral Stewardship in the United States, 1800–1865*. New Brunswick, NJ: Rutgers University Press and New York: Alfred A. Knopf.

Hall, David D. 1983. The uses of literacy in New England, 1600–1850. In William L. Joyce *et al.* (eds) *Printing and Society in Early America*, pp. 1–47. Worcester, Mass.: American Antiquarian Society.

Hammond, John C. 1978. *The Politics of Benevolence*. New York: Ablex.

Hatch, Nathan O. 1989. *The Democratization of American Christianity*. New Haven, Conn.: Yale University Press.

Hopkins, Samuel. 1793. *A Treatise of the Millennium*. Boston, Mass.: Isaiah Thomas & Ebenezer T. Andrews. Reprinted New York: Arno Press, 1972.

Humble, Bill J. 1952. *Campbell and Controversy: The Story of Alexander Campbell's Great Debates with Skepticism, Catholicism, and Presbyterianism* (no publisher).

Iyengar, Shanto and Kinder, Donald R. 1987. *News that Matters: Television and American Opinion*. Chicago: University of Chicago Press.

Johnson, Paul. 1978. *A Shopkeeper's Millennium: Society and Revivals in Rochester, New York, 1815–1837*. New York: Hill & Wang.

Lang, Edward M., Jr. 1972. *Francis Asbury's Reading of Theology: A Bibliographic Study*. Evanston, Ill.: Garrett Theological Seminary.

Langdon, Samuel. 1791. *Observations on the Revelation of Jesus Christ to St. John*. Worcester, Mass.: Isaiah Thomas.

Linden, Ingemar. 1978. *The Last Trump: A Historico-Genetical Study of Some Important Chapters in the Making and Development of the Seventh-Day Adventist Church*. Studies in the Intercultural History of Christianity, Vol. 17. Frankfurt-on-Main: Peter Lang.

McLoughlin, William G. 1978. *Revivals, Awakenings, and Reform: An Essay on Religious and Social Change in America, 1607–1977*. Chicago: University of Chicago Press.

McLoughlin, William (ed.) 1979. *The Diary of Isaac Backus*. Providence, RI: Brown University Press.

Miller, Glenn. 1976. "Fashionable to Prophecy": Presbyterians, the Millennium and Revolution. *Amerika Studien* 21: 239–60.

Miller, William. 1842. *Evidence from Scripture and History of the Second Coming of Christ, about the Year 1843*. Boston, Mass.: Joshua V. Himes.

Moorehead, James. 1978. *American Apocalypse: Yankee Protestants and the Civil War, 1860–1869*. New Haven, Conn.: Yale University Press.

Morse, Jedidiah, Worcester, Samuel, and Evarts, Jeremiah. 1811. Address to the Christian Public. In *First Ten Annual Reports of the American Board of Commissioners for Foreign Missions*, pp. 25–30. Boston, Mass.: Crocker & Brewster.

Noyes, John Humphrey. 1847. *The Berean: A Manual for the help of those who Seek the Faith of the Primitive Church*. Putney, Vt: The Spiritual Magazine. Reprinted New York: Arno Press, 1969.

Rhys, Isaac. 1983. Books and the social authority of learning. In William L. Joyce *et al.* (eds) *Printing and Society in Early America*, pp. 228–49. Worcester, Mass.: American Antiquarian Society.

Rogers, Richard. 1986. *Millennialism and American Culture: The Adventist Movement, 1831–1851*. Paper presented at the annual meetings of the Society for the Scientific Study of Religion, Washington, DC.

Rowe, David L. 1985. *Thunder and Trumpets: Millerites and Dissenting Religion in Upstate New York, 1800–1850*. Chico, Calif.: Scholars Press.

Ryan, Mary P. 1981. *Cradle of the Middle Class: The Family in Oneida County, New York, 1790–1865*. Cambridge: Cambridge University Press.

Shaw, Donald L. and McCombs, Maxwell E. 1977. *The Emergence of American Political Issues: The Agenda-Setting Function of the Press*. St Paul, Minn.: West Publishing Company.

Smith, Elias. 1808. *Sermons, containing an Illustration to the Prophecies*. Exeter, NH: Norris & Sawyer.

Smith, Elias. 1832. *A New Testament Dictionary*, ed. Robert Foster. Portsmouth, NH: Christian Herald Office.

Stout, Harry S. 1986. *The New England Soul: Preaching and Religious Culture in Colonial New England*. New York: Oxford University Press.

A Summary View of the Millennial Church, or United Society of Believers, commonly called Shakers 1848, 2nd edn., revised. Albany, NY: C. Van Benthuysen.

Sweet, William Warren. 1952. *Religion in the Development of American Culture, 1765–1840*. New York: Charles Scribner's Sons.

Talmon, Yonina. 1962. Pursuit of the millennium: The relation between religious and social change. *European Journal of Sociology* 3: 125–40.

Talmon, Yonina. 1968. Millenarism. In David L. Sills (ed.) *International Encyclopedia of the Social Sciences, vol. 10*, pp. 349–62. New York: Macmillan and the Free Press.

Thrift, Minton. 1823. *Memoir of the Rev. Jesse Lee*. New York: N. Bangs & T. Mason.

Toon, Peter. 1972. *Puritans, the Millennium and the Future of Israel: Puritan Eschatology 1600 to 1650*. Cambridge: John Clarke.

Tyler, Alice Felt. 1944. *Freedom's Ferment: Phases of American Social History from the Colonial Period to the Outbreak of the Civil War*. Minneapolis, Minn.: University of Minnesota Press.

Weber, Timothy P. 1979. *Living in the Shadow of the Second Coming: American Pre-millennialism, 1875–1925*. New York: Oxford University Press.

Wuthnow, Robert. 1987. *Meaning and Moral Order: Explorations in Cultural Analysis*. Berkeley, Calif.: University of California Press.

13

Materialism, ideology, and political change

Gene Burns

For most of the 1970s the general trend in political sociology was to avoid emphasizing ideological dynamics in the study of sociopolitical change. Motivating such a stance, to a significant extent, was a desire for theoretical distance from Parsonian, modernization, and social-psychological theories of social change. In the view of structurally oriented theorists, such models lacked supporting evidence, falsely emphasized value consensus and progressive social evolution rather than power and exploitation, and incorrectly implied that rebels were reacting to their own psychosocial maladjustment (Gamson 1975; Jenkins 1983; McCarthy and Zald 1977; Oberschall 1978; Skocpol 1979: 14–18, 168–71; Snyder and Tilly 1972; Tilly 1973).

In place of psychology, ideology, and values, there developed in the late 1960s and 1970s a general orientation in political sociology towards political and economic structures, the state, mobilization, and class. To some extent (especially in theories of the state and of revolution), Marxist influences became more pronounced. The discussion here begins with the premise that such a reorientation was an advance. Critics have effectively pointed out the theoretical errors and empirical limitations of such approaches as functionalism and relative deprivation, so that such approaches (or at least explicit appeals to them) have virtually disappeared from political sociology (Tilly 1984).

However, it became clear by the mid-1980s that a solely materialist orientation is not adequate to account for sociopolitical change. Traditional notions of "class" have come under criticism even from those neo-Marxists working in a field known as working *class* formation (Katznelson 1981; Katznelson and Zolberg 1986), and a substantial body of empirical evidence demonstrates incontrovertibly that there is not a direct, linear relationship between class and ideology or politics (for example, Calhoun 1981; Traugott 1985). The economism of Marxist theory has been effectively critiqued from within by the post-Marxists Laclau and Mouffe (1985). The critique of materialist structuralism has not, in addition, been limited to Marxism; even the most strident structuralists have retreated from what we might call orthodox structuralism (Skocpol 1982, 1985). In the field of development, there has even been some acknowledgement among sociologists influenced by dependency and world-systems analysis that not all of modernization theory was completely wrong (Evans and Stephens 1988: 741).

An explicit theoretical incorporation of ideological and cultural variables into a consideration of sociopolitical conflict and change became more fashionable, then, in the 1980s, at the instigation of sociologists, historians, and anthropologists (for example, Arjomand 1986; D. Hunt 1982; L. Hunt 1984; Sewell 1985; Skocpol 1982). (There has been a parallel development in the sociology of religion and culture, in which political effects have gained increased attention in the study of cultural change (for example, Fulbrook 1983; Lamont 1989; Wuthnow 1989; Zaret 1985). However, I will concentrate on political sociology.) But how does one reintroduce less materialist assumptions without returning to functionalist, modernization, and social-psychological theories? Translating an acknowledgment that ideology matters into a workable theory of sociopolitical change – one that does not abandon the insights of political sociologists of the last couple of decades – is not an easy matter. This, I argue, remains a central challenge for political sociology.

The main problem is reconciling structural analysis with a recognition that ideology matters. Analyses of political change have generally assumed an opposition between structural and ideological analyses (so that structures are primarily material forces of politics and economics). Where structure operates, ideology does not, and vice versa, but there is no clear analysis of why one or the other is dominant at particular times (Skocpol 1982; Wilsford 1985). Thus, ideology is commonly an *ad hoc* variable called into action when structural analysis fails. The difficulty of reconciling structures and ideas as causes of political change becomes clear, for example, in Lynn Hunt's interesting and accomplished (1984) study of the French Revolution. Hunt wants to argue, on the one hand, that political culture has a logic and life of its own, and, on the other hand, that class and regional differences influence political ideas. But, as Higonnet (1986) has pointed out, the book does not integrate these two arguments; Part II argues a materialist, reductionist approach to political culture that is at odds with the idealist causation of Part I.

Again, attempts to examine both ideological and material determinants of sociopolitical change are a definite advance within political sociology. As long as both are included, no longer will incorporation of class factors elicit automatic accusations of materialist reductionism; and no longer will discussion of ideology elicit immediate charges of functionalism or psychologism.

However, we must develop past an *ad hoc* approach and ask why material structures should sometimes, but not always, be dominant. We can ask the same for ideology. If we treat ideology and structure simply as opposites, there is no convincing way to answer these questions and provide a powerful empirical analysis of social and political change. There must be clearer theoretical and empirical arguments about the interaction between the two.

The most coherent approach to sociopolitical change which does posit a strong relationship between ideology and structure – so that the two are not simply distinct and independent – argues that ideology is "embedded" within social structure (although not all authors actually use the term "embedded-ness"). This approach originates in Marxist thought and continues to appear in sociological work. To understand how this model developed, its insights, and its flaws, I will discuss below its origins in Marxist theory and argue that it, also, is ultimately an unsatisfactory approach. Evidence and arguments to support the claim that ideology has a material existence are generally obscure or nonexistent; such a claim commonly leads to contradictory implications concerning the empirical role of ideology in sociopolitical change. I will then propose an alternative approach which, to avoid the Scylla and Charybdis of reductionism and extreme idealism, argues that we must emphasize the fact that spaces of ideological autonomy will always exist within social structures, owing to the very nature of such structures. In developing this position, I will examine the role of ideology in revolutions, especially through consideration of an interesting interchange between William H. Sewell, Jr., and Theda Skocpol on the relationship between politics and ideology in the French Revolution.

Marxist theory of ideology

Embeddedness and materialism

To say, within a Marxist framework, that ideology is embedded within social structure is to argue that ideology and structure are interdependent because both have a material existence. Thus one can discuss political culture and ideology and still claim not to be arguing for idealist causation. Marx's discussion of commodity fetishism (1972: 215–25) could easily be read to imply such a view. Marx argues that workers' experience with the means of industry and apparently impersonal economic forces (for example, the value of money, supply and demand) overwhelms recognition of the fact that economic forces are indeed products of social interaction and socioeconomic power. That is, the obscuring ideology of capitalism, in which impersonal economic laws – not people – control the market, is embedded in the complex nature of socioeconomic relationships.

This approach took a more developed form in Gramsci's discussion of "hegemony." Hegemony is an interlocking web of political and cultural forms of class dominance. The materialist approach ties ideology closely to other components of hegemony, so that ideological dominance, or ideology in general, is never really autonomous of other social forces. Hegemonic ideology, like all aspects of hegemony, has an embedded, material existence.

But, when we do examine Gramsci's discussion of the ideological component of hegemony, we can see how confused the "embeddedness" approach leaves the nature of ideologies. Gramsci distinguishes two types of ideologies, those that are "historically organic" (or, we might say, embedded) and those that are "arbitrary" or "willed," that is, exist only in thought. Organic ideologies have a basis in a given social structure, in that a hegemonic ideology cannot develop arbitrarily but must support the class leadership which is materially based. "Willed" ideologies are not a factor in hegemony; these cannot "create the terrain on which men move, acquire consciousness of their position, struggle" (1971: 161, 376–7). These "arbitrary" ideologies are eliminated fairly quickly in historical competition "whereas constructions which respond to the demands of a complex organic period of history always impose themselves and prevail in the end" (p. 341). Gramsci affirms that one's "real philosophy" of the world is that expressed in action, not intellectually; even thoughts contrasting with one's own action have a material political origin in intellectual sub- mission to another group (pp. 326–7). Thus Gramsci sees popular ideas as material forces (p. 165). Effective ideologies serve to "cement" a social group (p. 328).

Despite the ambiguity of some of Gramsci's major positions (see Anderson 1976/7), his distinction between "organic" and "arbitrary" ideologies does allow him to argue that effective ideologies are competitively selected by social-structural constraints. That is, he needn't argue a functionalist Marxism in which all ideologies automatically reflect dominant class interest. Nevertheless, he offers a contradictory view of ideology. While emphasizing the material basis of class rule, as well as the materiality of organic ideologies, he must argue that consciousness which is not expressed in a subordinate class's activity, but instead is derived from intellectual subordination to another class, serves to uphold the ruling class's hegemony (Gramsci 1971: 326–7, 333). It is true that he can still argue that the ideological subordination is materially based, but only in the activity of a *different* (that is, dominant) class than those (in the subordinate class) who hold that ideology. For the

251

subordinate class, that consciousness, or ideology, is a matter of beliefs and worldview, not of social practice; their (nonmaterial) subjectivity is central in the power of hegemony.

Likewise, Gramsci discusses the necessity of volitional initiation of resistance, but notes in the same passage that without such will, subordinate material conditions lead to subordinate "modes of thinking" (1971: 336), echoing Marx's dictum that social being determines social consciousness. But, in fact, he is arguing that subordinate groups should apply their will to the remaking of material conditions, that is, to use social consciousness to re-determine social being, not vice versa. Passivity and resistance exist under materially equivalent conditions, the difference being only a matter of will. Here, then, in contrast to his claims about organic versus arbitrary ideologies, willed ideology is not arbitrary or insignificant at all. In fact, it is ideology that reflects (or accepts) historically existing conditions – those he had called "organic" – that is politically quiescent. (This contradictory view of ideology reflects the contradictions between "scientific" and "critical" Marxism discussed by Gouldner (1980).)

Althusser is generally recognized as the next major Marxist theorist of ideology, and an influential one. Going beyond Gramsci, Althusser claims (1971: 167–70) that non-material ideas do not even exist; Gramsci allowed that they existed but said they were "arbitrary" and historically insignificant. But Althusser simply declares this view of ideology; if one looks closely it becomes quite clear that Althusser simply dismisses alternative views. He does not actually present any evidence or arguments to demonstrate that ideas have a material existence. Poulantzas (1969, 1973), following Althusser, takes a similar approach.

The question of the materiality of ideology may appear to be simply an abstraction, but it has important empirical consequences. Not only is such a claim unconvincing, but it does not allow a clear distinction between ideology and other social phenomena. Ideology becomes Gramsci's cement, taken to the extreme in Althusser's (1971) formulation where ideological "apparatuses" comprise essentially all of civil society, civil society in turn being simply an extension of the state (see also Anderson (1976/7: 34–9)). Althusser can see ideology only in terms of a function to control and reproduce labor power (1971: 133), that is, to train the proletariat into submission. He cannot see a politics that does not reduce directly to economic functions, nor can he see such an ideology. But his definition of ideology is not widely different from that of other Marxist theorists, including those to whom Althusser's rigid economic determinism is anathema. To see how persistent the materialist fallacy is, it is interesting to examine the very important radical reformulation of Marxist political theory by Laclau and Mouffe (1985).

Laclau and Mouffe are leading protagonists of the politics of discourse approach. Extending a Gramscian interpretation of Marxist theory, this approach emphasizes that political actors are made (and remade), not given, within the continuous process of social conflict. The discourse approach is an effective attack on economism, though it would not be appropriate to review here the complex theoretical critiques. However, it is subject to misinterpretation because the relation between discourse and ideology is, we shall see, problematic. While the discourse explanation initially appears to escape the reduction of ideology to material existence, this fallacy ultimately weakens its power.

It is easy to mistake the meaning of political "discourses" as signifying subjective interactions, that is, the development of new understandings, new consciousness. Thus, when Laclau and Mouffe use such examples as feminism (and Jones (1983) emphasizes English radicalism), discourses seem to indicate historically developed understandings around which subjects construct politics. Thus, a certain group might come to understand and pursue its political struggles not only along class lines, but also (or instead) along gender, regional, or other lines.

But, while politics necessarily involves the unending process of redefinition of groupings, so that the constituency and even the identity of conflictual groups constantly changes, discourses are essentially social locations or political frames that exist only within social practice. Laclau and Mouffe (1985: 108) argue that discourses do not occur along subjective lines; they disavow "the *mental* character of discourse. Against this, we will affirm the *material* character of every discursive structure." They go on (p. 109) to note approvingly (despite disagreement with earlier Marxists on many other points), "the progressive affirmation, from Gramsci to Althusser, of the material character of *ideologies*, inasmuch as these are not simply systems of ideas but are embodied in institutions, rituals and so forth." Even "all 'experience' depends on precise discursive conditions of possibility" (p. 115), that is, objectively existing and organized social conditions.

If we define ideology as a material phenomenon embedded in social practice, it ultimately becomes impossible to distinguish ideology from other aspects of social structure. This is true even if we see a society's ideology as its organizing principle (rather than a *consequence* of class interest, for example). Thus, Gareth Stedman Jones, including under the term "language" what others would call ideology or discourse, argues, "Language disrupts any simple notion of the determination of consciousness by social being because *it is itself part of social being*. We cannot therefore decode political language to reach a primal and material expression of interest since it is the discursive structure of political language which conceives and defines interest in the first place" (1983: 21–2, emphasis mine). Language – or, in my terms, ideology – is not determined by material conditions such as political structure, because it's *part* of politics; not only that, it's inseparable from social being.

Thus, despite their very effective critiques of Marxist economism and determinism, neither Laclau and Mouffe nor Jones provide a non-reductionist theory of the role of ideology in politics. While they consistently imply that resistance occurs when subordinated groups develop a new understanding of their position, there is in fact no theoretical place for "understanding": the subjective nature of understanding (ideology) is not granted an autonomous, non-material existence. Thus, just as it is easy to overestimate the idealism allowed for when Marxists discuss ideology, one mustn't mistake the central position of the concept "discourse" for an indication that subjectively understood interaction is crucial.

Thus even among theorists who have gone far from orthodox Marxism, there is a persistently obscure conceptualization of ideology, one which is implicitly reductionist.

Marxist functionalism: empirical shortcomings

In fact, what materialist theories of ideology end up arguing, as they emphasize a monolithic capitalist culture which incorporates all ideology via an unspecified mechanism, is a Marxist brand of functionalism. There is the problem that such an argument tends to become teleological: the dominant ideology is so pervasive – because it is inseparable from social practice – that all of social life seems to contribute to its reproduction. Resistance is then inconceivable. In pointing out this problem, Abercrombie, Hill, and Turner (1980) join a number of observers (Elster 1982; Giddens 1981: 15–19) who have noted the problematic tendency of Marxism to fall into a functionalist logic. (Cohen (1978: 249–96, 1982) has explicitly defended a functionalist interpretation of Marx.)

The only beginning of a break with this approach is in the conceptualization of ideology as one of the many "structured differences" within social life, those differences arising both because of the plurality of social life as well as the fact that in different social spheres (economic, political, ideological, and so forth), discourses necessarily take different paths. Althusser (1969) raised this idea in his concept of "overdetermination" by which different spheres simultaneously determine each other. Hall (1977) rejects Althusser's ambiguous attempt still to claim that the economic sphere is determinant "in the last instance" and emphasizes, like Laclau and Mouffe (1985) and Williams (1980: 40–3), that hegemony includes incorporation of ideological elements from subordinated classes. These elements would, then, necessarily not originally be products of dominant culture.

While acknowledging that a plurality of groups have some ideological autonomy, the "structured differences" approach does not go much further. Like too much of Marxist theory, it leaves unclear directions for empirical application, and once again, the ultimate purpose is to assert that dominant culture does ultimately incorporate all ideological strands, even if it does not necessarily give them birth. This approach gives little reason to study particular ideologies, since it implies that they are all eventually co-opted anyway. Yet there is no mechanism postulated by which capitalism does indeed incorporate these ideological strands, and the approach does not question the basic Marxist assumption that ideology has a material existence. Ultimately, then, Hall's and Williams' emphasis that dominant ideology must incorporate subordinate ideology becomes a postulated function rather than an explanation of process.

I would argue that truly empirical analyses of ideology necessarily abandon the claim that ideology has a material existence. In order to provide an empirically workable approach, Gitlin (1980: esp. 253–4) interpreted the concept of "hegemony" in a much more idealist way than did Gramsci. Burawoy's attempt to develop a Marxist theory of consent (as a non-subjective process built into the production process) is also worth noting in this context. He wants to retain the materialist perspective, yet he resorts to subjective explanations whenever distinguishing consent from (the experience of) coercion (1979: 132, 135, 223) and even, at times, to explain worker incentives for consenting (p. 85). He also vacillates between arguing whether class struggle is the cause or effect of consent (pp. 120, 186–9, 195). (See also Clawson and Fantasia 1983; Gartman 1983.)

The empirical analysis of ideology and politics

Many sociologists would of course agree that ideology is sociologically important only when embodied in practice; precisely at issue is developing an adequate conceptualization of the role of ideology in social practice and politics. But by refusing to look at the autonomous existence of ideology, the materialist formulation acknowledges ideology only once it has already been so embodied. It unconvincingly turns the question of the causal significance of ideology into a non-issue. We should be asking why certain (non-material) ideas affect social practice more than others, or at certain times and not others.

Still, we must remember the context that the "embeddedness" approach has by far been the most developed attempt to explain interaction between ideology and political change. The Marxist aversion to any element of idealist causation is based on reasonable theoretical and empirical concerns of avoiding the *deus ex machina* of ideas and beliefs identified, in an *ad hoc* fashion, as occasional but not consistent causes of social and political change. Political sociology as a whole has rarely explicitly addressed this question, so that ideology is commonly an *ad hoc* variable introduced when structural analysis falls short. The embeddedness approach is appealing enough that sociologists who are certainly not Marxists have borrowed from it (for example, Wuthnow 1985: 815).

In fact, what is arguably the most effective empirical study of the role of ideology in social and political change (Sewell 1985) explicitly draws upon the Marxist tradition. For Sewell, "[a]ll social relations are at the same time ideological relations"; ideology is constitutive of the social order (p. 61). Sewell, does not, however, argue for an ultimate material determination of ideology; instead, his position is close to that of Gareth Stedman Jones. Building upon his earlier work (1980), he identifies a pervasive ideology (or what others might call a political culture) as the most important determinant of social relations (not vice versa), and thus of the direction of the French Revolution. But the fact that Sewell can see the emergence of a new hegemonic ideology as the engine of the revolution, and yet still show such similarity to materialist views of ideology, is itself a telling comment on the embeddedness approach. Because the notion of embeddedness makes it difficult to distinguish ideology from other social phenomena, it is difficult to say what ultimately determines what. There emerge, then, as we shall see, certain problems in Sewell's analysis. But there also emerge many instructive strengths.

Sewell (1985) takes Skocpol (1979) to task for neglecting the role of ideology in social revolutions, particularly the French Revolution. Skocpol's earlier book, *States and Social Revolutions* (1979), had strongly asserted that ideology was not an important force in revolutions, mainly because outcomes never reflect the ideological program of particular groups. Even groups that take control of a revolutionary state encounter constraints, so that their policies commonly show little resemblance to their avowed revolutionary program. Sewell begins, appropriately, with this overly restricted definition of ideology that Skocpol had provided in *States and Social Revolutions*. Skocpol had equated ideology with voluntarism; but rejecting voluntarist explanations, Sewell appropriately points out, does not necessarily mean a rejection of a causal role for ideology.

Sewell offers, then, a more sophisticated view of ideology: the French Revolution had an overarching ideological frame within which there were various interpretations, or "ideological variants" (1985: 74–6). In that revolution, an ideology of Enlightenment replaced an old regime ideology of corporatism. Each ideology had its institutional expression (that is, was embedded in social practice). Corporatism existed in the monarchical government structure as well as in the actions and privileges of guilds, estates, *parlements*, and other corporations, so that there did not exist individual civic rights and responsibilities. Such rights and responsibilities depended instead on one's corporate memberships.

Sewell is less clear on the pre-revolutionary institutional expression of Enlightenment ideology. But he does insist both that ideology has an embedded existence (1985: 63–4) *and* that ideology played a causal role in the revolution. So, Enlightenment ideology had to have had a social expression *before* revolutionary conflict began; thus he notes that, within the French state, the growing rationalized bureaucracy had no clear place within corporate ideology (pp. 64–5). Presumably, then, the new forms of state bureaucracy that began with Louis XIV, and undermined the power of some corporate bodies, were a central antecedent to the revolution (see Sewell 1980: 63, 72).

However, just as there always exist ideological variants in a society, the existence of two opposing ideologies – corporatist and Enlightenment – does not in itself necessitate revolution. (Thus Sewell avoids a Durkheimian or Parsonian explanation of social disruption; Sewell's old regime could function without ideological consensus.) The revolutionary crisis emerged from the reality of state bankruptcy. But once "crisis had begun, ideological contradictions contributed mightily to the deepening of the crisis into revolution" (1985: 66–7).

Once there was a crisis, then, ideological commitments, not material necessities, drove the revolution forward. The calling of the Estates General, a corporate body, was reinterpreted in Enlightenment terms as an expression of the national will to revise the social contract. Thus, within months, even nobles within the Assembly, motivated by ideological rather than self-interested considerations, could support an elimination of seigneurial and other corporate privileges (pp. 68–9).

But the realities of the existence of competing social groups (such as peasants, *sans-culottes*, Jacobins) meant that while each drew upon the same general concepts – popular sovereignty, natural law, the general will – conflict emerged among groups committed to variant interpretations of those concepts. No one group could easily impose its particular ideological variant, a reality that led Skocpol (1979), erroneously, to conclude that ideology simply didn't matter (Sewell 1985: 74–6).

In a response to Sewell, Skocpol (1985) effectively identified the weaknesses of Sewell's approach. She criticized his "anthropological" conception of ideology as "constitutive of the social order" (pp. 89–91). Skocpol (in my opinion, correctly) states that occasionally the actual meaning of such an abstract formulation is not clear (p. 92). She argues that Sewell's approach too easily implies a tight, overarching ideology in which all social factions participate. (We might ask at what point Sewell's "ideological variants" becomes *distinct* ideologies.)

Indeed, what weaknesses there are in Sewell's approach are due to its origins in the embeddedness approach. In this approach, dominant ideology pervades society. Sewell occasionally implies that peasant revolts were inspired by Enlightenment ideology (1985: 68), but more often he suggests the more convincing view that peasants – hardly privy to the debates of *philosophes* and Jacobin clubs – revolted for independent reasons (for example, poor harvests in 1788 and 1789). It was the Assembly leadership, not the peasants themselves, that applied an Enlightenment discourse to peasant demands (pp. 69, 76–7). That is, he ultimately acknowledges that it's not empirically plausible to claim that all groups shared an Enlightenment ideology.

If one postulates an all-encompassing ideology, there is a temptation to argue not only that a powerful ideology pervades all social factions; it is also difficult to imagine any ideological change that is less than total. Thus Sewell's ideologies take on lives of their own, so that at times it is unclear whether French people mattered very much. We are told that "the calling of the Estates General was determined by the logic of the disintegration of the absolutist ideological synthesis" (1985: 68). And then, once "the Assembly was forced to destroy one complex of privileges, it was moved forward by an overwhelming urge for ideological consistency and destroyed them all" (p. 69; see also Sewell 1980: 63, 84–5). We must remember that Sewell himself (1985: 66, 1980: 74–5, 96–8) has argued and demonstrated that various political factions, both before and during the revolution, grafted Enlightenment concepts on to a corporatist worldview. He himself states (1985: 66) that people can live with ideological contradiction.

Sewell does, however, have a point that ideological concerns were sometimes higher priorities than were factional struggles over privileges or attempts to build a new revolutionary state. Skocpol cannot easily account for the great attention to such matters as the revision of the calendar and weights and measures (Sewell 1985: 77–8). Skocpol (1985: 92) argues that such changes can be seen as an attack on the social power and centrality of the Catholic Church, but did the attack on clerical power really necessitate changing the length of the week and the names of all days and months? More significantly, Skocpol does not challenge the empirical specifics of Sewell's central point that people who clearly stood to lose from the abolition of seigneurial privileges nevertheless enthusiastically supported such reforms at the Assembly meeting of August 4, 1789. Support for these changes, though partly a response to peasant rebellion, did not come about in an atmosphere of resignation, but was more closely one of celebration in which delegates' interests appeared relatively unimportant.

Still, Skocpol's response is a thoughtful one which raises some central questions. Skocpol argues that the ideas that influence revolutions (what she calls "cultural idioms") are more free-floating and less specific than Sewell would lead us to believe, and she notes that many developments in the revolution cannot easily be attributed to ideological causes. Skocpol's perspective could more easily account for the fact that some groups, such as peasants, do not seem to share much ideologically with other rebels, and the fact that the direction of the revolution was often strongly determined by war, famine, or other events that were hardly of an ideological origin.

However, Skocpol's approach allows us to deal with ideological influences only in an *ad hoc* fashion: it is unclear why revolutionary actors draw upon cultural idioms sometimes and not others. And such free-floating idioms are of questionable explanatory power. For an ideology to matter in revolutions, there must be some limits to divergent interpretations; there must be some degree of shared meanings among those who draw upon it. If a "cultural idiom" is subject to infinitely broad interpretation – and Skocpol does not discuss any limits – it really is not a social influence or constraint.

How, then, can we reconcile and reinterpret the many insights provided by Sewell and Skocpol? To begin, there is no particular reason to insist that to be influential, an ideology must captivate *all* revolutionary actors. Some people can spread ideas to others, who act on them collectively, even though much of the society has not been exposed to the same beliefs. We fall into the trap of expecting an all-encompassing ideology only when we accept that ideology must be "constitutive of the social order." Ideas are just that – ideas. They are not material forces. It is true that we care about ideas only when they affect people, when people act upon them. But the empirical question then becomes why do people act upon and reinterpret ideas some times and not others?

To answer this question, we should consider another insight provided by Skocpol and Sewell. It is interesting that Skocpol (1985: 86–7), in responding to Sewell, greatly retreats from her strictly determinist view of revolutions. She allows for the ability of revolutionary actors to reconstruct structures, implicitly accepting Sewell's (1985: 60–1) view, following Giddens, that structures are enabling as well as constraining. One way to apply this insight is to emphasize that no structure is all-encompassing. There will always be some room for some actors to maneuver; some will have some degree of autonomy from social-structural constraints.

If we treat ideologies as material forces, we need to identify specific changes in social practices to account for ideological changes. There must always be a correspondence. But if ideas are subjective, it makes more sense to consider when people might gain *autonomy* from material constraints and thus be able to consider and apply new ideas more thoroughly than they had before (cf. Wuthnow 1989). The financial crisis of the French state, a crisis Sewell and many others identify as the spark of the revolution, was just such an event. The interesting thing about theories based on embeddedness is that they must try to identify an ideology "constitutive of a social order" even when social orders are tumbling down in revolutions! The financial crisis, the assembled Estates General, and peasant rebellions all weakened the French state and French elites; as a result, radical ideological challenges could develop much more quickly than would normally be the case. Surely, some of these ideas had a long history; there are always some people with enough leisure and autonomy to develop, publicize, and digest new ideas. And the fact that some ideas are publicized better than others will affect the ideological pool that other people can draw upon. But more important, at least in revolutions, is the autonomy available to apply those ideas to politics.

We would be mistaken, then, to think that the germ of any revolutionary ideology has to be fully formed before a revolution can even begin. The ideological direction of a revolution, or any sociopolitical change, will depend upon which social powers are weakened, which are strengthened (that is, acquire increased autonomy), and which ideas are accessible to those strengthened groups. Also important are the *types* of autonomy (political, economic, and so on) and the timing of such changes, which can influence which groups (temporarily or otherwise) are ideologically compatible, and which groups (or institutions) are most vulnerable to attack. Ideological reconstruction involves the flexing of muscles; it is central to political reconstruction.

In the French Revolution, peasant ideologies were most unlikely to dominate, given the peasantry's relative disadvantages in developing or enforcing a coherent program. It was too geographically dispersed and could not ultimately compete, for example, with the army's coercive abilities. *Sans-culotte* ideologies could have the greatest impact when Parisian revolts were enough to threaten revolutionary governments and social order. The power of *sans-culotte* ideology was, then, often associated with unstable military situations (due to war and regional counter-revolution) from 1792 to 1794. This more radical period was the height of ideological influence of this most radical faction.

August 4, 1789, must be seen as the result of both collapse of the political economy and a search for new ideological commitments in the wake of such changes. In the turbulent, yet (for many) promising, summer of 1789, ideological commitments altered rapidly. And the autonomy of popular groups vastly expanded. Old ideas that justified a social order that, to many appeared already to have disappeared, could themselves evaporate.

Conclusion

This short discussion can only be suggestive of new directions for the analysis of ideology's role in sociopolitical change. By discarding the empirically unworkable premise that ideology exists only materially, we can build upon the insights of such sociologists as Sewell and Skocpol. Materialist conceptions easily imply that ideologies correspond to all-encompassing social structures. But rare is the life that is completely constrained in all its aspects; rare is the society that provides no autonomy for some members to develop new perspectives. Revolutions are a particularly fruitful area in which to study ideological change, given the rapid disintegration and reconstruction of social-structural constraints. Only recently have empirical analyses appeared which emphasize that the direction of revolutions is not predetermined but can partly be directed by groups able to construct a unifying ideology within the constraints that limit them (Moghadam 1987). By emphasizing the spaces of autonomy that exist in any social structure, we can continue to develop empirically workable theories of the relationship between ideology and social change.

References

Abercrombie, Nicholas, Hill, Stephen, and Turner, Bryan S. 1980. *The Dominant Ideology Thesis*. London: George Allen & Unwin.

Althusser, Louis. 1969. *For Marx*. London: Allen Lane.

Althusser, Louis. 1971. Ideology and ideological state apparatuses (Notes toward an investigation). In *Lenin and Philosophy and Other Essays*, trans. Ben Brewster, pp. 121–73. New York and London: Monthly Review Press.

Anderson, Perry. 1976/7. The Antinomies of Antonio Gramsci. *New Left Review* 100: 5–78.

Arjomand, Said Amir. 1986. Iran's Islamic Revolution in Comparative Perspective. *World Politics* 38: 383–414.

Burawoy, Michael. 1979. *Manufacturing Consent*. Chicago: University of Chicago Press.

Calhoun, Craig. 1981. *The Question of Class Struggle*. Chicago: University of Chicago Press.

Clawson, Dan and Fantasia, Richard. 1983. Beyond Burawoy: The dialectics of conflict and consent on the shop floor. *Theory and Society* 12: 671–80.

Cohen, G. A. 1978. *Karl Marx's Theory of History*. Oxford and Princeton, NJ: Princeton University Press.

Cohen, G. A. 1982. Reply to Elster on "Marxism, Functionalism, and Game Theory." *Theory and Society* 11: 483–95.

Elster, Jon. 1982. Marxism, Functionalism, and Game Theory. *Theory and Society* 11: 453–82.

Evans, Peter B. and Stephens, John D. 1988. Development and the World Economy. In Neil J. Smelser (ed.) *Handbook of Sociology*, pp. 739–73. Newbury Park, Calif.: Sage.

Fulbrook, Mary. 1983. *Piety and Politics*. Cambridge: Cambridge University Press.

Gamson, William. 1975. *The Strategy of Social Protest*. Homewood, Ill.: Dorsey.

Gartman, David. 1983. Structuralist Marxism and the labor process. *Theory and Society* 12: 659–69.

Giddens, Anthony. 1981. *A Contemporary Critique of Historical Materialism*. Berkeley, Calif.: University of California Press.

Gitlin, Todd. 1980. *The Whole World Is Watching*. Berkeley, Calif.: University of California Press.

Gouldner, Alvin W. 1980. *The Two Marxisms*. New York: Oxford University Press.

Gramsci, Antonio. 1971. *Selections from the Prison Notebooks*, ed. and trans. Quintin Hoare and Geoffrey Nowell Smith. New York: International Publishers.

Hall, Stuart. 1977. Culture, the media and the "ideological effect." In James Curran (ed.) *Mass Communication and Society*, pp. 315–48. Beverly Hills, Calif.: Sage.

Higonnet, Patricie. 1986. Review of Lynn Hunt, *Politics, Culture, and Class in the French Revolution*. *Journal of Social History* 20: 192–4.

Hunt, David. 1982. Village culture and the Vietnamese revolution. *Past and Present* 60: 131–57.

Hunt, Lynn. 1984. *Politics, Culture, and Class in the French Revolution*. Berkeley, Calif.: University of California Press.

Jenkins, J. Craig. 1983. Resource mobilization and the study of social movements. *Annual Review of Sociology* 9: 527–53.

Jones, Gareth Stedman. 1983. *Languages of Class*. Cambridge: Cambridge University Press.

Katznelson, Ira. 1981. *City Trenches*. New York: Pantheon.

Katznelson, Ira and Zolberg, Aristide R. (eds). 1986. *Working-Class Formation.* Princeton, NJ: Princeton University Press.

Laclau, Ernesto and Mouffe, Chantal. 1985. *Hegemony and Socialist Strategy.* London: Verso.

Lamont, Michèle. 1989. The power–culture link in a comparative perspective. *Comparative Social Research* 11: 131–50.

Marx, Kárl. 1972. *The Marx-Engels Reader,* ed. Robert C. Tucker. New York: Norton.

McCarthy, John D. and Zald, Mayer N. 1977. Resource mobilization and social movements. *American Journal of Sociology* 82: 1212–41.

Moghadam, Val. 1987. Socialism or anti-imperialism? The Left and revolution in Iran. *New Left Review* 166: 5–28.

Obserschall, Anthony. 1978. Theories of social conflict. *Annual Review of Sociology* 4: 291–315.

Poulantzas, Nicos. 1969. The problem of the capitalist state. *New Left Review* 58: 67–78.

Poulantzas, Nicos. 1973. *Political Power and Social Classes.* London: New Left Books.

Sewell, William H., Jr. 1980. *Work and Revolution in France.* Cambridge: Cambridge University Press.

Sewell, William H., Jr. 1985. Ideologies and social revolutions: Reflections on the French case. *Journal of Modern History* 57: 57–85.

Skocpol, Theda. 1979. *States and Social Revolutions.* Cambridge: Cambridge University Press.

Skocpol, Theda. 1982. Rentier state and Shi'a Islam in the Iranian revolution. *Theory and Society* 11: 265–83.

Skocpol, Theda. 1985. Cultural idioms and political ideologies in the revolutionary reconstruction of state power: A rejoinder to Sewell. *Journal of Modern History* 57: 86–96.

Snyder, David and Tilly, Charles. 1972. Hardship and collective violence in France, 1830 to 1960. *American Sociological Review* 37: 520–32.

Tilly, Charles. 1973. Does modernization breed revolution? *Comparative Politics* 5: 425–47.

Tilly, Charles. 1984. *Big Structures, Large Processes, Huge Comparisons.* New York: Russell Sage Foundation.

Traugott, Mark. 1985. *Armies of the Poor.* Princeton, NJ: Princeton University Press.

Williams, Raymond. 1980. *Problems in Materialism and Culture: Selected Essays.* London: New Left Books.

Wilsford, David. 1985. The *conjoncture* of ideas and interests. *Comparative Political Studies* 18: 357–72.

Wuthnow, Robert. 1985. State structures and ideological outcomes. *American Sociological Review* 50: 799–821.

Wuthnow, Robert. 1989. *Communities of Discourse.* Cambridge, Mass.: Harvard University Press.

Zaret, David. 1985. *The Heavenly Contract.* Chicago: University of Chicago Press.

Index